ADULT EDUCATION AND SOCIAL PURPOSE

A History of the WEA Eastern District 1913 to 1988

V. Williams & G. J. White

Published for the

Workers' Educational Association Eastern District

by

Graham-Cameron Publishing, Cambridge, England

© 1988 V. Williams & G. J. White   ISBN 0 947672 16 8

i

ii

CONTENTS

LIST OF ILLUSTRATIONS

FOREWORD

The danger of being asked to write a foreword to the District's history is that contemporary events cannot be seen in their historical context. Only a later considered assessment will show whether the concerns expressed at the time proved to be unfounded. Nevertheless, a contemporary analysis of the WEA could show that the seventy-fifth year of the Eastern District's history marked a watershed in its affairs.

The passing of first Megan Mothersole and, a few months later on 14th July 1988, Frank Jacques certainly marked the end of an era. For many generations of WEA members these two names were synonymous with all that was best about the WEA in the Eastern District. The fifty years service of Frank Jacques and the thirty-two of Megan Mothersole will also be associated, in many members' minds, with a period of certainty about the role and function of the WEA.

We now seem to have entered a period of great uncertainty for the WEA in so many areas of previously stable relationships. The public funding the WEA receives through the Department of Education and Science has a large proportion related to the new efficiency criteria of 'effective students', and there are also allocations for Special Activities and Tutor Training. The salary and related costs of field staff are no longer guaranteed, but are dependent upon the less certain grant income based upon student enrolments.

At the same time, the WEA is being asked to be increasingly concerned with identifying the disadvantaged in society and meeting their educational needs and aspirations. Within the WEA the shift of resources necessary to achieve these objectives is creating tensions which will not be easily resolved.

The longstanding relationship between WEA Districts and University Extra-Mural Departments, which has maintained a programme of Joint Committee classes since the inception of the WEA, is now under review. The new funding arrangements for University Extra-Mural Departments, together with the removal of 'Responsible Body' status from the older departments, raises serious long-term questions about the future of WEA Joint Committee provision.

The Education Reform Act 1988, has implications for the WEA in terms of the long-term future of Local Education Authorities. The traditional support the WEA has received from the LEA sector has not only been the grant-aid but equally important, the provision of accommodation for its classes, and both these could be at risk in the future.

When reading the history of the Eastern District, I am conscious that such fears and concerns are not new and that the WEA has had to face up to crises many times in its history. It could be said that each new District Secretary felt he had taken over at a period of crisis. As the Eastern District has only had three District Secretaries in seventy-five years my five years' service would certainly qualify me to be termed new!

What clearly emerges from this history is that the WEA has always been able to meet each new challenge and draw the best out of its voluntary officers and members. It is inevitable that an official history tends to draw upon the records and papers available in the District Office and, understandably, less from the limited records kept by branches and individual members. In this sense it is unable to record fully the countless hours of voluntary work undertaken by the thousands of voluntary officers and members who have served the WEA Eastern District in its seventy-five years. Their tribute is recorded in the thousands of classes provided throughout the District over this period and those countless students who have derived enjoyment and intellectual stimulation from a WEA class in their community.

It is to that 'vanguard of the anonymous', as Professor R. H. Tawney described them, that this history is dedicated.

REG CARNELL
District Secretary

PREFACE

In writing a history of the Eastern District of the Workers' Educational Association the authors throughout were conscious that it reflects some of the major policies and events which have shaped the history of the National Association during the past eighty-five years and which await further detailed scholarly research. It is believed that this history of the Eastern District during the first seventy-five years of its existence will contribute substantive material to a national study of the Association in conjunction with histories of other Districts, published in recent years.

The study of the Eastern District arose from the disparate but related interests and experiences of the authors. One had been an education officer in one of the LEAs in the region during the 1960s and the other a tutor-organiser on the staff of the District a decade later. Both have been Individual Members of the District for many years. Their joint interest in the history of the District led to a proposal by Frank Jacques, then District Secretary, that a published record of this, geographically the largest WEA District in the country, should be undertaken. The decision to publish was taken by his successor, Reg Carnell, and by his District Executive, with the intention that the book should mark the seventy-fifth anniversary in 1988 of the formation of the Eastern District.

During the research for, and preparation of, the text, the authors were provided with free and unfettered access to the large collection of archival material in Botolph House, Cambridge, and were given much encouragement and full co-operation by both District Secretaries, by the late Assistant Secretary Megan Mothersole, and by their colleagues voluntary and professional. To accommodate their personal interests the authors agreed that the earliest period from 1913 to 1952 would be covered by Vivian Williams and the years from 1953 to 1988 would be the responsibility of Graeme White. They have, however, worked in close collaboration with each other where topics have overlapped, and in such other preparatory work as the joint editing of the text.

Their gratitude for the support and goodwill of both District Secretaries, their staffs and their Executive Committees, and to all those who have helped in so many ways in the production of this book, is unreserved. Much if the research would scarcely have been possible but for the work of Anne Shiel, former archivist to the Eastern District, in sorting and filing the papers in the basement of Botolph House. To Alan Bishop the authors are grateful for his advice and skilled compilation of the index, not least for reducing it to manageable proportions. They are grateful, also, to Mike Graham-Cameron for the cover design and for his advice and execution in the publishing process. The authors owe much to the voluntary and professional members of the Eastern District, past and present, who have willingly answered queries and have commented upon drafts of particular sections of the book. Special thanks are due to Kathryn Coles for her patience and skill in turning the authors' much-modified drafts into the final typescript for the publisher. Gratitude to all who have helped to produce this book is exceeded only by indebtedness to the authors' immediate families: they have given unqualified support and encouragement to the research and writing, and have shown considerable forbearance over prolonged and frequent absences from home.

Finally, the authors would not wish to claim that this is a definitive account or analysis of the history of the WEA Eastern District. The views expressed are essentially personal ones. Although glimpses of occupational categories are provided at various points in the text, much more research is required, for example, into the socio-economic backgrounds and motivational influences of the thousands of students who have enrolled in the District's classes and courses during the past seventy-five years. Comparatively little appears to have survived from the inter-war period, as many District records were lost when an enthusiastic but misguided member of the clerical staff gave much material to a waste-paper collection in aid of the war effort in the early 1940s. Further, few WEA branches seem to have kept detailed records of their activities or meetings. During this research, only Bedford WEA branch responded to an appeal by Frank Jacques for such material. Nevertheless, the authors believe that the main framework of the history of the Eastern District has now been constructed. It will be necessary for others to undertake further research before it will be possible to make firm judgments about the social and educational influence of the WEA on the lives of individuals and communities within this and other Districts of the National Association.

Vivian Williams
Wootton, Woodstock
May 1988

Graeme White
Chester

The WEA Eastern District

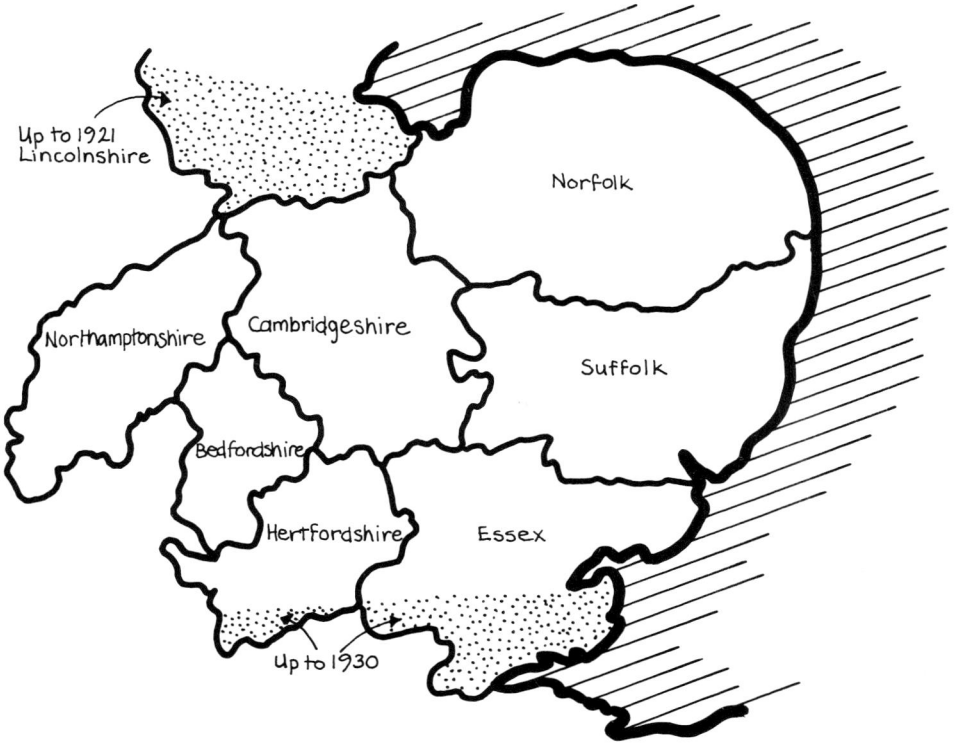

Up to 1921
Lincolnshire

Norfolk

Northamptonshire

Cambridgeshire

Suffolk

Bedfordshire

Hertfordshire

Essex

Up to 1930

Design & Production: Graham-Cameron Publishing, Willingham, Cambridge
Indexing: Alan Bishop, 23a Guest Road, Cambridge
Cover Design & Illustrations: Helen Herbert, Willingham, Cambridge
Typesetting: Goodfellow & Egan Ltd, French's Mill, Cambridge
Printing: Target Litho, Cottenham, Cambridge

CHAPTER 1

THE EASTERN DISTRICT: FORMATIVE INFLUENCES AND EARLY YEARS 1913–18

Preparing the Foundations

The early vigorous growth of the WEA following its establishment in 1903 is well-documented, and it is unnecessary to go over that historical ground here. It is sufficient to say that its creation reflected the confluence of experience, achievement and, ultimately, continuing dissatisfaction with existing provision and the inability to respond to the growing demand of societal and political pressure for increased access to educational opportunity at many levels and was not exclusively an issue about the education of adults. For adult education, the WEA represented a gathering momentum of demand based on experience during the latter part of the nineteenth century and reflected a natural development rooted in the university extension movement from which the WEA emerged.

For the history of the early WEA one need look no further than Mansbridge's own accounts, the Oxford Report of 1908, and Price's little text, all of which provide first hand, largely contemporaneous personal perceptions of the immediacy of events.[1] Longer and more analytical perspectives are available in Mary Stocks' celebration of the WEA's Jubilee, Kelly's comprehensive sweep of the history of adult education, and the more recent forensic, evaluative work of Fieldhouse and Jennings.[2]

In 1905, eight WEA branches existed and a rudimentary district organisation was evident in the formation of area committees in the North West and South West regions following conferences of adult students at the universities of Manchester and Exeter respectively. Each area committee functioned through the appointment of honorary secretaries. By 1908, three areas had appointed full-time salaried secretaries (North West, the Midlands and South Wales) and a district organisational pattern had been established. The majority of the existing fifty WEA branches were attached to a district organisation while the remainder continued the original links directly with the small, two-room central office of the WEA in Adam Street, London. In October of that year *The Highway* was also launched which stimulated and fostered a sense of unity, partnership and a cohesive national movement.

Encouraged by the tireless Mansbridge as the energising nucleus of a steadily expanding organisation, the pattern of central support of local autonomy was established and was given shape through further revision of the WEA's constitution in 1907 to provide for a central council of the Association composed of representatives of its Districts as its governing body. There was also a recognition of the pivotal position of the office of District Secretary to the Association's activities and the policy of creating district organisations with full-time salaried secretaries was adopted. Through the regional organisation, the key principle of local autonomy of student groups and branches was established and sustained by providing a facilitating organisational and administrative framework. An organisation of this kind was also deemed necessary to stimulate and channel existing and potential 'demand' requirements of adherents and members through branches and match it to the 'supply' of teaching by the universities. Further, the crucially important issue of financial support required meticulous attention and a recognised, credible and accountable mechanism in order to qualify for grants available under Board of Education regulations, from the newly established Local Education Authorities (LEAs), charitable organisations, university authorities and, not least, from individual philanthropists.

In hindsight, it is difficult to imagine how these complexities might have been co-ordinated effectively without the creation of the post of District Secretary and it is unsurprising to find that in the histories of other WEA Districts, the key role of district secretary is invariably given pre-eminent significance as the single most important reason for the relative success of those Districts in their formative periods. As in all voluntary organisations, the WEA has continued to rely heavily on the organisational, administrative and personal skills of its district secretaries. The Eastern District reflects this tradition as its history, probably unique in the WEA, is above all a record of the endeavours of two District Secretaries who held office over a span of seventy years: George Pateman, 1913–35, and Frank Jacques, 1935–83.

In the early years of the WEA, the first group of district secretaries worked largely in *ad hoc* ways, pragmatically seizing opportunities as they adventitiously arose. They were required to interpret and rigorously observe Board of Education regulations, a difficult task as these were not designed originally to include grant-aid for liberal adult education. They had to persuade newly established LEAs to provide financial support for classes and courses which the local authorities neither organised nor

2

provided; to negotiate with trade unions for support over enrolment and fee remission for their members (and for whom liberal adult education was not regarded as a central priority or proper function by some of the unions); to enlist the participation of university academics in the provision of short courses as well as three- year Tutorial Classes. It was also important to persuade industrialists, manufacturing companies and many charitable organisations as well as individuals to provide funds or offer donations, or act as guarantors, for non-statutory adult education enterprises to secure liberal adult education for working people. In addition, they were required to possess a variety of skills enabling them to attract, encourage and sustain the support of those adults for whom the WEA existed through the organisation of educational opportunities for student groups or WEA branches scrupulously observing local autonomy within self-governing, self-maintaining local and district organisations. It was a tall order, and through the office of District Secretary, each District occupied in Tawney's phrase 'the strategic position' in the WEA.

The District, through its democratic, participative, and largely autonomous organisation, reflected from its earliest experience both its major virtues and an inherently serious disability. The autonomy of the branches led to widespread parochialism in its earliest years and undoubtedly made more difficult the development of the WEA as a nationally recognised organisation. Financial support for district and national organisation was infrequently given as at branch level the relevance of their functions was not widely acknowledged. Thus, at both district and national levels the funding of their activities became a perennial problem and the 'perpetual headache of . . . finance'[3] weakened the status and negotiating position of both district and national organisations in their relationships with local authorities and central government as well as with other providing and funding bodies. In the history of the Eastern District, the ambivalence of such virtues and disabilities underlined the relative success and failure in its growth and development and provided a continuous set of recurring themes from its creation to the present day.

The Eastern District – A Deliberate Strategy?

As in so many other ways in the early years of the WEA, Mansbridge was the main architect of district organisation. It is contended that the establishment of the Eastern District was a direct outcome of his wider strategy and initiatives with Cambridge University in 1913.

The precise circumstances surrounding the establishment of the

3

District are not entirely clear simply because documentation appears not to exist and there is no record of a declared policy plan for its formation. However, it seems reasonable to infer that following the lead taken by Oxford in 1907 it was imperative for Mansbridge to seek to establish similar arrangements at Cambridge, the original source of university extension and where there was an outstanding record of experience and endeavour in serious study opportunities for adult students. Perhaps because of this record, there appears to have been less enthusiasm for WEA Tutorial Classes than existed at Oxford. Certainly, arising from its unique role in, and commitment to, university extension from 1873, the introductions of WEA Tutorial Classes at Cambridge were seen as:

> . . . a legitimate development of the old University Extension System, but they were more intensive than most of the older courses.[4]

This was the view of D. H. Cranage, Secretary to the Cambridge Syndicate from 1902, and although welcoming WEA Tutorial Classes as a new development he believed they fell within the university's existing provision for university extension and did not require separate arrangements through a new joint committee of WEA and university representatives which had been recommended in the 1907 Oxford Report and adopted by other universities. It is probable that this view endured until May 1913 when a joint Tutorial Classes Committee was formed at Cambridge and reflected a university reluctance to differentiate within its own provision for university extension. As Cranage and Mansbridge were the joint secretaries of the new committee, it seems likely that the agreement also reflected the success of persuasion by Mansbridge over a period of some years. As suggested later, there is some evidence to indicate that Mansbridge had planned to establish a WEA District in Eastern England in 1911 or 1912.

Nevertheless, it is important to recognise that the formation of the WEA in 1903 had been welcomed, and supported, by the university and members of its Syndicate. James Stuart, G. F. Browne, J. B. Paton and D. H. Cranage all made personal donations to central or local WEA funds. In 1905, the Syndicate agreed to donations to the WEA and in 1906 offered scholarships (essentially in the form of remission of fees) to members of the WEA to enable them to attend the Cambridge Summer Meetings for adult students and in 1913 the support was extended to the introduction of the Cambridge Summer School for Tutorial Class students and some fifteen students were enrolled. In 1909, WEA Tutorial Classes were offered at Cambridge Extension Centres in Leicester, Portsmouth and Wellingborough and for these new courses

Mansbridge was given considerable freedom by Cranage to organise them and others through the nomination of tutors, selection of students recommended by local WEA branches and who paid only nominal class fees as the Syndicate generously made up the fee-deficite from its own funds.[5] In 1912, the first two of these centres were included in the Board of Education's specially commissioned, and subsequently celebrated, report on fourteen Tutorial Classes inspected by HMI.

Thus, by 1913 WEA Tutorial Classes had become an established feature of the Syndicate's work, supported by Board of Education grant-aid as well as through annual grants from several Cambridge colleges (notably Trinity) and individual donations. In May 1913, the reality was given constitutional status through the establishment of the Tutorial Classes Joint Committee composed of five representatives from each of the WEA and Syndicate parent bodies. Mansbridge had secured the objective of a formal, regularised association with Cambridge University and his other, and earlier, activities also matured which were to lead to the formation of the Eastern District. Although scanty, the evidence for concluding that Mansbridge had, at least, a personal strategy for the Cambridge connection is corroborated by Bernard Jennings' perception of Mansbridge as a 'skilful manipulator with a subtle mind' which accurately reflected his orchestration of an apparently fortuitous conjunction of people and events.[6]

Although the absence of firm documentary evidence allows a subjective interpretation of the ways in which the Eastern District was established it appears that by 1912 at the latest, Mansbridge was developing a plan, the shape and timing of which may have been influenced by fortuitous factors, to which attention must now be given.

Early in 1912, George Pateman, a Mancunian carpenter, moved to Letchworth in search of improved health and regular employment in the first of the planned 'New Towns' and boarded with an uncle who had preceded him. Then aged 24, Pateman had been a member of the first Tutorial Class held in Manchester in 1909. Some years earlier he had been an active member of the Independent Labour Party (ILP) and of his union (the Associated Society of Carpenters and Joiners) and had been so impressed by reports of the WEA and Mansbridge's activities for improved educational provision for working people that he had joined the WEA. In the Manchester Tutorial Class Pateman had met a young printer, William Lowth, who was to play an indirect but decisive role in shaping Pateman's later career when they met again in 1912 in Letchworth, to which Lowth had also moved in search of employment. Among many active new voluntary societies, Letchworth had a vigorous

WEA branch which Pateman joined and of which he became honorary secretary in that year. In 1912, Pateman first met Mansbridge when he attended a WEA meeting in London – possibly at the Southwark branch. Like many others, Pateman was profoundly influenced by the dynamic, mercurial Mansbridge and became a devoted admirer, friend and colleague. He regarded Mansbridge as 'the lynch-pin in the development of the Movement'; a view he held unswervingly throughout his life and which subsequently coloured his views of Mansbridge's successors, especially Mactavish.[7]

As secretary to the Letchworth branch, Pateman invited Mansbridge to speak at a meeting in the new town, at which Pateman again met Lowth. Mansbridge invited both men to join forces with him in working for the WEA mainly to extend and consolidate its growth through the formation of a new District in Eastern England, apparently at that time, 1912, without any clear geographical delineation. Both agreed to his proposal but in the event Mansbridge chose only Lowth for the new venture.

In Pateman's view the choice of Lowth was both appropriate and correct. At that stage in the development of the WEA it was vital to attract the attention and enlist the support of trade unions, a matter in which the WEA had not been really successful in its formative years and over which Mansbridge had been criticised. Apparently, Lowth was of greater value than Pateman in such matters as his father was then general secretary of the Associated Society of Railway Servants. Lowth moved to the central office of the WEA in Red Lion Square, London, as acting pro tem secretary of the new District in late 1912 or early 1913 and began to develop a skeletal communication linkage with existing branches in a dauntingly large area from the outer fringe of the London District, formed in 1912, through East Anglia and extending to Lincoln.

In the initial conversation with Mansbridge and Lowth at Letchworth in 1912, Pateman had expressed some doubts about the concept of district organisation and believed the strength of the WEA lay with its branches rather than at a district tier of organisation. Further, he thought Mansbridge's envisaged District would be difficult to establish, organise and maintain. He told Mansbridge 'it would break the heart of the first man, but the second man might succeed'.

Nevertheless, with Lowth's assistance Mansbridge pressed ahead with the formation of the new District and by March 1913, the few existing branches in the nascent District had been visited by Lowth and then circularised about the proposed new district organisation. The eight branches involved at this formative stage were: Colchester, Ipswich,

Kettering, Letchworth, Lincoln, Luton, Norwich and Wellingborough – all important urban manufacturing centres with some owing their origins to university extension as centres under the Cambridge Syndicate and others under the aegis of the Oxford Extension Delegacy, viz. Luton and Wellingborough.

The first record of a District meeting (although there may have been an earlier one in 1913) was on 29 March 1913. It was held at Trinity College, Cambridge, and was attended as was customary at that time by the secretaries of existing branches. Pateman thus represented Letchworth but in 1965 was unsurprisingly unable to recall any details of the meeting except that it was agreed to proceed with the formal establishment of the new District. However, he did remember that it was his first visit to Cambridge and, even more vividly, the unique pleasure of taking tea in an undergraduate's room at Trinity!

His failure to recall some fifty-two years later any details of the meeting, of which no minuted record exists, is hardly surprising. He regularly attended many meetings at that time, some in connection with elementary education provision in Letchworth, others for political reasons through his membership of the ILP and even more in connection with his increasingly important trade union activities. In 1912–13, the WEA was not amongst his most important or pressing concerns. The greatest claims on his time were in association with his union activities in which he was becoming a prominent figure in Letchworth. In 1913 he was elected chairman of the local trades council as well as secretary of the local branch of the Associated Society of Carpenters and Joiners, in which capacity he arranged practical classes for his fellow members to improve their skills as craftsmen. As a member of the ILP he was active in local politics, narrowly failing to win a seat on the parish council in May 1913 – a more important office then than today. Also, in May 1913, he became 'President' of a strike committee of Letchworth carpenters as a result of which he organised a march of his members who were in dispute with their employers, the New Town Corporation, and a little later gave evidence to the conciliation council established to resolve the dispute and which was chaired by Sir George Asquith. Pateman eventually negotiated an end to the dispute having secured an increase of ½d. in the hourly rate, which he regarded as an honourable compromise as the original claim had been for an increase of 1d. on the hourly rate.

About the same time, he was appointed a member of the Managing Body of Norton Elementary School, Letchworth. The appointment is significant in its indication of the value which Pateman, even then as a young bachelor, placed upon educational provision and over which he differed from other contemporaries of similar political persuasion. The managing body of the school held their meetings in the afternoons and although Pateman 'lost time' and therefore wages, he believed 'it worthwhile as education was the key to everything' – an appropriate sentiment of a disciple of Mansbridge.

A further indication of his political activities was his support of women's suffrage and at Letchworth he first met Clara Rackham at a public meeting. She was a prominent non-militant suffragette, a Cambridge academic, subsequently a WEA tutor and chairman of the Eastern District and Pateman could not have foreseen that some years later they would work closely together in the cause of adult education at Cambridge.

Despite all these demanding responsibilities and interests, Pateman gradually became more closely involved in the work of the WEA. At Mansbridge's invitation, he joined the council for the South East District in January 1913 and in the following month, again at Mansbridge's suggestion, he returned to Manchester to attend a meeting of the Central WEA. That he should have accepted Mansbridge's invitation to participate more fully in the work of the WEA is perhaps comprehensible only because of his attendance at the Summer Meeting at Balliol College, Oxford, in July 1912 when he achieved a long-held ambition to attend a summer school. He was much impressed with the concourse of adult working men and women with distinguished Oxford tutors. To attend the Oxford summer meeting, he cycled from Letchworth, a distance of some fifty miles, and the Oxford experience made such a deep and lasting impression on him of the value of summer study opportunities that when in due course he became District Secretary he channelled his energies and enthusiasm into the organisation of the Cambridge University summer schools for many years.

At Oxford, Pateman again met Mansbridge and E. S. Cartwright, the organising secretary of the Oxford Joint Committee and who had been a student in the first Longton Tutorial Class. He also met Zimmern and Tawney, perhaps the two most distinguished Oxford tutors in the early years of university support for Tutorial Classes. The most enduring recollection of Oxford, however, was Pateman's first meeting with Reuben George of the Swindon branch. With Mansbridge, George appears to have had a profound effect on Pateman's developing attitudes over the potentiality of the WEA's role and contribution to the education of working adults, denied access to extended educational opportunities beyond the then circumscribed, rudimentary system. Many years later in recalling these early experiences, Pateman considered George '. . . a wonderful man . . .' who was '. . . the best example of a working man who wanted to know'. According to Pateman, Archbishop Temple shared his own admiration and officiated at George's funeral some years later.

Thus, it appears reasonably certain that in the summer of 1912 Pateman's interest and involvement in the WEA was no longer peripheral. He had met the major figures in the Association, had attended his first summer meeting for Tutorial students, and had been impressed by the genuine interest, support and sense of mission shown by those Oxford University tutors who contributed so much to the early growth and credibility of the early WEA. It seemed therefore reasonable that he accepted willingly the office of honorary secretary of the new Eastern District as successor to Lowth in 1913. He was unaware of the reasons behind the invitation but believed it was at Mansbridge's suggestion. Certainly he knew that Mansbridge wished Lowth to devote more of his energies and time to extending his activities in developing links between the Association and the trade unions.

In recalling the circumstances more than fifty years later, Pateman resisted the temptation of claiming any prescience about the future growth of the District. He had neither sought the office of honorary secretary nor was he pushed into it. He simply believed he could be of assistance in the growth of the new district organisation, which included his own branch, and quite natural that he should offer his talents and experience to help Mansbridge achieve his objective. Further, and of considerable importance to Pateman's own existing commitments, the immediate responsibilities of the office appeared undemanding. He envisaged the role as one of providing information for a few branches; as a reference source for existing and parturient branches, and acting as a linking-pin for them with the central organisation at the London office.

Although there is no documentary evidence, it is possible that Mansbridge had sensed the growing interest and closer involvement of Pateman in the WEA – indeed he may well have stimulated it. He was clearly aware of Pateman's influential position in trade union affairs in Letchworth which could have been used to stimulate and extend links with other unions at local and, possibly, at regional levels. Further, there appears to be no evidence that Mansbridge had gained an early foothold in the Cambridge area with recognisably working class organisations. With Pateman as a member of the University/WEA Joint Committee for Tutorial Classes, also established in 1913, it was possible that as District Secretary the young trade unionist might prove to be influential in the growth of the Association from an artisan base which would match and emerge as a parallel force with the university's own involvement. If this confluence of influences were achieved then Cranage's firm view that Tutorial Classes were merely an element in the university extension provision would require modification and Mansbridge was acutely aware that Cranage had been 'especially instructed to emphasise the experimental and temporary character of the scheme'. Although other universities were increasing the number of Tutorial Classes, Cambridge had only four at this time, mainly organised by Mansbridge, who from 1912 acted with Cranage as joint secretary for their administration.[8]

In addition to the existing Wellingborough Tutorial Class in English Literature, tutored by A. J. Wyatt, two further Tutorial Classes were arranged in the region by the Syndicate, with Mansbridge's encouragement, prior to the formation of the Eastern District. In Michaelmas Term 1912 the Norwich WEA branch began its three year course in Economic History with Frank Salter, Fellow of Magdalene College, as its tutor. A term later, the Ipswich WEA branch began its course in the same subject and was tutored by W. G. Constable, St. John's College. Some years later Frank Salter became the District's honorary treasurer from 1918–31 and was a member of the Syndicate and its successor body the Board of Extra-Mural Studies from 1914–57.[9]

As Joint Secretary to the Oxford Delegacy's Joint Committee for Tutorial Classes, Mansbridge was also aware that the Delegacy had arranged a Tutorial Class in Economic and Social Problems in Luton in 1910. The tutor here was J. G. Newlove who was to become the District's first salaried tutor in Norfolk in the nineteen twenties. Further, in 1912 the Delegacy arranged two further Tutorial Classes, in Economic and Constitutional History both tutored by Miss Helen Stocks, at Kettering and Lincoln.

Thus by 1913 it was clear that '. . . tutorial classes were a permanent part of the Syndicate's work'.[10] Mansbridge clearly saw the opportunity for the new District to be established with immediate representational and organisational functions for adult education in the area he had earlier discussed with Lowth and Pateman and arising from developments which he probably encouraged and orchestrated.

The Early Years

As honorary secretary for the new and largely undefined District, Pateman faced a variety of problems and opportunities from the outset. The establishment of the Syndicate's Joint Committee for Tutorial Classes in May 1913 precipitated Pateman into an important role before he could have really considered his functions as District Secretary. In this respect he must, at least in retrospect, have thought himself fortunate. He was provided with an immediate opportunity of encountering the working of university committees and observing at first hand the attitudes of significant figures in the university and the WEA especially Mansbridge who was, with Cranage, Joint Secretary to the committee. He also learned of the ways in which policies and regulations shaped the provision of Tutorial Classes under the aegis of Cambridge and how the relationship between the supply and demand elements were co-ordinated. It must have been both a stimulating yet intimidating experience for the young carpenter from Letchworth.

He saw the impressive diplomatic and political skills of Mansbridge in negotiation with Cranage and the committee, heard from Layton and Angus of their experiences in tutoring classes, learned from Goodman (another WEA member of the committee) of the developments in the London District of the WEA and became aware of the wider issues raised at the Central Joint Advisory Committee, on which Goodman represented the Syndicate's Tutorial Classes Committee. Another member was St. John Parry who enjoyed a considerable reputation for his published work on adult education and, of course, there was Cranage himself. In such distinguished company, Pateman perceived himself as a '. . . watcher and listener' and discovered yet again in his early years in the WEA that he 'was the youngest involved wherever I went'.[11] He freely acknowledged his indebtedness to that early experience as a member of the Syndicate's Joint Committee.

To Cranage, Pateman owed particular gratitude. The cordial personal relationship between Mansbridge and Cranage prepared the way for his own association with the latter. He believed Cranage openly welcomed the participation of the WEA in adult education and fostered the Association's growth and development in the Eastern District. The relationship between them from 1913 until Cranage's appointment as Dean of Norwich in 1928 was unfailingly 'open and cordial'. Cranage, the senior man by some twenty years to Pateman freely provided the considerable guidance Pateman required not only about the provision of adult education but, more urgently, about the ways of the university. As Pateman later confessed about the extent of his personal problem: 'I did not know what a college was, or a Master, or even how important Cranage was' when referring to his first year as Secretary of the District.[12]

Until Mansbridge was forced through ill-health to withdraw from active involvement in the work of the Syndicate's Joint Committee in 1915, Pateman acted as his adjutant; constructing a network of

11

contacts, building good if deferential relationships with members of the committee, encouraging groups and branches to consider Tutorial Class commitments and interpreting the demands of the WEA to those who approved classes, provided tuition and the necessary finance. As an accepted member of the Joint Committee he gradually increased his value and prestige, not least through his enthusiasm and efforts in connection with the University's Summer Schools, organised by the Joint Committee, which eventually led to a largely unfettered hand in their arrangement. For his services in organising the summer schools Pateman initially received a modest fee which increased significantly as part of his salary when some years later the District encountered severe financial difficulties. It is therefore unsurprising that throughout his life, Pateman respected and admired the work of the Syndicate which was rooted in his relationship with Cranage and his early contribution to the activities of the Joint Committee. These and other difficulties, considered in later chapters, undoubtedly weighed heavily in his decision in 1935 to accept an appointment with the Syndicate's successor body – the Cambridge Board of Extra-Mural Studies.

But all these considerations lay ahead of the young Pateman who was re-elected at the first annual general meeting of the Eastern District in July, 1914. The meeting was held at the Passmore Edwards Settlement, Tavistock Place, London, and attended by officers of the existing WEA branches. Although not all were active in 1913, representation came from eight formally constituted branches at Colchester, Ipswich, Kettering, Letchworth, Lincoln, Luton, Norwich and Wellingborough. Of these, Ipswich and Wellingborough had Tutorial Classes arranged by the Syndicate. Norwich, established in 1912, also arranged a Tutorial Class under the Syndicate at Cambridge. Luton and Kettering had arranged classes under the Oxford Delegacy, the latter becoming active again in 1913, after a brief lapse, because of local WEA member- stimulus. Other branches arranged a variety of activities; from single lectures to short courses and preparatory classes from which it was hoped Tutorial Classes would emerge. Study circles also existed as part of preliminary activity for more substantial courses and the formation of new WEA branches, such as at St. Albans where lecture courses were arranged in conjunction with an existing Adult School.

At the time of the first annual general meeting in July 1914, Pateman was ill and was re-elected in his absence. His inability to attend was caused by a combination of overwork and a physical pre-disposition to ill-health – a clear indication of the difficulties he encountered through engagement in his wide interests during the first year as District Secretary.

The review of the District's first year was not entirely promising. Individual membership of the District had increased from 189 on its formation to only 224 at the end of the year and some anxiety was expressed about the District's future. Any misgivings were, however, swept aside by the outbreak of war in the following month. That there was little District activity during the summer of 1914 was attributable not so much to the war as to Pateman's continuing illness during a period when the planning of lectures and classes should have been undertaken for the following session.

Worse was to follow. Pateman was a convinced pacifist and during the early months of the national emergency he experienced considerable personal difficulties. Some of these are revealed in his letter to Dorothy Jones, Mansbridge's secretary, on the 26 October 1914:

> I feel uncertain as to the future, things are very bad here and I may have to move; while there are married men walking about I shall be out of work. The only work ... is building Military Huts on Salisbury Plain and elsewhere and my conscience keeps me away from Military centres. A result of refusing work at one of these my unemployment benefit has been suspended so I am living on my savings. That of course cannot go on, so if I do not get work locally soon I must consider moving. Should this happen I would ask you to look after my district until my return.[13]

The sense of commitment and personal identification with the Eastern District conveyed by the sentiment in the final sentence is a clear indication of the development of Pateman's attitude during the previous year. In November 1914 he volunteered to work in a non-combatant unit of the Society of Friends and early in 1915 was posted to central France where he was employed in the construction of hutted accommodation for refugees from embattled areas.

As he had requested, his duties as District Secretary were assumed by Dorothy Jones, in addition to her other duties at the central office of the WEA. At this time, Mansbridge was in Australia and thus Miss Jones was in a position to undertake the additional work of the new District. In 1916, Pateman returned briefly on leave and gave time to the growing activities of the District. For example, he spoke at a public meeting in Bedford, called to consider the formation of a WEA branch, and which by the end of the war had become the largest in the District. Before returning to France he had a meeting with J. M. Mactavish who had succeeded Mansbridge as the General Secretary of the Association in February 1916, to discuss his future role as District Secretary. Pateman's recollection of this first meeting was that he was '... a real Scot: fiery

. . .'. It was not a congenial encounter and they were destined not to co-operate amicably in future years.

Pateman returned finally from France where he had worked for the War Victims Relief Committee to a temporary post at the London office of the Society of Friends and on 1 September 1917 he was appointed as the first full-time salaried Secretary of the Eastern District of the WEA. The appointment stemmed from an earlier undertaking given by Mansbridge who, although still convalescing, had attended the second annual general meeting of the District held at Queens' College, Cambridge, in July 1915. At that meeting, Mansbridge had committed the Central Council of the WEA to favourable consideration of such an appointment subject to the continued growth of the District and an improved financial position of the National Association.

Unquestionably, Mansbridge was conscious of the importance of a well-founded District working in close association with Cambridge university – certainly the modest growth of the District during the early years of the war would not have otherwise warranted such favourable consideration. In 1917, Mactavish honoured the undertaking given by Mansbridge in 1915 but before accepting the appointment, Pateman discussed the role and its implications with Mansbridge. Arising from their discussion Pateman became conscious of the importance of moving to Cambridge to establish the District office in the city and the establishment of formal relationships with the University's Syndicate and the Tutorial Classes Committee all of which had been important Mansbridge objectives. Pateman was in a position to accept the appointment because having appeared before the War Service Tribunal on at least two earlier occasions he was granted the relatively rare absolute exemption and registered as a conscientious objector.

The outbreak of the war created particular difficulties in the new District. Of the existing eight branches, Colchester suspended its activities almost immediately in 1914 as the town became the most important military base in eastern England and there were many restrictions. In 1915, Norwich and Letchworth became inactive but the others continued and even expanded their activities through seizing opportunities arising from the national crisis. For example, Wellingborough and Ipswich made 'educational conferences' a regular feature of their programmes in the form of evening or weekend meetings to consider war-related topics. Ipswich introduced lecture series for soldiers who were stationed just outside the town. A particularly ambitious event was a tri- partite branch meeting at Ipswich in October 1914 when members of the Ipswich, Norwich and Colchester branches were addressed by the national WEA President, William Temple. The success of this meeting led to a successful winter session in 1914–15 at Ipswich where branch membership increased and Tutorial Class activity was extended.

The following table summarises the growth of the District throughout the war years and indicates the stimulation to WEA activity provided by the serious issues arising from that conflict; a trend reflected elsewhere in the country.

Table No. 1

Branch	Membership 1914–15	1915–16	1916–17	1917–18
Bedford			85	216
Braintree				51
Chelmsford				34
Colchester		Suspended activities		
Halstead			24	54
Hitchin			46	58
Ipswich		57	80	118
Kettering		8	51	110
Letchworth		Suspended activities		
Lincoln		10	8	23
Luton		16	28	18
Norwich			30	35
Wellingborough		57	49	74
Totals		148	401	791

Ipswich, Norwich and Colchester were originally university extension centres under the Cambridge Syndicate. Wellingborough arranged its first Tutorial Class under the Syndicate in 1909 and Luton in 1910 under the Oxford Delegacy. Thus, the early branches of the new District had their roots in university extension with apparently only Letchworth and Kettering directly influenced by the growth of the WEA; the former to the stimulation of Pateman and the latter by the formidable presence and enthusiasm of Miss Helen Stocks.

By the end of the war, thirteen branches existed, of which Colchester and Letchworth maintained a nucleus of organisation but without any organised activities. But from 1916, public interest in the WEA increased and much of it was stimulated by two pressing national issues both of which were taken up by the National Association as major policy issues.

These were: Post-war Reconstruction and the new Education Bill. In addition, the growth in interest and strength of the branches shown in the table was partially attributable to Pateman's appointment as a full-time salaried Secretary from 1917 when he was able to devote his time to promote the growth of WEA activity in the District. He visited regularly the more accessible branches such as Bedford, Halstead, Hitchin and Kettering and by 1918 most of these were flourishing branches. For example, the growth in 1917–18 was reflected in the formation of eighteen new study circles, more that seventy single lectures, most on the two major topical themes mentioned above and several short courses of lectures and discussions were also arranged dealing with post-war reconstruction or the Education Bill.

Post-war reconstruction was perhaps the more important as it arose from a government committee which was elevated to a Ministry of Reconstruction in 1917. The other topical issue arose from the Education Bill published in 1917. In both cases, the WEA launched national and conspicuously successful campaigns to press for adult educational development and improved educational opportunities in the then rudimentary statutory system of education. National publications by the WEA were widely distributed; local, regional and national conferences were held in late 1917 and early 1918 which fuelled the debate. All the active branches in the District arranged conferences on one if not both issues. For example, those on the Education Bill were held in conjunction with other interest groups such as the National Union of Teachers. In Ipswich, in both 1917 and 1918, a jointly arranged meeting attracted an audience of more than 250 and debated the issues raised in the national WEA pamphlet *What Labour Wants From Education*.

In Bedford, a similar meeting organised in conjunction with the NUR led to the trade union branch supporting the recommendations of the WEA which was circulated to all NUR branches throughout the country and other meetings on either or both of these topics were held at Halstead, Hitchin, Kettering and Norwich.

This ferment of activity reached its peak at a national conference on Educational Reconstruction held in London in May 1917, addressed by Temple, which adopted a whole range of recommendations for expansion of educational opportunities. The recommendations were swiftly printed and distributed to all WEA branches throughout the country. At this conference the Eastern District was well represented through the attendance of the District Chairman, S. J. Hutley, an Ipswich teacher, Miss Jones, who substituted for Pateman who was then in France, and six other representatives from the District's branches as well as others from the University Syndicate. The momentum generated by this and other conferences, significantly assisted in the growth of the National WEA as well as at local level and helped to publicise the radical attitude of the Association in connection with programmes for social and educational reform and, incidentally, to expanding the influence of the WEA as a democratically representative organisation. For the District, the national and regional influence of these two major issues, were important in publicising its existence and led to increased membership, a rise in the number of societies affiliated to the District, and the establishment of links with kindred organisations such as trades union branches, local co-operative societies and teachers' organisations.

A glimpse of the influence of this activity is reflected in the record of a meeting of the District Council in September 1917. While there was a general welcome for the Fisher Education Bill as a measure for the establishment of a national system of education, it was regretted that nursery education could not be made available to all children. Further criticism of the proposals pin-pointed problems such as an absence in the Bill of guidance on the maximum size of classes in schools, the discretionary attitude to medical treatment of pupils, the failure to prohibit the employment of children and the absence of educational provision for pupils who had left school under the age of fourteen before the Bill was enacted.

In all these hectic months of late 1917 and throughout 1918, Pateman was closely involved. In that period he addressed some forty meetings of adult schools, trades councils, co-operative societies and also a meeting of senior pupils at Holt Grammar School, Norfolk, and the Cambridge University Conference of History Teachers. He also spoke at many branch meetings and study circles, exhorting his audiences to believe in an educated democracy in its search for improved educational opportunities and the recognition of adult education provision as part of the national fabric of education through the WEA in alliance with Cambridge University.

On balance, the growth of the District even under the adverse circumstances of the war years and much affected by the toll of that conflict was encouraging. Although some decline in three-year Tutorial Classes occurred, the District established a network of branches and other preparatory centres for post-war growth and in 1916 its optimism was reflected in the adoption of its first constitution at the annual general meeting which incorporated changes made in the national constitution in October 1915.

Under the 1915 revision of its constitution, the National WEA became representative of the corporate interest rather than that of individual members. Thus, the national committees were composed of, governed by, and financed through the Districts and nationally affiliated bodies. In effect it meant that from 1915, the organisation of the WEA was based on collective control by Districts with the result that the organisation of the National Association was dependent on the effectiveness and financial strength of the constituent Districts – a matter in which the Eastern District, by no means the only one, was to fail consistently in the years following the war. This degree of devolution was entirely within the spirit of the WEA tradition, but it presupposed sound constitutional and financial bases at District level. At that time, some Districts were not financially self-sufficient: indeed the Eastern District was administered and financed through the WEA Central Office. Following the 1915 amendment to the national constitution, which enhanced the importance of district organisation, it became necessary to consider defining the geographical extent of the Eastern District. It was agreed that it should be delineated as covering the nine counties in eastern England from the northern fringe of London to the northern boundary of Lincolnshire, a distance of some 150 miles; and from the east coast to the western limits of Northamptonshire, a lateral distance of some 130 miles. It was the largest geographical District in England and apart from the later transfer of Lincolnshire to the East Midlands District when it was established in 1921 and the subsequent inclusion of south Essex and south Hertfordshire in the London District in 1930, the boundaries of the District were identical to those of the present time. Pateman must have frequently recalled the doubts he expressed to Mansbridge in 1912 about the formidable tasks facing the District Secretary of such a large area.

Nevertheless, the confidence of the District in adopting its 1916 constitution was reflected in the chairman's report at the annual general meeting:

> In the light of the present needs of the Eastern District it may seem a little too complicated and drawn upon too large a scale, but it has been prepared with an eye to the future when the Eastern District, the most difficult of all the Districts to organise and co-ordinate with its widely scattered and comparatively weak branches, shall have become what we all desire it to be . . . [14]

The objectives were simply that there should be a WEA branch in every town and many villages after the end of the war. For Hutley, Pateman and others the District's functions were conceived as performing a linking mechanism for the mutual help and support of all branches, affiliated societies and individual members in the geographically large District, made more difficult because of its predominantly rural character and lacking an extensive public service communications network. In addition, there was the important function to provide advice, arrangements and assistance to branches in securing for them educational study opportunities.

The simplicity of District organisation in 1916 did not require the office of District Treasurer as its financial affairs were handled by the National Association, although provision was made for such an appointment in the 1916 constitution. Similarly, the activities of the District were so limited that a District Executive Committee was not required until 1919, when the 1916 constitution was modified to allow its formation. Until then, business was dealt with at the twice-yearly District Council meetings.

However, the appointment of Pateman as a salaried officer of the District entailed an inescapable commitment to raise funds to meet that charge, at least partially, as the National Association's undertaking over his salary had not been given in perpetuity. The National WEA encouraged all its Districts to achieve financial self-sufficiency as quickly as possible – a matter which led to difficulties between it and the District a few years later. More evident was the early recognition of a need to increase income substantially if the District's activities were to be developed and sustained after the war. Future difficulties were foreshadowed early. The initial response to fund-raising in the District was not encouraging and in 1918, the total income from 128 affiliated societies and 867 individual members produced only some £40 with a further £10 contributed by branches in the region.[15] Troubled by this poor response, the June 1918 annual meeting agreed that a levy of 1d. in every shilling received from classes arranged by branches should be contributed towards District funds. Even so, the inadequacy of these new arrangements was almost immediately apparent by January 1919 when the District rejected a levy on it of £30 suggested by the National WEA towards the costs of central organisation of the movement on the grounds that the amount proposed would consume some 40% of the existing income of the District. It was obvious that at the end of the war a District Treasurer should be appointed and the District more energetic in its efforts to achieve financial self-sufficiency, excluding Pateman's salary, by the end of the 1919–20 financial year. The first District Treasurer appointed in late 1918, was F. R. Salter, Fellow of Magdalene College, and an experienced tutor for the Cambridge Syndicate, of which he was also a member. Salter had also tutored the Norwich

Tutorial Class in 1912–13 and was a staunch supporter of the WEA. He was well-known to Pateman as both were members of the University's Joint Committee for Tutorial Classes. Immediately, Salter was faced with a daunting prospect of finding new, more successful ways of increasing District income in its search for financial independence, and the end-of-year accounts prepared by the central WEA in May 1919 revealed the extent of the difficulties. The credit balance was less than £40 and even this modest balance concealed the reality of the financial problem as the National Association had paid Patemen's salary of £125 from its own funds as promised. It had also provided a loan of £25 to the District as a goodwill gesture; had accepted the District's rejection of the £30 levy and a reduction to the lowest acceptable minimum of ten guineas as the District's affiliation fee to the national WEA. The District was bracketed with the two publicly acknowledged 'depressed areas' in the country, the Scottish and Welsh Districts, an unenviable distinction for a District associated closely with the prestigious Cambridge University, and one with ambitious objectives for the growth of its activities in the post-war period.

Thus, by the end of the war and notwithstanding the foreshadowing of financial problems, it was considered that the Eastern District was reasonably well-founded and it faced the post-war period with bounded optimism. Its constitutional position was clear; a salaried District Secretary was in post, now married and living in Cherryhinton Road, Cambridge, which served as the District Office, and one of Mansbridge's central objectives to establish a WEA presence in close association with the 'other' university in a partnership of co-operation and amity, if not yet equality, was within foreseeable realisation. Less certain and clear were the initial steps taken to establish the District as a self-sufficient organisation although guarded optimism was evident through the appointment of a distinguished university tutor as its honorary treasurer. Pateman was bustling around the District and in addition to the anticipated growth in the number of Tutorial Classes during post-war reconstruction, the number of branches had begun to grow towards the end of the war. In 1918, there were thirteen branches with new ones formed at Braintree and Chelmsford in the final year of the war; revival of older branches occurred at Colchester, Letchworth and Norwich and the smallest branches at Lincoln and Luton offered a promise of continued growth during the period immediately following the Armistice in November 1918. The future was not unpromising.

George Pateman,
District Secretary 1913–35

Frank Jacques,
District Secretary 1935–83

NOTES

1) See for example:

Albert Mansbridge: *University Tutorial Classes* (1914)
An Adventure in Working Class Education (1920)
The Trodden Road (1940)

T. W. Price: *The Story of the Workers' Educational Association* (1924)

The Oxford Report: *Oxford and Working Class Education* (1909)

2) Bernard Jennings: *The Oxford Report Reconsidered* (1975)
Albert Mansbridge and English Adult Education (1976)

Roger Fieldhouse: *The Workers' Educational Association: Aims and Achievements, 1903–1977* (1977)

Tom Kelly: *A History of Adult Education* (1970)

Mary Stocks: *The Workers' Educational Association, the First Fifty Years* (1953)

3) Mary Stocks: ibid. p.51

4) D. H. Cranage: *Not Only a Dean* (1952) p.96

5) Edwin Welch: *The Peripatetic University: Cambridge Local Lectures* (1973) p.109

6) Bernard Jennings: op.cit. (1976) p.13

7) Williams: conversation with George Pateman. The following sections about the establishment of the District are derived from conversations in October and November 1965.

8) For example, in 1914 London provided 30 Tutorial Classes, Oxford had 18, Manchester 17 and Liverpool 16 in that year.

9) Reports on all three Tutorial Classes provide much interesting detail about the quality of work submitted by students and their occupations. The reports were printed in the Cambridge Local Examinations and Lectures Syndicate Reports on Tutorial Classes, 1909–1911 (for Wellingborough) and 1912–1913 (for Norwich and Ipswich).

10) Edwin Welch: op.cit. p.113

11) Williams in conversation with Pateman November 1965.

12) ibid.

13) G. H. Pateman's Letter Book, Botolph House.

14) District Annual General Meeting, 1 July 1916:

Chairman's Report by S. J. Hutley, Minute Book No.1, Botolph House.

15) Annual Report: Statement of Accounts, 1917–18, Botolph House.

CHAPTER 2

CAUTIOUS OPTIMISM AND MAJOR PROBLEMS:
1918–24

A Contextual Background

The period following the end of the war in November 1918 brought many changes which were unforeseeable prior to its outbreak. The diffusion of national wealth in the shape of purchasing power as a result of 'war wages' made life somewhat easier for working people immediately afterwards but this amelioration was linked to an uneasy realisation that earlier values, ethical standards and social stratification were being transformed as the certainty of the Edwardian period rapidly crumbled. These changes, not dissimilar from those accepted as inevitable after the Second World War, were unprecedented in 1919 and were reflected, in part, through the election of a coalition government under Lloyd George. Significantly, as a result of electoral reform and the enfranchisement of women over the age of thirty, the Labour Party for the first time became the official opposition. It is also possible to infer that with the growth in political power of the people and experience of direct political action by trade unions and the suffragettes the earlier interest in education as a routeway to power declined relatively with a new perception of the expanding provision of education as the main avenue of social mobility.

For example, Lowndes, writing in 1937, estimated the rapid growth in the number of schools as an increase in excess of 100% between 1914 and 1921 which in his view reflected 'the changes that had been going on in the previous twenty years – the multiplication and increasing accessibility of schools, the growth of appreciation among parents, the example of others – had been working silently and unsuspected beneath the surface to create a new desire for education'.[1] These factors together with the stimulation of the Balfour Act of 1902 and the generation of interest in the issues of the Fisher Act of 1918, were important contributory factors in the awakening of interest in wide sections of the population to the importance of, but hitherto inaccessible, possibilities of educational opportunity.

Earlier reference has been made to the activities of the WEA at

National and District levels in the campaign for increased educational provision in 1917 and 1918. Some of these were in conjunction with teachers' organisations in the elementary and secondary sectors of education in addition to its own campaigning in alliance with universities for improved access to adult educational opportunities. Thus, the WEA played an important role in the leavening of public opinion and in the formation of attitudes leading to a demand for increased educational provision while at the same time drawing attention to itself as an educational movement with general objectives as well as specific ones for the education of adults.

As a result of these activities post-war optimism was high. The National Association increased its financial resources briefly after the war; activities of its Districts and branches briefly expanded and a temporary period of rapid growth spurred on by public interest in national reconstruction occurred. However, the early 1920s proved to be a difficult period with social and economic conditions creating problems of similar magnitude, if for different reasons, to those of the war years. Both Price and Stocks have provided a clear outline of this period as one of growth for the WEA under difficult and testing conditions at National level through a combination of much activity but lacking adequate funding to support it. This pattern was reflected in the Eastern District and was exacerbated through conflict between the Association's General Secretary and Pateman. The District experienced major difficulties over its survival which were not resolved with any degree of confidence until the Adult Education Regulations were introduced in 1924, which marks the end of this chapter.

As noted earlier, Pateman, now married, moved to Cambridge in late 1918 and set about the task of establishing the work of the District on a permanent footing in co-operation with the university through the Joint Tutorial Classes Committee, of which he became joint secretary with Cranage at that time, in succession to Mansbridge who, in turn, was elected Vice-Chairman of the committee. He was also aware of the National Association's expectation that all Districts would become organisationally and financially self-sufficient within three years of their formation. Although this was never defined in calendar terms for the Eastern District, it was assumed that the three-year period began with Pateman's full-time appointment in September 1917.

With the framework of the 1916 District constitution as his guide, and conscious that district organisation occupied a pivotal position in the WEA's structure, Pateman undertook a demanding programme of visits to existing and potential WEA branches. He also engaged in the search for subscriptions from a great variety of people, institutions and companies; cajoled local branches of trade unions to support the work of the new District, and gave lectures and talks on the aims, objectives and progress of the WEA on two or three evenings every week. Rough notes and outlines of his talks have survived, well thumbed through much use and amended as fresh ideas and material arose, all of which indicate that his style was that of an evangelist rather than a logician. His passionate belief in the inalienable rights of just, democratic citizenship which education would bring to those hitherto deprived of educational opportunities in earlier life is evident from them. The model for success which he offered relied heavily on the past achievements of the co-operative movement and trade unions in the nineteenth century in that the mobilisation of the opinion of working people had led to 'strength in unity'. He argued further that the accumulation of social and political knowledge was an essential preliminary step which required harnessing to skilful leadership to carry working people towards the promise of an educated democracy. From these notes there appears to be no evidence of any reference to his mentor's belief that education might be conceived as a tenable objective *per se*. Mansbridge might well have been disappointed.

As Pateman interpreted his role and considered the formidable tasks before him in the new District, the demographic characteristics and the limited public service transport facilities at a time when the motor car was a novelty of a privileged elite, it became obvious that while not eschewing opportunities for growth in rural areas, his priorities would be in developing the work of the WEA in the industrial zone of Northamptonshire, in the larger market and administrative centres such as Bedford, Lincoln and Norwich, and in the extra-metropolitan fringe of Essex and Hertfordshire. These were also the centres in which the District's activities were developing and which had, in some cases, experience of an adult education tradition prior to the formation of the District. On the other hand, the rural communities in Cambridgeshire, Huntingdonshire, Norfolk, Suffolk and North Essex appeared for the immediate future to lie beyond the reach of the slender resources available to Pateman and the practical possibilities of securing tutors for any classes for which a demand might exist, or be stimulated.

With this concentration of focus, Pateman was able to capitalise on the novelty of, and enthusiasm for, the new District. Substantive links with, and support from, the Syndicate developed mainly through an early increase in the number of Tutorial Classes arranged – some directly as a result of his proselytising work – and his status and effectiveness gradually increased in the period immediately following the end of the war.

The National Association was generally disappointed with the 1918 Education Act as most of the issues on which it had campaigned had been omitted. However, the Act imposed a duty on each Local Education Authority to prepare educational development schemes for improvements in the education service. Economic problems in the 1920s prevented much effective progress but provided the WEA with opportunities to continue to campaign for improvement in educational provision within the maintained system; to voice community concerns in a collective way and to maintain vigilant overviews of LEA proposals. For example, the Ipswich branch was invited to nominate members to sit on three borough committees for educational development under the 1918 Act and the Lincoln branch formed its own committee to consider the implications of the Act which met with an LEA committee to discuss the planning of adult education provision in the city.

As LEAs were charged with a responsibility for future planning of adult education provision, the publication of the government's 1919 Final Report on Adult Education became an important document in WEA campaigning.[2] In the Eastern District the majority of the LEAs were largely rural and it was natural that the focus of attention should extend beyond the urban areas, in which some WEA development had already occurred. Further, the District had encountered considerable difficulty in establishing itself in rural areas either as provider of educational opportunities for adults or as a cohesive movement promoting social change.

The 1919 Final Report and Rural Adult Education

The special problems of rural areas were considered in the Final Report of 1919 and the Committee concluded that a re-creation of rural communities was necessary through the development of new social and cultural traditions. In the furtherance of this formidable task the role of adult education was central and the Committee advocated the case for new statutory regulations for adult education and improved levels of grant-aid as essential stimuli for its provision. Significantly, the 1919 Report conceived the main effort should be through the establishment of a corps of resident tutors in rural areas whose functions would be to organise and provide educational activities, commonly found in urban, industrialised centres but absent in most rural regions. The conditions in the latter reflected the social and economic conditions of the previous century and the position had been exacerbated by the continuous drift of young people to the new urban areas and consequent rural depopulation, a trend accelerated during the war.

Before 1914, agriculture was in a depressed, stagnant, isolated condition: long hours of work, low wages and the 'tied cottage' system with its concomitant insecurity of tenure, combined with little development of road and rail networks produced a sense of social introspection and acceptance by many in dispersed communities of farm workers locked into pre-industrial social stratification. In these conditions, with only rudimentary trade union organisation among agricultural workers, there was little prospect for the development of adult education. Further, the universities and the WEA had neither the staff resources nor adequate finance required to stimulate and satisfy any incipient demand for adult education. The war brought a clear recognition of the importance of agriculture to the national economy, its well-being and even survival and inevitably brought into sharper focus the social and economic conditions of rural life. Not only was it an important matter for the Ministry of Reconstruction but the National WEA gave specific attention to the problems of rural adult education from 1917 onwards through the formation of a sub-committee on rural education. Pateman as the recently appointed District Secretary for the region which contained the 'granary' of England and which extended over the largest rural area in the country, was the natural choice to become its secretary.

In July 1918, the sub-committee produced the WEA's short report *Rural Reconstruction* outlining its policies for the development of adult educational provision.[3] It anticipated the 1919 Report in its particular emphasis on the importance of resident tutors for future development who would organise the provision and teaching within groups of rural communities. The recommendations were not unique. Similar small-scale arrangements had been made in Sussex and Warwickshire in earlier years. Immediately after the war, Warwickshire had appointed staff tutors for rural education, but the WEA report of 1918 established its policy for rural areas and one which has continued to the present time. It was a policy which was to dominate the future planning of provision in the Eastern District during the following seventy years through its staffing and organisational strategies for resident tutors and county federations of WEA branches.

The reality of such a policy had major implications not merely for finance and accessibility of rural areas but also for the degree of freedom over the selection of subjects for study and tutors, which had been perceived as centrally important to the success of the WEA's early development. Nevertheless, the WEA sub-committee was sufficiently convinced that these limitations were of a lower priority than the urgent objective of providing opportunities for sustained study in rural areas and believed villages would welcome the organised provision of adult education and accept some measure of constraint on their freedom in the selection of subjects for study and tutors. Initially, this assumption provided to be correct, but as the work in rural areas developed, difficulties over the central tenet of freedom for branches to exercise choice arose and persisted until improved public transport and wider car ownership gradually emerged during the 1930s. In the Eastern District the difficulties and solutions were exemplified through the experience of J. G. Newlove and H. C. Shearman, considered later in this chapter and in the following one.

Unsurprisingly, Pateman developed a deep and enduring interest in the development of rural classes and courses: initially in Norfolk and Cambridgeshire, and, later, in Bedfordshire, East Suffolk and Essex. Funding for the establishment of resident tutor-organisers was, however, difficult to secure and in January 1920 Pateman reported at the District Council meeting that schemes could not be introduced simply because the National Association lacked finance to initiate or underwrite its policy. He thus devised his own improvised, practicable solution to attempt to break new ground in rural East Anglia.

He assembled sets of lantern slides, and wrote or borrowed accompanying notes, much in the style of the later school film-strip kits, to provide a comprehensible commentary. These were packaged in stout wooden boxes which, on request from a village, were despatched to the nearest railway station for pre-arranged collection by a local clergyman or teacher who would then arrange a meeting in the village and provide the illustrated talk before returning the box to Pateman at Cambridge. The most widely used box appears to have been a set of glass slides illustrating the changing pattern of the rural countryside from Saxon times to the Seventeenth Century which was subsequently modified and improved as 'English Rural Life in the Middle Ages' with the notes revised by a Cambridge University historian. It proved to be a timely and felicitous choice of topic and was much in demand for village and small rural town audiences, laying foundations for several subsequent rural WEA branches. For example, in one unidentified village, at least seven miles from the railway station, an evening talk was given by the vicar in a crowded classroom in a village school to which many villagers carried their own chairs and following which more requests for lectures were made. But Patemen had difficulty in responding to the request in 1920 at the start of the enterprise, and it is not known if any further provision was made at that village.

Pateman gave many talks to more accessible rural audiences but conceded that although valuable in stimulating and reflecting the extent of considerable interest in relatively isolated communities, they inevitably suffered from the superficiality of single 'popular' lectures about which much criticism had been made of university extension, and over which the WEA itself had been trenchant. Eventually, he accepted that the 'village lecture' did not in many instances lead to a measurable expansion in serious, sustained study to which the WEA had a commitment and the real growth in One-Year courses and Tutorial Classes in rural areas had to await the appointment of resident tutors and improved communication networks before rural adult education could become a reality in the District.

One other brief attempt to provide adult education in rural areas was made in 1919–21 by the Ipswich branch. With Pateman's encouragement, this established, active and flourishing branch arranged a series of meetings in outlying villages in the hope of stimulating interest in the WEA through the formation of study groups. It was hoped some, if not all, of these would provide a basis for the creation of new branches and more formal study opportunities. But after a year or so, the problems of organisation, of finding leaders and volunteer tutors among the membership of the Ipswich branch led to a loss of enthusiasm which, coupled with a limited response from villagers, appears to have been insurmountable and the experiment was abandoned.

The Norfolk Scheme – I

Nevertheless, the apparently distant goal of appointing resident tutors in rural areas became an immediate possibility when in April 1920, the Norfolk LEA invited the District to submit a proposal for a pilot-scheme of one-year classes for adults in the north of the county. For Pateman and the District's Executive Committee the problem was to find a tutor who would be prepared to undertake the work as the LEA had guaranteed financial support for only one year and the District itself could provide no financial aid for the scheme. Further, the National Association was at that time experiencing a major financial crisis and even though the Norfolk initiative was an attractive prospect, it was unable to offer any financial support to the District.

Fortuitously, the problem over the tutorship resolved itself through the availability of John Newlove, an experienced former Oxford Joint Committee tutor, who was at that time convalescing at Nayland Sanitorium, near Colchester. Faced with the prospect of almost certain unemployment on discharge, Newlove was keen to accept the tutorship on its temporary basis and he was appointed by the District following a satisfactory medical examination. The agreed salary, paid by Norfolk LEA, was £200 a year and a further £50 was to be made available from District funds to meet anticipated expenses in connection with the scheme. In the event, the latter sum was not paid, because of the District's perennial financial difficulties. With Newlove, Pateman devised the scheme for the LEA involving classes at five centres, each to be visited by Newlove on a different evening each week. Thus they had to be close to each other and accessible by rail. After local consultation, the five centres were: King's Lynn, Wells, Melton Constable, Fakenham and East Dereham and they all followed the same course of study on 'Industrial and Social History Since 1760', extending over a period of twenty weekly meetings during the autumn of 1920 and the spring of 1921. Attendance at all centres was excellent. At Wells, for example, twelve students attended all meetings, a further eleven missed only one week and some cycled several miles from surrounding villages to attend. Unfortunately, no personal records of the students have been found and no registers of classes appear to have survived, but it is known that at Melton Constable, then an important regional railway centre, the class consisted largely of railway employees, some of whom often left the classes to work their night shifts.[4]

Newlove's account of his weekly itinerary of class meetings hardly suggested that of a patient recovering from serious illness who lived at the Nayland Sanitorium throughout the pilot year. On Monday mornings he caught the train from nearby Colchester to King's Lynn to take the class there that evening. This class is known to have enjoyed the active support of the Society of Friends in the town and, subsequently, three of his students became county councillors and one, mayor of the borough. Each evening after the classes, Newlove stayed overnight with a class member, leaving the following morning by train to his next centre. In these ways he worked his way around north Norfolk to the East Dereham class on Friday evenings, correcting written work submitted while travelling on the train before returning to Nayland on Saturday mornings.[5]

That Norfolk should have been the first LEA in the District to initiate a scheme is, perhaps, a reflection of the conscious recognition of the importance of adult education established as a traditional attitude by the Society of Friends in the previous century. It would appear that its approval by the LEA was almost entirely attributable to the support given to the proposal by the Vice-Chairman of the county's education committee, Alderman Sam Peel, a Quaker, who knew of Pateman through the Society of Friends and with whom he had corresponded in earlier years about the work of the new District. The Peel family were to become staunch supporters of the District's work in Norfolk over many subsequent years.

The pilot scheme's programme was a resounding success and the interest which it stimulated led to its continuation and, in the case of Wells and East Dereham, to the provision of two three-year Tutorial Classes, each with Newlove as its tutor, and based on the encouraging standard and amount of written work undertaken during the first year, although there had been no requirement for students to submit any. With the approval of the Cambridge Tutorial Classes Committee; the status conferred by that body's imprimatur and its greater security over finance and duration, Newlove moved to live in Wells following his discharge from Nayland. Norfolk LEA continued to provide financial support and three further one-year classes were organised: at King's Lynn, Melton Constable and at Wymondham, the last named replacing Fakenham as a new centre. The LEA increased its funding through a salary increase for Newlove with a further £120 in recognition of responsibility for two Tutorial Classes. In addition, £40 was made available for each one-year class to support their activities and slightly smaller sums were provided for advertisement of the classes, printing of leaflets about the classes, administrative costs in connections with Newlove's duties for the classes as well as a small sum to supplement books obtainable from the Central Library for Students. Most generously, the LEA also allowed class fees to be retained by the centres for local use in connection with the development of their educational activities. All this financial support was on a scale unmatched by other LEAs in the District for many years.

Thus, by 1924, the Norfolk scheme was well established and the first two Tutorial Classes had successfully completed their three-year study programmes. During the four years, 1920–24, the Norfolk LEA had provided funding of about £1,500, a sum which easily outstripped the financial support for adult education by all the other local authorities in the District's region. This unprecedented support also demonstrated the immediate, beneficial effect of a resident tutor in a large rural area and where in earlier years the WEA had managed to establish itself only in Norwich, some thirty miles to the south.

For Pateman, the Norfolk scheme was the crucial first major step in his ambition to organise adult education provision in rural areas. It enabled him to demonstrate that not only was he, as secretary of the

31

WEA's national sub-committee on rural education, in the forefront of the Association's enterprise, but through its introduction had reached the very apex of the WEA's educational endeavour – successful Tutorial Classes in two centres serving a rural area. But his critics might have questioned the accuracy of 'rural area'. In reality the Norfolk scheme was based on urban populations in five small towns with additional class members drawn from surrounding villages. Nevertheless, important new developments had occurred: the scheme had been successful because of LEA financial support to launch and sustain it. The scheme had also demonstrated the value of the provision of preliminary courses of study before attempting the very demanding regime of three-year Tutorial Classes. In its early achievements the Norfolk scheme was a considerable success for the communities in which it was based; for the demonstration of the degree of co-operation between the LEA, the University Syndicate and the WEA; and not least for pointing the way forward for further development some five years later when the first genuinely rural adult education scheme was introduced in Bedfordshire. The glimpse of the possibilities in Norfolk in the early 1920s, became a reality elsewhere in the District a decade later.

The Norfolk scheme ended in 1926, largely as a result of the further illness of John Newlove. The LEA continued to accept full financial responsibility for Tutorial Classes in the following years but the original pioneering scheme lapsed in that year. Following a partial recovery, Newlove resumed as tutor to the Wells Tutorial Class, but the scheme had run its full distance and early enthusiasm had been lost. There were criticisms of Newlove as a tutor both in north Norfolk and within the Syndicate – he was the only non-graduate tutor employed by the Joint Committee for Tutorial Classes, but it must be said that he had proved to be a successful tutor during the early years of the scheme and had in many ways exemplified the aspirations of the early WEA and the hopes expressed in the Oxford Report, 1908.[6]

The Kettering and District Scheme – I

In addition to the Norfolk scheme, and contemporaneous with it, the District was developing its urban organisation for adult education and from 1919 its main focus centred on Kettering. The initiative here came through the National Association which had endeavoured to attract financial support for pioneering adult education activities. In 1919, the Cassell Trust offered to fund the appointments of five tutor-organisers to initiate adult education provision among working people over a period of three years.[7] Resident tutors were appointed in Hampshire, the East

Riding, South Wales, Scotland, and Kettering and District in 1919–20. The choice of Kettering stemmed from two considerations. First, an active interest in the WEA had been sustained from its earliest years and classes had been provided under the Oxford Delegacy some years before the District was formed; at Northampton, Wellingborough and Kettering. The industrial centres for boot and shoe manufacturing were dispersed with the largest employer being the Co-operative Society. Further, the high level of female employment and the well-organised trade union organisation made the area prominent in the provision of classes for both men and women with, occasionally, segregation of the sexes. Secondly, Miss Helen Stocks had established a considerable reputation as an Oxford tutor over several years and in 1915 had organised all-female classes as a preliminary step towards a full three-year Tutorial Class for women. Her work in Kettering had attracted national attention and when the District was offered a Cassell Trust funded appointment, Miss Stocks volunteered to act as guarantor for a further £100 a year to promote the work of adult education with an emphasis on the development of classes for women.

Further, in her first all-female class in Kettering, Miss Stocks much admired Miss Sophie Green, an employee at the Co-operative Society's clothing factory. Her tutor regarded the caring young woman and devoted student as an example of a working woman who could and should be developed as a leader of women in industry and as someone who recognised the value of adult education in the continued emancipation of women. Miss Green enjoyed considerable status within her peer working group and although it is doubtful if she was seriously regarded as a proletarian counterpart of the redoubtable Maude Royden, she was apparently cast in a similar mould. As a person of considerable influence, it is probable that it was Helen Stocks who had suggested to the Cassell Trust the idea of funding pioneering initiatives and also proposed that Miss Green should be one of the tutor-organisers and it is equally probable that these were decisive factors in the choice of Kettering. In the final consideration of the nominations, Kettering was selected and it was unanimously agreed that Miss Green should become the tutor-organiser.[8]

She began her duties in November 1919, returning almost immediately to the Co-operative clothing factory which she had left only a few weeks earlier in order to conduct a women's class in English Literature. With the full approval of the factory manager, the scheme was launched under the most propitious of circumstances and although many difficulties arose in later years, Miss Green was to serve the District continuously in the industrial triangle of Northampton-Corby-Rushden until the onset of the war in 1939.

Initially, Miss Green's activities were centred on Kettering and the district within a twelve mile radius of the town, a decision taken on the accessibility by public transport of potential centres for development. Her work was under the direction of Pateman, and her salary was almost identical to his and more securely funded. Although her work was not exclusively with women, it was with those of her own gender and background that she was most at ease and successful. Initially, she was somewhat limited as a tutor both in terms of her own educational background and in undertaking a teaching role. She attempted to overcome these major disadvantages through attending tutor training courses at Hollybrook House, Reading; at a variety of summer schools and, later, studied at Bryn Mawr College, Pennsylvania. Her academic achievements were never remarkable but she did possess considerable native ability, intelligence, commitment and sincerity – all of which she brought without reservation to her work. Her main virtues lay in a genuine concern for, and great sensitivity with, her adult students and she gave freely of her time in the provision of individual tutorials at her home to encourage confidence and assist with written work in addition to the prescribed two-hour weekly class sessions. Whatever shortcomings she may have had in the strictly academic and pedagogic sense, there was widespread gratitude from many of her students for her sincere and devoted attention to their individual needs. She was much appreciated as a tutor who understood and sought to meet the genuine needs of her students – an important WEA precept.

Her main interests as a tutor in the Kettering district were English Literature and Industrial History and she was apparently successful over many years in teaching introductory, preliminary short courses and one-year classes in both subject areas. She was, of course, encouraged constantly by Helen Stocks who provided a mentor role over her work and progress as a tutor. Miss Stocks must have been gratified by the unsolicited praise for Miss Green's efforts which came from members of her classes. For example, it was not uncommon for several women to meet at her home on a tutorial or study group basis during the summer months when no classes were programmed with much of the activity being given to preparation for study either at summer schools in Cambridge or in anticipation of the following autumn's classes. A few members of her classes went to Girton College for a term's residence where, in a masterly under-statement in the District's annual report for 1921–22, 'they were able to acquaint students with conditions in industry'. Four others followed in 1923–34 to Newnham College and an established pattern of residence at Newnham's summer school for working women began which continued up to 1939.

Undoubtedly, Miss Green achieved much in the Kettering area for women who had considerable ability but who had been denied, like herself and so many of her generation, opportunities for secondary and higher education. It was for such people that the WEA proved to be attractive in the 1920s; providing opportunities for serious, sustained study which no other form of adult education could offer at that time. Miss Green was herself a remarkable woman and in more generous times would almost certainly have proceeded to a college or university education. Helen Stocks clearly recognised the latent ability and sought to employ it away from the factory bench. Miss Green undertook a formidably demanding programme, but additionally, was secretary of the Kettering WEA branch and served in a similar capacity to the Co-operative clothing factory's education committee. On her appointment as tutor-organiser in 1919, George Chester, later to become General Secretary of the National Boot and Shoe Operative Union, described her as 'the ideal person . . . sympathetic, studious, not afraid of hard grinding work and . . . displays a vision which few people reach'. Daniels, the manager of the Co-operative clothing factory at Kettering, and her previous employer, believed she had been 'the inspirer of educational work among the workers which had developed in a very fine manner' before her appointment as the District's tutor-organiser.[9]

As a result of her qualities and energetic activities the number of short courses and study circles expanded considerably. However, her highly individual, personal way of meeting everyone interested in arranging courses or classes and her commitment to individual tuition led to a less than full teaching programme and questions arose at District and national levels during the first year about her work-load. Pateman resolutely defended her, conscious that the organising functions of her work made considerable demands on time and effort, often for scant visible reward. His own experience as District Secretary was not dissimilar and he said so in a letter to Helen Stocks in 1921 '. . . organising comes out badly on paper'. Pateman showed an avuncular liking for Miss Green, regularly visiting centres in her area, corresponding in a variety of helpful ways on a weekly basis, usually over matters of administration and routine work in connection with her classes. He also well knew and understood many of her difficulties as the factory-hand turned tutor. Miss Stocks was also aware of the difficulties and regularly consulted Pateman about them. The correspondence in these early years indicates that on occasion, pretentious working people who were members of reading and study circles and employed as clerks and shop assistants considered themselves socially superior to their tutor and their attitudes to Miss Green were as deeply wounding as they were unjustified.

Although Miss Green received the wholehearted support of Pateman and Miss Stocks, they were realistic about her abilities and the limitations of her role. For example, when it was mooted that she might be the tutor for a three-year Tutorial Class for men at Irthlingborough in 1920–23, Miss Stocks vetoed the proposal on grounds of suitability and competence to meet the exacting, sustained academic standards required of tutors at that level. Nevertheless, when the District submitted an application to the Cassell Trust for the renewal of her salary grant Miss Stocks, with the active support of Tawney, instructed Pateman to inform the Trustees that they 'ought to be thankful to get Miss Green . . . (she) . . . is capable of doing first rate educational work and it would be a great pity not to give her a really good chance' through renewing the grant-aid to enable her to consolidate and extend the valuable pioneering work undertaken during the initial period.[10] Pateman agreed; did as he was asked and the Kettering scheme was financed by the Cassell Trust for a further three years.

However, the issue over her teaching load led to a major difficulty in 1921, and with hindsight it is difficult to escape the conclusion that it was Miss Green herself who created the crisis. It was ironic that Pateman unwittingly provided the flash-point. A mildly worded request from him, undoubtedly relayed on behalf of the District's executive committee, that she should consider the possibility of increasing the number of classes taught by her produced an anguished response wholly disproportionate to the matter. The District, local branches in the Kettering district, the National Association, Tawney and Miss Stocks were all swept into a verbal convulsion in the defence of Miss Green with the unfortunate Pateman at its centre – and its target. It is clear from the correspondence that Miss Green had misconstrued Pateman's original request as one which called into question the standard and quality of her work as tutor-organiser. Undoubtedly, the physical demands of her commitment to the development of adult education in Kettering and district as organiser and tutor, her unstinting support given to individual women students, her personal sensitivity to others and, perhaps above all, an inner tension about her own confidence in her role meant that she was under considerable pressure during the initial phase of her appointment. The upshot was that in April 1921 she tendered her resignation,

36

crucially at a time when the renewal of grant-aid was under consideration by the Cassell Trust.

The origins of the difficulty lay not with Miss Green or Pateman but in the terms of appointment. The Cassell Trust had provided funds for the appointment of a tutor with the not unreasonable expectation that a large proportion of the duties would entail teaching classes of adults. The District had appointed Miss Green as tutor-organiser, seeking to stimulate development through classes and courses in the industrial villages around Kettering to which Pateman had been able to devote little time and energy – particularly as at that time he was involved in the development of the Norfolk LEA scheme. With a dual responsibility, it is unsurprising that the number of classes taught by Miss Green was lower than those of other tutors supported by the Cassell Trust. It is almost certain that the discrepancy was noted at the WEA central office when the details of the activities of all five tutors were collated for reporting to the Trust. At that time, Pateman feared that unless Miss Green increased the number of classes and courses taken by her, renewal of the Cassell grant would be jeopardised – a matter of considerable gravity as both the National Association and the District were in severe financial difficulty. Without securing renewal of the Cassell funding the Kettering scheme would have been abandoned. The prospect in late 1920 and early 1921 was bleak, and concern was expressed over future relationships with the Cassell Trust if it were discovered that funds intended for tutoring had been used for the organisation of demand for courses and classes.

Miss Stocks was also alarmed at the possibility of termination of the Kettering scheme. It and Miss Green's appointment had been actively promoted by her and it had been only with considerable difficulty that she had raised the personally guaranteed £100 a year to support the scheme; much of that sum coming from her own resources. In correspondence with Pateman in early 1921, it is clear that Miss Stocks was determined neither to lose her protege nor abandon the Kettering scheme and its potential in furthering the cause of women's education. Eventually, in June 1921, Miss Stocks in concert with Tawney and Pateman persuaded Miss Green to withdraw her resignation and, apparently, without the Cassell Trust becoming aware of the District's crisis the grant was renewed for a further three years with Miss Stocks again acting as guarantor for £100 a year.

With the difficulty resolved, Miss Green's self-confidence increased and she also recognised the need to demonstrate both her tutoring and organising achievements more overtly. Her pioneering work had been recognised, she was a prominent figure in the Kettering branch and a respected member of the local community, while her work with individual students was widely admired as being in the finest tradition of the WEA and much approved by Tawney. Through her continuing trade union membership she had established personal links with Newnham College and had used that contact to provide opportunities for women members of her WEA classes at summer schools and through periods of residence in Cambridge. Following the renewal of the Cassell grant, she reaped the benefits of earlier spadework in the Kettering area and beyond, through the establishment of new branches at Corby, Desborough, Rothwell and Thorpe Malsor during 1921–23. In addition, she extended her programme of talks and short courses with local Adult Schools, Young Co-operators and Women's Co-operative Guilds. She also consolidated her work and position through taking one-year courses at Kettering, Desborough and at Corby. At Corby, developing as a major iron and steel centre, she overcame a number of local difficulties to establish a branch in 1921–22 and in addition to her own pioneering one-year course, she added in the following year a fortnightly class in Economics conducted by Mr. Wallis, a former member of an earlier Tutorial Class in the subject held at Kettering.

By 1924, the Kettering scheme was firmly established and confirmed the importance of the struggle to retain it in 1921. The loss of Miss Green's appointment would have been a serious setback for the District in its development of the resident tutor principle. The experience gained in both Norfolk and Kettering was valuable and laid foundations for later, more secure development of adult education in the District.

District Development

It is important to record that there were other encouraging developments in the provision of adult education in the District during the period 1918–24, and these are now considered. The distribution and scale is summarised in Table 2.

As mentioned earlier, even before Pateman's full-time salaried appointment in September 1917, modest growth had occurred in the District (Table 1.). By the end of the 1918–19 session, individual membership of branches exceeded 1,200 and a further four branches had been established in Cambridge, Stowmarket, Woodbridge and Castle Hedingham increasing the District total to fifteen. Castle Hedingham, in north Essex, was thought to be a significant breakthrough in that it was the first 'village' branch in the District, but although apparently well-founded with forty registered members, it appears not to have organised a class

Table 2. Eastern District: WEA Branches/Centres 1918–24
Tutorial (T) and Other Classes (OC)

	1918–19	1919–20	1920–21	1921–22	1922–23	1923–24
*Bedford	OC-3	–	T-1 OC-1	T-1 OC-1	OC-2	–
*Bourne	–	–	–	OC-1	OC-2	OC-1
*Braintree	OC-1	–	–	–	–	–
*Cambridge	OC-2	OC-3	OC-7	OC-5	T-1 OC-5	T-1 OC-5
*Chelmsford	OC-1	OC-1	–	–	–	–
*Corby	–	–	–	OC-1	OC-2	OC-3
Desborough	–	–	–	–	–	OC-2
*East Dereham	–	–	OC-1	T-1	T-1	T-1
Fakenham	–	–	OC-1	OC-1	–	–
*Halstead	OC-1	OC-1	T-1	T-1	T-1	OC-1
*Hitchin	OC-2	OC-1	OC-4	OC-1	–	–
Holt	–	–	–	–	OC-1	–
*Ipswich	OC-4	– OC-3	T-2 OC-4	T-2 OC-4	OC-4	OC-4
*Kettering	T-1 OC-6	– OC-10	T-2 OC-9	T-2 OC-8	T-2 OC-8	T-2 OC-6
King's Lynn	–	–	OC-1	OC-1	OC-1	–
*Letchworth	–	OC-1	OC-1	–	–	–
*Lincoln ‡	T-1 OC-5	– OC-4	T-2 OC-3	–	–	–
*Louth ‡	–	–	OC-1	–	–	–
*Luton	–	–	OC-1	OC-1	OC-2	OC-1
Melton Constable	–	–	OC-1	OC-1	OC-1	OC-1
*Northampton	–	OC-1	–	–	T-1	T-2
*Norwich	OC-1	OC-2	OC-1	T-1	T-1	T-1
*Peterborough	–	–	OC-2	OC-4	OC-2	OC-3
*Raunds	–	–	T-1	T-1	T-1	T-1
Rawreth	OC-1	–	–	–	–	–
*Rothwell	–	OC-1	–	OC-1	–	–
Saffron Walden	OC-1	–	–	–	–	–
*St. Albans	–	OC-1	OC-2	OC-2	OC-3	OC-4
*Spalding	–	–	–	OC-1	OC-1	OC-2
*Stowmarket	–	–	–	OC-1	–	–
Thorpe Malsor	–	–	–	OC-1	OC-1	–
*Wellingborough	OC-1	–	OC-1	OC-1	–	–
*Wells	–	–	OC-1	T-1	T-1	T-1
*Woodbridge	–	OC-3	–	OC-1	–	–
Wymondham	–	–	–	OC-1	OC-1	OC-1
TOTALS 35	T=2 OC=29	T=5 OC=32	T=9 OC=42	T=10 OC=39	T=9 OC=36	T=9 OC=34

* = WEA Branches
‡ = Branches which were transferred to East Midlands District in 1921

and was disbanded within a year of formation.

As Table 2. indicates, during the period 1918–24, and in spite of serious difficulties, the growth of the District's activities was encouraging, if not spectacular, both for its quantitative increase and the stability of sustained development under severe social and economic difficulties which affected most of the country. In 1919–20, the number of branches rose to eighteen; in 1920–21 to twenty-two with a slight decline to twenty in the two following years. Of these branches, eleven had established themselves on a continuative, self-sustaining and largely sound organisational basis with responsible, conscientious branch officers who observed the requirements of their constitutions, approved by the District under its 1916 constitution, and with a continuous record of educational activity reflected in the number and variety of courses provided. The eleven WEA branches with these commendable characteristics were: Bedford, Cambridge, Halstead (See Appendix C), Hitchin, Ipswich, Kettering, Luton, Norwich, Stowmarket, Wellingborough and Woodbridge. Of the other, nine were either of recent origin and suffered through inexperience of branch organisation or from uncertainty about purpose at that time viz. Bourne, Corby, Northampton, Peterborough, Rauds, Rothwell, St. Albans, Spalding and Wells. The remainder were classified as branches which had failed to maintain their earily enthusiasm and waned during the difficult years following the war: Braintree, Castle Hedingham and Chelmsford. Two other branches, Lincoln and Louth, were transferred to the new East Midlands District in June 1921, when the District's northern boundary was more closely defined, as extending from the mouth of the Welland westwards to Witham.

There was a corresponding growth in the number of Tutorial and other classes of sustained study. For Tutorial Classes the early signs were encouraging. It will be recalled that during the war, these classes were suspended under the Cambridge Joint Committee arrangements but the Oxford Delegacy continued to arrange classes on a restricted scale and two of these were conducted by Miss Stocks at Kettering and Lincoln. By the end of the 1923–34 session, eight Tutorial Classes were arranged by the Cambridge Joint Committee; the Oxford Delegacy was responsible for one, at Kettering, the other at Lincoln having been transferred to the East Midlands District. As shown in Table 2. Tutorial Classes were held at widely dispersed branches during this period: Bedford, Cambridge, East Dereham, Halstead, Ipswich (2), Kettering (2), Lincoln (2), Northampton (2), Norwich, Rauds and Wells. Kettering was a long established branch and at this time the centre of the Cassell funded scheme, but it was also unique in the District in that it organised

Tutorial Classes under both university joint committees. In 1922–23, the Oxford Delegacy arranged a women's class in Ancient History and in the following year the Cambridge Syndicate provided a class in English Literature. The pattern continued until 1931 when the Cambridge University Board of Extra-Mural Studies assumed responsibility for all Tutorial Classes in the Eastern District.

Although impressive initially, the demands of the WEA's unique contribution to adult education through the Tutorial Class concept were difficult to maintain. The commitment to Tutorial Class study was acknowledged as demanding but the National Association resisted attempts in the post-war period to modify either the efforts required of the tutor or those of the student, a stance which had been reinforced following publication of the encomium in the Hobhouse and Headlam Report 1910.[11] It was never conceived that the Tutorial Class would appeal to, or become a reality for, the majority of adult students. Thus, the Tutorial Class was at the apex of educational achievement for students and branches and in the District it was acknowledged that in most cases branches required time and experience to establish a tradition for extraordinary dedication and sustained effort by students before embarking on the considerable work of a three-year Tutorial Class. In this context, it was a substantial achievement by branches in a new District to undertake some fifteen Tutorial Class commitments during the period under consideration.

Other, more attractive alternatives became popular following the war, arising at least partially from the limited opportunities available during war-time restrictions when the arrangement of public lectures and short lecture-based courses proved to be successful between 1914–18. Some branches such as Bedford and Ipswich found attendances at such single or serial public lectures very encouraging and the atmosphere redolent of earlier university extension short courses except that the themes were related to topics about the war, or politics or sociological concerns rather than those traditionally provided under earlier university extension arrangements. The other characteristic feature of branch activity during the war was the arrangement of reading circles and study groups, in many cases intended to maintain the fabric of the organisation and an educational momentum.

The effect of these improvisations and *ad hoc* arrangements extended into the post-war period and led to a significant increase in requests for, and provision of, shorter courses. A new membership, mainly women, was attracted to WEA courses and the appeal was more easily recognised by those for whom a pledged commitment to the rigorous three-year Tutorial Class was too demanding. The trend in the District is revealed in Table 2. and was encouraged both because of its scale of growth and also in the hoped-for building of interest in adult education which might become a launch-pad for more serious, sustained study offered through the Tutorial Class. Several of the latter arose from one-year preparatory classes which, in turn, not infrequently stemmed from earlier experience in study circles or short courses. From the existing records it is clear that following the war, the original premiss of branch formation to provide local organisation and momentum to sustain three-year Tutorial Classes exemplified by the pioneering work in Reading, Rochdale and Longton was modified in response to demand by potential or existing branch members. It also marked the beginning of a dilution in the sense of commitment to a social movement endeavouring to create an educated democracy – a central tenet in the original objectives of the National Association.

The interest in, and requests for, short, less demanding courses of study gradually increased and the range of contemporary issues and problems – political, economic and social related to the war, its causes and post-war solutions – powerfully stimulated interest. Pateman, through the District's organisation, provided information on speakers, syllabuses and topics to enquiring groups and branches in order to promote the expansion of the District's activities and to use the initial interest to stimulate the local organisation of demand as a nucleus around which a WEA branch might grow. The objective continued to be educational through the formation of WEA branches but no longer principally for the purpose of ultimately arranging Tutorial Class study opportunities. This was a recognition of the expressed needs of working people and a latent demand for serious study in relatively small classes over shorter time-scales of six, ten, twelve or twenty-four class meetings and without a prescribed commitment to undertake written work.

Further, there were obvious and immediate benefits for the District. The increased range and flexibility in provision was perceived as valuable to the National Association's and the District's public visibility and esteem in that it encouraged a much wider section of the community to participate in and benefit from voluntary educational activities. The District tackled these new opportunities with vigour and confidence as they offered it, and the National Association, a field of untrammelled activity, independent of university committees and regulations and occupying a stratum of educational provision between that offered by LEAs and the universities. Here, the WEA created new opportunities for liberal adult education which were attractive across the spectrum of social class and occupational structure, in addition to those already existing through Tutorial Class provision which some members of short courses subsequently found attractive.

For example, in 1918–19, the Bedford branch arranged two one-year courses in European History and Public Speaking; a reading circle on Shakespeare and a one-day conference on the recently published Whitley Report and its implications for the national industrial system. At the Ipswich branch in 1920–21, and in addition to two Tutorial Classes, a series of lectures was provided on International Relations as well as a class for trade union officials and three study circles. These examples illustrate the range of interests in communities which the WEA attempted to serve as well as to stimulate interest in itself as a voluntary democratic educational movement, in the absence of initiatives taken by the LEAs.

The Role of the Local Education Authorities

The role of LEAs was defined with greater clarity in the Education Act of 1918 in respect of their statutory provision for elementary and secondary education and clarified their powers and duties over the education of adults seeking vocational and technical training. For liberal adult education provision, no significant development occurred, so much so that the Final Report of the Adult Education Committee, 1919, commented trenchantly on the attitudes generally held by members of LEA education committees:

> It is to be feared that there is still a number of education committees who are unable to understand a desire for education of no utilitarian value, unless it be for the purpose of personal accomplishment, and who suspect dark motives in the minds of those who desire such education. More especially is this so where the demand is for study of problems which are controversial. It is within our knowledge that there are even today town councillors to whom the term 'economics' is synonymous with 'socialism'. The majority of those who most desire to study do so probably because of the interest they have already taken in industrial or other public affairs. They include, for example, a large number of active trade unionists and local trade union officials. This is presumably the basis for the charge sometimes made by Local Authorities, and suggested even by some members of universities, that the classes 'encourage discontent and socialism'.[12]

There were exceptions to this acerbic observation among which were the London County Council's non-vocational afternoon/early evening institutes established in 1913, but most provided evening schools exclusively for vocational instruction and training. Where LEAs supported the activities of WEA Districts and branches it was commonly in the form of grant-aid for Tutorial Classes or through the provision of rooms in educational premises without charge. Earlier, financial support had been given to offset the costs of university extension courses, usually in the form of modest annual subscriptions, for example in Kent and Staffordshire. Initially, a few local authorities had adopted a similar practice towards the WEA. In the District, the attitude of the Norfolk Education Committee was amongst the most enlightened of local authorities in that it recognised the existence of social and individual needs of its largely agricultural and dispersed rural population. There was a fortunate conjunction in Norfolk of key people who were supportive of the objectives and purpose of the WEA. As mentioned earlier, the most significant of these was Alderman Sam Peel but recognition must also be accorded to Lamport Smith, who was Assistant Secretary to the County Council over a period of several years. The rapport and trust established between the District and the local authority was reflected in the early development of the Norfolk scheme in 1920 and by 1923 the respective responsibilities of LEA and Eastern District were understood and succinctly put in a letter from Lamport Smith to Pateman on 26 November 1923. Over the provision of a short course at Aylsham he stressed that he would accept the recommendation of Pateman and Newlove '. . . to tell me exactly what you propose to do. Although the County Council is paymaster, the organisation really remains with Cambridge . . . I regard the question of organisation as entirely in your hands and all I can do is to advise as to places and as to financial possibilities'.[13]

Lamport Smith was also helpful to the District over suggestions about the possibilities of new centres for WEA classes making useful comments about avoiding towns where Cambridge University extension classes were well established; for example Cromer, Thetford and Hunstanton. He strongly supported the continuation of WEA classes at Melton Constable as '. . . this is the only piece of industrialism in Norfolk and I think we should go on with the WEA here as long as the Railway situation remains unchanged'. He advised against an attempt to organise a WEA class at the King's Lynn technical institute as it was a well established centre for evening vocational courses, but urged Pateman to consider classes for those in the peripheral areas of the town. For some years the attitude of the Norfolk Authority and its officers was unique in the District and it established a tradition of mutual trust and confidence which has continued to the present time.

Other LEAs were also supportive, if not as munificent. By 1922, Bedfordshire, East Suffolk, Cambridgeshire, Hertfordshire and Northamptonshire were modestly grant-aiding one-year courses arranged by the District and all LEAs in the region were supporting Tutorial Classes in their authorities through grant-aid to the University Joint Committee on an *ad hoc* basis. Practice varied more widely in respect of grant-aid for other types of classes and courses and the District subsisted with unremitting difficulty in the funding of these which were increasing significantly throughout the period 1918–24. Under a variety of amendments to the Regulations for Technical Schools a limited range of grants could be earned for liberal adult education classes in addition to specific arrangements made in 1908 and 1913. These grants were earned *post hoc* from the Board of Education if classes and courses complied with the Regulations and enabled the District partially to offset the costs of courses. However, it was necessary to supplement the grants through subscriptions and donations as well as enrolment and tuition fees from those attending. In an attempt to attract as wide an attendance as possible the District levied uneconomically low fees with the shortfall intendedly matched by income from the sources mentioned above. Although the deficits were hardly ever covered in this way and the District was perpetually in financial difficulty, the position only became serious with an accumulation over recurring deficits which arose as the expanding programme of courses and classes other than Tutorial and successful one-year courses (on which grant-aid could be earned) became the major focus of activity.

Financial and Other Crises

The District experienced a major financial crisis within a year of assuming financial responsibility for its own activities, and continued to suffer from several debilitating problems until the introduction of the Adult Education Regulations in 1924. Until 1918–19, the year in which the District formally became responsible for its financial affairs, the National Association had met deficits incurred in the development of the new District, in which the appointment of Pateman was seen as the cornerstone of its future success and he had quickly become the indispensable factor in the planning and assumptions of the Association and District.

For the National Association, the undertaking to find Pateman's salary presented a particular problem and commitment for its own slender resources which reached the first critical level in mid-1919. An attempt was made to persuade the District to accept responsibility for resourcing Pateman's salary through a loosely arranged compact between Pateman and Mactavish. It was agreed that the national WEA should invite Mrs. Ruth Dalton (wife of Hugh Dalton, later Chancellor of Exchequer in the post-1945 Attlee government) to undertake a special fund-raising campaign in the District. The rather vague agreement was on an understanding that her salary and expenses would be the first charge on the sum raised; a further £200 would be available for the development of work in the District, and any sum raised above these two commitments would be divided equally between the National Association and the District. This agreement was to become the basis of a rancorous division between the National Association and the District personified through animosity surfacing between Pateman and Mactavish. The compact agreed in October 1919 envisaged a campaign target of £400 and the appointment of Mrs. Dalton who described herself in a letter to Pateman the following month as 'beggar for the District. I am quite nervous about it as I realise the difficulty of the task'.[14] The task was indeed formidable and urgent. The National Association was in arrears on Pateman's salary and some of his planned visits within the District were cancelled simply because there were no funds for railway fares. Pressure on the National Association from the District in late 1919 for financial support produced an aggressive reaction from Mactavish who extended the intentions of the compact to include '. . . a certain portion of money towards the payment of your (i.e. Pateman's) salary'. Thus, by late November 1919, the main idea of a fund for the expansion of the District's activities appears to have been modified and in the following month to have been discarded. In a further letter to Pateman from Mactavish the appeal fund was aimed at '. . . relieving the Central Funds of its present responsibility in regard to your salary'.[15] This was a considerable surprise to Pateman and an alarming reversal of his understanding of the central objectives for development of the District's work. His reaction to Mactavish's unilateral decisions and blustering correspondence is revealed in Pateman's letter to the District Chairman, S. J. Hutley, on New Year's Day 1920, '. . . I do know that he (Mactavish) has upset several District Secretaries recently . . . Alround- (sic) there is general dissatisfaction . . .'.[16]

For Pateman, the attraction of the appeal fund was the availability of resources which would enable the District's work to expand and lead to its objective of becoming a significant provider of adult education in partnership with the University of Cambridge so that the latter's university extension classes and those of the WEA would be seen as complementary elements in the provision for liberal adult study in ways similar to those already established through the Joint Committee for Tutorial Classes. He also hoped that much needed clerical assistance might be financed through the appeal fund so that more of his time would be freed for his pioneering activity especially in rural areas in which he was then becoming more closely involved at District and National levels. But above all, the apparent change in attitude by Mactavish was reprehensible as its stark implication was that the appeal fund would enable the National Association to shed its responsibilities for Pateman's salary, a commitment which it.had undertaken less than three years earlier. Here again, Pateman saw the promise made by Mansbridge in 1915, reluctantly implemented by Mactavish in 1917, now to be discarded at the first opportunity and at a time when the District would be wholly incapable of meeting the charge for his salary, let alone having resources to finance the much-needed development of educational work other than that available through the Joint Committee for Tutorial Classes – all at a time when the interest in, and demand for, shorter courses and classes was clearly increasing.

Mactavish, as he was to admit later that month, wrote a direct, bluntly phrased letter to Pateman on 10 December 1919, stressing that the first charge on any District was its secretary's salary as part of a drive to achieve financial autonomy. He reminded Pateman that the National Association had paid his salary for more than two years without, in his view, the District having made any real effort to contribute towards the commitment. The letter dispelled any doubts about the vagueness of the October agreement that in offering the assistance of Mrs. Dalton the objective of financial self-sufficiency was at the heart of the fundraising appeal. Objectively, although the personal antipathy between the two men cannot be ignored, Mactavish was applying general WEA policy in that financial support for Districts should be limited to a three-year span and if by the end of that period financial autonomy had not been achieved the District should be allowed to 'fail' and its work placed on an alternative footing, but there is no known record of this policy ever being implemented.[17]

Whatever Mactavish's intentions, Pateman's response was immediate and he submitted his resignation to Hutley, the District Chairman. Pateman knew there was no practicable way in which the District's existing finances could meet his salary let alone resolve its other difficulties over finance. He was distressed that his salary had been a burden to the National Association, had been accepted with reluctance in the past and was clearly unacceptable in the future – a position from which he made the not unreasonable extrapolation that both he and the office were expendable. His barely concealed dislike of Mactavish now became publicly visible. Notwithstanding the reasons for and rectitude of his resignation on 14 December 1919, it is possible that Pateman had taken a calculated risk based on his excellent standing with the District Council, his status with the Cambridge Syndicate and Cranage's support, and his knowledge of Mansbridge's conviction of the importance of an active, vigorous District in close partnership with the University. Further, in submitting his resignation neither he nor Hutley informed other members of the District Executive Committee. Fortunately, Hutley wisely refused to act hastily. He assumed there had been a misunderstanding between Mactavish and Pateman, adopted a conciliatory role and wrote to both men. Mactavish's response was to agree to a meeting with Hutley to clarify and resolve the problem. However, and although Hutley had written in unequivocally supportive terms to Pateman on 16 December 1919 '. . . I am sure the District Council will wish to retain your services at all costs as your leaving us would mean the break up of the District organisation, so far as I can see', he was discomfited by Pateman who proved to be unbending and intractable. Although Hutley confined the dispute to the trio, Pateman somewhat unwisely outlined the problems to Mrs. Dalton. Additionally, he either misunderstood arrangements for, or deliberately avoided, a meeting with Hutley and Mactavish in Ipswich intended to resolve the difficulties and also refused to meet Mactavish a little later in London, in a further attempt to settle their personal differences.

For his part in the creation of the crisis, Mactavish appears to have been contrite and on 18 December 1919 he wrote to Hutley and in agreeing to a meeting in Ipswich offered to strive to arrive at a compromise:

I feel that would settle the whole matter if Pateman, you and I met first and had a downright heart to heart talk. I am inclined to think that the misunderstanding is due to two over-tired men discussing by letter a problem from two different angles. I certainly let myself go a bit when I wrote Pateman last, and am more than sorry if as a result he has got the unfortunate idea that his salary is a burden. That is not what I meant to convey. I wanted him to see the dimensions of my worries over the Centre's financial problem and to get him to co-operate with me in helping to solve it. But there. I will be better able to go into the whole matter when I meet you.

The two men met on 31 December and Hutley learned for the first time the central purpose of Mrs. Dalton's fund-raising activities and her attempts to secure annual subscriptions guaranteed for three years to support the Eastern District and the creation of a Development Fund to expand the provision of opportunities for liberal adult education. Hutley recognised that it was possible to interpret these objectives in different ways to achieve financial self-sufficiency and had been impressed by Mactavish's '. . . most friendly attitude and (he) quite convinced me of his sincerity'. This impression he conveyed to Pateman in a letter on 2 January 1920 and claimed that Mactavish had accepted that '. . . the only way to place the District on a self- supporting basis is to *spend more* money on development. This he now guarantees will be done'.[18]

By January 1920, the District Executive Committee knew of Pateman's intended resignation, and some but not all of the circumstances which had prompted it. They pressed him to withdraw the letter as it was hoped the matter might yet be resolved. Similar sentiments were also expressed by Mrs. Dalton in an early January 1920 letter to Pateman and she, in turn, interpreted the objectives of her appeal, begun in November 1919 in Cambridge and elsewhere in the region, as one in which the first priority was the £200 for expansion of the District's educational activities with a lower priority attached to the objective of relieving the National Association of responsibility for Pateman's salary.

The affair dragged on until in March 1920; the overtures of individuals and the District's Executive Committee, and the compromise solution offered by Mactavish reduced Pateman's resentment and he withdrew his letter of resignation. As a result of this protracted and, at times, unpleasant difficulty, Pateman emerged vindicated and publicly indispensable. His position was considerably strengthened because the District had refused to consider the possibility of a new part-time or honorary secretary or having no secretary at all as the viability of the existing District would have been an extremely doubtful proposition. Pateman's new confidence in his position was reflected through his immediate resignation as secretary of the National Association's Rural Sub-committee, a decision for which he openly held Mactavish responsible, and his agreement with the District's officers that he would no longer undertake any of his own duties around the District on Sundays!

By June 1920, the problems were resolved – at least superficially. Mrs. Dalton's appeal aggregated a net sum of £350 of which, as agreed in Mactavish's compromise, £200 was retained by the District for expansion of its educational work and the residue was remitted to the funds of the National Association. The District's share of £200 was placed in a Development Fund to support pioneering activities and to finance village lantern lecture schemes for a period of three years – a set of decisions which did not quite match the recommendations of Mrs. Dalton.

She had raised most of the money in the Ipswich, Norwich and Northamptonshire areas and when concluding her work for the District in June 1920 strongly advocated that significant sums should be devoted to expansion in these areas as a substantial proportion of the monies had been donated by engineering firms in Norwich and Ipswich who hoped the District would attract some of their employees into liberal adult education courses and classes. Similar hopes had been expressed by boot and shoe manufacturing companies in Northamptonshire and she believed that in all three areas efforts should be made to strengthen the presence of the WEA through the development of visibly higher profiles of provision so that the monies donated could be seen to be applied and thus create a supportive attitude for subsequent applications for donations in future years. It is apparent that she was more successful in obtaining donations than guaranteed subscriptions and thus the strategy of securing funding over a defined period was not realised and the original difficulties were merely masked in the short term.

It is also possible that the open breach in the relationship between Pateman and Mactavish led to a local disinclination to pursue the District cause of financial self-sufficiency as the District and National Association emerged with a mutual antipathy. The animus between Pateman and Mactavish existed for many years and had repercussive long-term effects. For example, Pateman's indiscretion in writing to Mrs. Dalton about his difficulties with Mactavish in December 1919 apparently led to a loss of support from King's College, Cambridge, where Hugh Dalton was a Fellow. According to Frank Jacques, Hugh Dalton confided in him in 1937–38 that the apprehension felt over, and loss of confidence in, the ways in which the District and the National Association were at loggerheads in 1919–20 extinguished possible support for the WEA by that college for several years.

In addition, it appears not unreasonable to speculate that other than the agreement to support the Kettering Scheme by the Cassell Trust in 1919, and agreed before the schism between Pateman and Mactavish, no further National Association initiatives were channelled into the District's development until 1927 when the Bedfordshire scheme was launched. It is perhaps significant that this was also the year in which Mactavish effectively surrendered his office as General Secretary of the WEA to J. W. Muir who became Acting General Secretary for a period until the former's formal resignation in 1928. It is also possible that the schism led to Hutley's resignation at the 1920 Annual Meeting of the

District. Almost single-handed he had achieved the compromise agreement between Pateman and Mactavish, but after mid-1920 he disappeared from the counsels of the District, although continuing to be a prominent and active member of the Ipswich branch. He was replaced by Mrs. Clara Rackham as District Chairman.

Although Pateman's value as District Secretary was readily acknowledged, even without the testing experience of the Mactavish episode, it is surprising to discover that his salary was increased in May 1920 from £235 to £275 a year; a second increase on the original salary of £200 agreed in 1917. It is possible that this increase was directly related to that of the £200 a year offered to Newlove on appointment as resident tutor under the Norfolk scheme in that month. Nevertheless, the precarious position of the District's finances must have been known at that time and was formally reported by Salter, the District treasurer, a few weeks later. In brief, Salter's annual report indicated an estimated deficit of £300 for the 1919–20 financial year.

At the June 1920 Annual Meeting of the District Council, and in the light of Hutley's resignation and Salter's gloomy financial report, a series of urgent measures were agreed. As Mrs. Dalton's appeal had just finished, it was agreed she be asked to continue a second phase of the fund-raising campaign. An immediate appeal was also made to branches and subscribers for increased financial support and the existing branch levy of 1d. for every shilling of income was doubled to 2d. Every branch was urged to recruit more members and to seek new group affiliations and individual subscribers.

However, little was achieved. Mrs. Dalton firmly declined the invitation to continue with the appeal and the other fund-raising efforts proved to be disappointing. In April 1921, Salter reported that the appeal to branches had produced an increase of a mere £10 and only £53 had been donated by individual members and well-wishers. During the period between June 1920 and April 1921, the National Association provided a loan of £245, of which only £55 was repaid. By the end of the financial year, 1920- 21, the deficit had risen to £360 and the National Association was yet again approached for further financial assistance. Surprisingly, at the Annual Meeting in June 1921, there was unquestioned acceptance of the National Association's new salary scales for WEA District Secretaries. For the Eastern District, this fixed Pateman's salary at £310 rising in annual increments of £10 to a maximum of £400. In agreeing this further increase the District called yet again for branch and individual support to increase its annual income by a further £350, the sum estimated to meet its additional responsibilities over

Pateman's salary and to place the District on an independent financial basis.

With the benefit of hindsight it seems extraordinary that the District's Executive Committee, Council and officers failed to appreciate the gravity of the financial position and their inability to meet existing financial commitments let alone new ones. It is impossible to avoid concluding that the District's officers, including Salter, did not understand rudimentary accountancy or recognise the causal relationship between the expansion in non-Tutorial Class activity and the increasing deficit. Many years later, Clara Rackham confessed that in June 1920, when she became District Chairman, everyone was '. . . baffled by the financial problems, and Salter was as puzzled as the rest!'.[19]

The financial position inevitably deteriorated further and in the autumn of 1921, Wimble, then Financial Secretary to the National Association, met the District's Executive Committee in Salter's rooms at Magdalene College and apprised them of the National Association's critical financial position and the impossibility of offering further assistance to the District. In future, no assurance of general funding could be made by the National Association and Districts requiring financial help were to submit monthly applications which would be considered competitively on merit and necessity. Yet again, the District agreed to the familiar but ineffective three-point financial plan: appeals to branches, new affiliation subscription fees from groups and individuals in the District, and the establishment of a special fund to extinguish the deficit on the current financial year's estimates. All branches and members in the District were circularised about the acute financial position at District and national levels and a fresh appeal for funds launched.

In the interim, the Development Fund of the Dalton appeal was used to reduce the District's deficit by withdrawing £120 of the £200 it contained. Pateman's salary was yet again in arrears as the National Association had been unable to issue any cheques during November and December 1920. But during the autumn of 1920 and into 1921, the number of District short courses, classes and lectures had increased and the expenditure on these led inevitably to a further increase in the annual deficit.

The National Association and all Districts reflected the difficulty in establishing and maintaining a significant public profile through the provision of opportunities for liberal adult education in the post-war period prior to the introduction of the Adult Education Regulations in 1924. Until these were introduced, the criteria for the recognition of

WEA classes other than those provided under the separate regulations governing three-year Tutorial Classes, were inappropriate for many of the activities which the Association promoted during the period 1918–24. Thus, the majority of its pioneering classes relied on income derived from class fees. Understandably, these were deliberately kept at minimal levels to attract those earning low wages and the accountancy equation of class fees being balanced by lecturers' fees and expenses relied heavily on donations from subscribers, affiliation fees from local or national groups and organisations notably trades councils, co-operative societies and trade unions. For example, about 25% of the Eastern District's total income in 1921–22, some £550, came from these sources but the overall expenditure amounted to £790. The deficit was largely caused by payments for tuition to part-time tutors plus their travelling expenses to and from classes, payment of advertisements announcing the intended provision of classes in local newspapers or through printed leaflets, the use of rooms and payment of caretakers. In the District at that time, only Norfolk County Council provided full financial support to meet all expenses incurred in the provision of classes. Although not a charge on District funds, the Cambridge Syndicate also incurred working deficits on the provision of Tutorial Classes. For example, in its final year before being replaced by the University's Board of Extra-Mural Studies, the Cambridge Syndicate in 1923–24 had a deficit of £470 which was met from a £2,000 government grant towards the extra-mural work of the University.

For the District, the problem of finance was, of course, essentially related to the growth in its educational activities. The twenty-five branches and centres at which the District organised and arranged One-Year and other classes had fixed fees and membership subscriptions for branches at the lowest possible levels, often at pre-1914 rates of 6d. or 1s. 0d., in an endeavour to ensure that no one should be excluded on financial grounds. However, by 1920, it was difficult to consider increasing fees to more realistic levels as unemployment was rising rapidly and many others were in short-time employment. It was feared that an increase in fees to more cost-effective levels would precipitate a dramatic decline in enrolments, a position which the National Association would not accept and the District could not envisage as a newly established area of the WEA seeking to gain support, credibility and to extend its influence in a large area of rural England. Table 2 indicates the pattern of growth in the District while *The Highway* for August 1920 reported a remarkable national growth curve. In 1919–20 there was a 30% increase in the number of branches, an increase of 50% in

Tutorial Classes while the number of One-Year courses increased by a remarkable 125%. In aggregate, the national picture in 1919–20 indicated that the number of students attending WEA classes had increased by 228% on the 1918–19 statistics. There was nothing to suggest to the National Association that 1919–20 was to be a 'boom' year and, with the exception of Tutorial Classes, a decline was to begin in 1921.

In its growth both at National and District levels, the WEA was not geared to an explicit formula of matching expenditure with income. Thus, the more extensive the provision, the greater the expenditure and the deficits which had to be met from income other than fees. The lack of an explicit financial policy presented few problems when the Association had been relatively small because of the agreement between the universities and the Board of Education, reflected in the Tutorial Classes Regulations of 1913. Income from affiliated societies and individual subscriptions, many of which later disappeared either because of, or during, the war had been sufficient to meet the minor deficits of a small number of classes, mostly Tutorial, and thus were seen as unproblematical by the Association. However, with the rapid post-war expansion in classes other than Tutorial and the increase in the number of part-time tutors required and employed, neither the existing regulations nor the officers of the Association proved to be sufficiently responsive and flexible. In search of employment many tutors were taking up WEA work and were unable, or disinclined, to return fees earned as donations for the further development of WEA provision. Accordingly, the largest single item of expenditure in the provision of the rapidly expanding classes was that of lecturers' fees and expenses.

Further, as the organisational complexity of the Association's activities increased, so did the administrative requirements. The necessity of appointing clerical staff to undertake essential managerial and administrative tasks to facilitate organisational arrangements for increased educational activity was unavoidable. Their activities did not generate any income but further increased expenditure. The position was neatly summarised in *The Highway* in August 1920:

> . . . all organisations dependent upon voluntary financial support are suffering in the same way as the WEA. The WEA, however, is in a peculiarly difficult position. Many people and many Trust Funds are willing to grant money for actual educational facilities, but are unwilling or unable to subscribe towards the expense of the organisation and administration, without which the former cannot be provided.[20]

This was clearly a reference to restrictions placed upon grant-aid to the WEA by the Cassell Trust and which involved the District in some difficulties in supporting the work of Miss Green in the Kettering scheme. It was a perpetual difficulty which the District encountered on subsequent occasions in its relationships with LEAs, notably Bedfordshire and Cambridgeshire, and invariably through limitations placed upon grant-aid by the Board of Education Regulations. Until the late 1930s, it was a requirement that organisational and administrative work had to be financed solely from the WEA's own funds.

The circularity of the financial dilemma was not resolved until the Board of Education introduced the Adult Education Regulations in 1924. During the period covered by this chapter, the position in the District deteriorated following the 1920–21 financial crisis. The national economic crisis, with reductions in public expenditure on education which were introduced in 1921, led to a decline in adult education provision at national and local levels. From 1922, the national membership total fell by some 1,350 members and in the District the decline was reflected in membership totals of 1,704 in 1922 and 1,220 in 1923, i.e. a reduction of almost 30%. This decline adversely affected and exacerbated the already serious financial position which had existed from 1919.

Nevertheless, because of its policies for educational expansion and refusal to consider a sharp increase in course fees, the District actually showed a growth in class members overall. Enrolments in Tutorial Classes declined slightly in the early twenties, but enrolments in One-Year and shorter courses rose and in 1922 the District's class membership exceeded 1,000 students for the first time. Thus, in terms of its educational development, the District's record was encouraging, largely because of the Norfolk and Kettering schemes, and contrasted sharply with the decline evident in the national position.

However, the decline in individual membership reflected the pressure which the District attempted to impose on its branches and subscribers from 1921 in an attempt to ease the financial problems. The 1921 financial appeal produced little by way of additional income and it was clear that branches were simply not capable of generating the new income required to overcome the District's financial difficulties despite vigorous efforts through special events undertaken by a few of the larger branches such as Ipswich, Bedford and Cambridge. The continuing problem of Pateman's salary was partially overcome when the Cambridge Syndicate agreed to pay for his hitherto free services as Joint Secretary to the Tutorial Classes Committee and for his organising role in the University's annual summer school. But the relief was not immediate as the District did not receive the contribution to Pateman's salary until 1924, when the Board of Extra-Mural Studies replaced the Syndicate.

In April 1922, a more immediate further crisis arose over the finances of the National Association and on the twenty-eighth of that month a lengthy meeting of the Central WEA Executive Council, attended by Pateman and Salter, led to a series of draconian measures from which the District recognised that subventions from the Association were finally at an end. In essence, it was clear that the National Association's practice of deficit budgeting was to be discontinued and under a new policy, only small pre-determined and fixed grants would be made to dependent Districts. Among other considerations, the key question that finally had to be faced by the District was the continuation of Pateman's post as secretary. It was raised publicly through a District circular sent in May 1922 to all branch secretaries for discussion with members.

Three options were presented in the circular letter:

... firstly, to accept the national recommendations for increased Branch contributions to District and National funds of 1/- and 6d. per member respectively. A further effort would be required by Branches to secure the sum of £200 for the District if the services of the District Secretary were to be retained on the existing salaried basis.

Secondly, to adopt the national recommendations in respect of the level of contributions to District and National funds, and to raise sufficient, but unspecified, additional funds to retain the services of a District Secretary on a half-time basis.

Thirdly, to limit the level of contribution to the recommendations of the National Association and dispense with the services of a salaried District Secretary, and re-organise the work of the District to enable it to continue through a District Council and an Honorary Secretary.[21]

The expectation was that every branch council would arrive at a clear decision by the following month and have it confirmed by holding a general meeting of the branch on the matter. In June, only eight replies were received out of twenty-five branches, Of these, only two branches were not clearly in favour of the first, and most expensive, option. The others pressed for the first option and the adoption of new fund-raising efforts to ensure the retention of a full-time salaried District Secretary. As the eight branches from which replies had been received were Bedford, Cambridge, Ipswich, Kettering, Norwich, Peterborough, Stowmarket and Woodbridge and represented more than 50% of the total District membership, it was unanimously agreed by the District Executive Committee to adopt the first option as the basis for future policy planning. However, the promises from branches to find the £200 necessary for its implementation exceeded performance and eventually only £80 was firmly guaranteed.

In May 1923, the funds promised under the first option yet again failed to materialise and as the financial deficit was some £150 Pateman's position was once more in jeopardy. However, there was some measure of relief for Pateman in that during the academic year 1922–23, he was awarded the first James Stuart Exhibition, established by Trinity College, Cambridge, to enable a WEA student to spend a year's study in residence at the college. The District willingly agreed to release Pateman following its continuing embarrassment over the difficulties of his security and tenure as Secretary. The arrangements were that although a student on a full-time basis during full university term he would undertake twenty-four hours of District work each week, reverting to his full-time secretarial role during university vacations. The Exhibition carried a scholarship worth £50 which was viewed by the District Executive Committee as a supplement to his salary, which was almost constantly in arrears, and in recognition of his acceptance of a notional reduction earlier in 1922 in agreeing to forego implementation of the new national salary scale of £310 by remaining on his existing salary of £295. Nevertheless, the National Association was surprised that the District had not reduced Pateman's salary when he entered Trinity College in October 1922, particularly as it was only too well aware of the existing financial predicament.

Because of the continuing financial problem, it was a major relief to the District's Executive Committee when Pateman was offered a second year at Trinity in 1923–24 to continue his studies in social history and economics. In turn, he sought and gained assurances over his salary position from the District which continued to be in arrears throughout both years. The arrears persisted even though the District had negotiated a bank overdraft of £100, had withdrawn all monies remaining in the Development Fund to reduce the deficit and was conducting a virtually continuous appeal campaign with WEA branches and subscribers to enable it to function; a situation which persisted throughout the 1920s.

In 1924, the National WEA celebrated its twenty-first anniversary at Oxford in July. On a smaller scale, a 'Coming of Age' celebration was held in Cambridge the following month in the Fellows Garden at Trinity College. Even on this occasion, the District over-reached its negligible financial resources. A souvenir booklet was printed and sold at 1s. 0d. per copy, but it is doubtful if sales amounted to 500 copies of the 1,000 the District ordered, and contributed to further financial deficit. Of the WEA's first twenty-one years, the District had contributed to its growth for one half of that period, but the possibility must have occurred to some who attended the celebrations that the District might not survive to celebrate the silver jubilee of the National Association.

WEA branch members from the Bedford area on a summer ramble to Elstow, c.1924

NOTES

1) See G. A. N. Lowndes: *The Silent Social Revolution* (1937) p.114

2) The 1919 Final Report is an abbreviation of the Ministry of Reconstruction's *Adult Education Committee Final Report* (HMSO 1919) (Command 321). It was the first government report on the provision of liberal adult education, and was described by R. D. Waller in 1956 as 'probably the most important single contribution ever made to the literature of adult education . . . it has served two generations as a store of information and ideas'. (*Design for Democracy, p.16*)

3) Printed in pamphlet form by the WEA, this was an interim report but little was achieved because the then existing financial constraints of the National Association precluded the launching of any WEA funded schemes.

4) Eastern District's Annual Report, 1920–21, Botolph House

5) Williams in conversation with John Newlove, 5 August 1965. Newlove wrote an article of his work in *The Highway*, March 1921, 'Prospecting in Broadland'.

6) The Oxford Report (1908) is the usual shortened name for *Oxford and Working Class Education*. It was the first of the four major reports on liberal adult education so far this century and is notable for the formulation of the relationships between the University of Oxford and the WEA characterised through arrangements made for University Tutorial Classes. An interesting account of the evolution of the Tutorial Class system and the Oxford Conference of 1907 is given by Mary Stocks in *The Workers' Educational Association, The First Fifty Years*, Chapter 4

7) A general account of the five schemes is provided in *The Highway*, September 1922

8) Eastern District Minute Book No.1, Botolph House.
   Details reported at a District Executive Committee meeting, 15 November 1919

9) Eastern District Letter File, Botolph House.
   Chester's letter to Pateman, 7 November 1919, and a letter from Daniels on 10 November 1919

10) Eastern District Letter File, Botolph House.
    Miss Stocks' letter to Pateman, 2 February 1921

11) On behalf of the Board of Education, J. W. Headlam, HMI, and Professor L. T. Hobhouse inspected fourteen Tutorial Classes throughout the country and which were reviewed in the *Special Report on Certain Tutorial Classes in Connection with the Workers' Educational Association* (HMSO 1910). The importance of this Report lies in its approval of the method, spirit and achievement of the classes which, in the opinion of the authors, confirmed that the standard of lecturing and teaching corresponded to the spirit of university teaching. For example, they believed 'The best third-year students would, we think, be quite in a position to read for Oxford Diploma in Economics, and would, probably, after a year's full work obtain it without difficulty. Here and there, work of a still higher standard is to be found.' The commendatory nature of the Report undoubtedly influenced the Board's decision to issue its special Regulations for University Tutorial Classes in 1913.

12) Op.cit. the 1919 Final Report pp.206–207

13) Eastern District Letter File, Botolph House.
Lamport Smith's letter to Pateman, 26 November 1923

14) Eastern District Letter File, Botolph House.
Ruth Dalton's letter to Pateman, 24 November 1919

15) Eastern District Letter File, Botolph House.
Mactavish's letter to Pateman, 24 November 1919

16) Eastern District Letter File, Botolph House

17) Eastern District Letter File, Botolph House.
The WEA policy is quoted by Mactavish in his letter to Pateman on 10 December 1919

18) Eastern District Letter File, Botolph House.
S. J. Hutley, Chairman of the District, to Pateman, 2 January 1920

19) Williams in conversation with Clara Rackham, November 1965

20) See *The Highway*, August 1920, p.199

21) The Eastern District Minute Book No.1, Botolph House, has a reference to the details of the circular letter

CHAPTER 3

PROGRESS, CONSOLIDATION AND NEW DIRECTIONS: 1924–35

Context

The period covered in this chapter marked a watershed in the development of the WEA at national and District levels. During these years, the status of the WEA as an 'Approved Association' and its Districts as 'Responsible Bodies' were confirmed through legislation and the first set of Board of Education Regulations specifically designed to provide financial support for liberal adult education provision. The earlier sought opportunities for growth and development of liberal adult education became available on a scale hitherto impossible for voluntary organisations, and for the universities through their extra-mural functions.

Under the Adult Education Regulations of 1924, all existing sixteen Districts of the WEA became eligible for direct, specific grant-aid from the Board of Education and the status of the WEA as an integral part of the national framework in a putative educational system was recognised. Not only did the WEA have providing rights and responsibilities in negotiations with the Board of Education and LEAs but it enhanced its position and status in seeking funds from philanthropic bodies to support pioneering, experimental schemes for the provision of adult education, particularly in rural areas. This latter development led to the breaking of new ground and organisational maturity through the introduction of well-founded resident tutor projects which characterised much of the activity in the Eastern District during this period and which flowered in the following and subsequent decades. In addition, recognition of the WEA's Districts as Responsible Bodies also strengthened its national status as the major voluntary organisation in the provision of liberal adult education – in recognition of the vigour and influence of its earlier activity and the quality of the provision made through its Tutorial Classes and other courses. Further, tacit acceptance of its reputation and credibility in that role was visible through the disinclination of most LEAs to assume direct and full responsibility for liberal adult education and their acceptance of the legitimacy of the provision already being made by the WEA and the universities. Of course, many LEAs actively supported the work of the two major providers, but even without explicit support the field of liberal adult education was not seen as attractive territory for LEA participation or control until the implementation of the Education Act 1944 in the early nineteen fifties.

The period was also notable for the creation of new university extra-mural departments in recognition of the importance of liberal adult education as an integral, natural and legitimate function of universities. The WEA fully supported these developments which had earlier occurred on an *ad hoc* basis in universities. Close, mutually supportive partnerships existed through the joint responsibilities for Tutorial Classes and between WEA courses and university extension provision from its own establishment in 1903, and the identification of shared objectives developed through the 1908 Oxford Report. For the Eastern District, the partnership had existed through the Cambridge University Syndicate's Joint Tutorial Classes Committee from 1913.

Nevertheless, in these stimulating developments of the mid-twenties lay several, although initially dormant, problems for the WEA. Firstly, the attitude of the Board of Education was later to favour the provision made by university extra-mural departments, whose functions developed rapidly during this period, rather than the WEA. Secondly, and particularly in the Eastern District, the former, mutually supportive relationships between the Cambridge Board of Extra-Mural Studies and the District gradually shifted to become uneasy collaboration when the 1924 Regulations were interpreted and applied more flexibly as provision expanded. The culmination in the favouring of university provision is clearly recognisable in the 1932 Adult Education Regulations through the approval of the appointment by universities of Article 11 tutors for rural areas. Undeniably, the Board's regulations of 1924 and 1932 exerted a powerful beneficial influence on the nature and extent of provision for liberal adult education throughout the period and proved to be a major factor in facilitating the rapid increase in the scale of activity. They also powerfully helped to shape the subsequent roles and responsibilities of the major providers during the period in the District.

A Note on the Regulations for Adult Education, 1924 and 1932

Prior to 1924, the Board of Education's Regulations for University Tutorial Classes, 1913, defined the standards and requirements for grant-aid for these classes. But other courses provided through university extension and WEA initiatives were discretionally grant-aided by the Board and LEAs under regulations linked to the Technical Instruction

Act 1889 and modified by others arising from the Education Acts of 1902, 1918 and 1921. No clear, specific regulations for these adult education classes and courses existed before 1924.

Under such improvised arrangements, the Adult Education Committee's Final Report, 1919, had confidently predicted that:

> We do not think that local authorities will, generally speaking, take bold steps to provide facilities for the study of non-vocational subjects. Indeed, we believe that they are more likely to provide vocational studies.[1]

By 1922, the accuracy of this view was confirmed by the Board of Education's own Adult Education Committee which claimed that no scheme submitted by any LEA under the terms of the 1918 Education Act had included an extensive programme for liberal adult education.

The reluctance of LEAs to use their powers under the 1918 Education Act to make direct provision for liberal adult education and the Board of Education's powers under the 1921 Education Act to grant-aid university and national voluntary organisations providing liberal adult education led the new Ramsay MacDonald minority government to issue, somewhat hastily, the 1924 Adult Education Regulations effective from 1 August of that year.[2] As a nationally 'Approved Association' under the 1921 Act, the WEA's Districts were recognised in the 1924 Regulations as 'Responsible Bodies' because they organised, controlled and provided courses and classes, as did the universities. Thus, each District became accountable to the Board of Education for the observance of the Regulations, for the efficient conduct of instruction together with the organisation of the provision which included approval of tutors and syllabuses. In addition, each District was required to submit annual financial statements to the Board; a major increase in the administrative workload and responsibility for district secretaries. The grant-aid formula for Responsible Bodies provided 75% of fees paid to tutors but no contribution was made through grant-aid towards the costs of administration, organisational expenditure or other promotional educational activity at District level.

The Regulations were presented in five 'chapters'. Chapter II dealt with university extra-mural provision while Chapter III applied to those courses arranged by Approved Associations. Under Chapter II, the Regulations also subsumed the 1913 Regulations for Tutorial Classes but reduced the maximum size of classes from thirty-two to twenty-four students. To earn full grant-aid the student attendance requirement of 66% of the possible total was continued as was that for written work at a university honours course standard. For the first time, Preparatory

Tutorial Classes became eligible for grant-aid and the Advanced Tutorial Class extending into a fourth year was formally recognised for financial support. The overall responsibility for all these classes continued as a joint University/WEA partnership.

More significantly, under Chapter II university extension courses were now recognised as eligible for grant-aid – after an existence of more than fifty years. The importance of their eligibility lay in the opportunities which became available to universities, stimulating new policies for, and provision of, adult education. As extra-mural departments were established at several universities during the mid-nineteen twenties, the conjunction of the new Regulations and the entrepreneurial activities of departments such as Nottingham and Cambridge (where the Board of Extra-Mural Studies replaced the Syndicate in 1924) led to a rapid growth in both scale and range of university provided courses.

Under the 1924 Regulations, university extension courses which aggregated tuition over a minimum of eighteen hours were eligibile for grant-aid and were somewhat similar to WEA Terminal courses. Additionally, other university extension courses extending over forty-eight hours and comprising twenty-four meetings were almost identical to WEA One-Year courses, matters which were to become of concern to the WEA in subsequent years.

The Regulations for Chapter III prescribed arrangements for Approved Associations. Undeniably, they offered possibilities for assured if modest financial support for the WEA, a position which it had sought for several years. With the introduction of the Regulations in August 1924 the District saw a solution to its perennial financial problems and believed attractive prospects existed for expanding provision in its large geographical area through the three types of courses eligible for grant-aid: One-Year, Terminal and Vacation.

One-Year courses represented a prestigious category and the formal requirements for grant-aid were similar to those for Preparatory Tutorial Classes without the expectation that they would be precursors of three-year Tutorial Classes. For full grant to be earned, One-Year courses extended over twenty-four weeks, each meeting of two hours' duration with an equal division between instruction and class activity. The maximum permitted enrolment was thirty-two students and written work was an explicit expectation. In the District, many of these One-Year courses stemmed directly from earlier Terminal courses and some, in turn, led to three-year Tutorial Classes. The increase in the number of One-Year courses during the period under review was a gradual one in the District, averaging twenty-five to twenty- seven courses a year between 1925 and 1935.

Significant growth in the District following the introduction of the 1924 Regulations occurred in the Terminal course category. This category was clearly intended to introduce and promote study opportunities in liberal adult education. To earn full grant-aid, Terminal courses had to extend over a minimum of twelve meetings, and aggregate twenty-four hours of attendance for a minimum of twelve students. Although encouraged, written work by students was not a formal requirement. In the District, recognition of its Terminal courses in full or truncated form, provided new opportunities for expansion of its provision and were particularly attractive for the development of pioneering, exploratory adult education activity in towns and villages.[3] Through these courses, nucleii of students were created, some of whom proceeded to undertake more rigorous and extended studies following the formation of WEA branches.

However, prospect was more encouraging than reality. From the early years following the introduction of the 1924 Regulations, experience showed that the net income derived from grant-aid, coupled with the District's policy of setting its student fees at the lowest possible level to encourage enrolments, failed to lead to financial self-sufficiency and the District's financial difficulties, although eased initially, were not eradicated. The annual statements of accounts indicated that the costs of organising and mounting courses were frequently in excess of the combined income from total grant earned and student fee- income. Nevertheless, Terminal courses increased steadily throughout the following decade, doubling in total numbers between 1925 and 1935 and reaching a total of fifty in the latter year. They represented the main category of course provision in the District and provided the major area of growth in student numbers and geographical expansion. Above all, they facilitated particularly the development of resident tutor-organiser initiatives within the District in the decade following 1924, and consolidated the independent, autonomous status of the District as a provider of liberal adult education.

Finally, the distinctions between Chapter II and Chapter III extended into the category of Vacation courses. Originally, these were developed in connection with university extension courses in the late-nineteenth century and established the tradition of summer meetings for study at Oxford, Cambridge and at other universities. Later, vacation courses were extended to provide intensive residential study opportunities for Tutorial Class students which expanded in post-1918 with the growth in provision of these three-year courses. Under Chapter II, grant-aid was available for these arrangements and similar but separate arrangements were introduced for vacation studies and 'summer schools' attended by students who had attended WEA classes and courses under Chapter III regulations. In the District these were organised and developed by George Pateman at Cheshunt College for several years, and became a distinctive feature of summer programmes.

Thus, with the distinctions made between Chapters II and III, the Board of Education sought to establish clear, demarcated responsibilities for each of the two main providers of liberal adult education; with the universities engaged in more academic levels of study. However, in the years following 1924, some universities, among them Cambridge, extended their activities into Chapter III course provision and encroached on territory which the WEA perceived as its own. The encroachment in the District occurred notably over the resident tutor-organiser scheme in Bedfordshire in 1930 and further overlapping and competitive situations arose following the issue of the revised Adult Education Regulations in 1932.[4]

The Adult Education Regulations of 1932 addressed a major problem which had not been resolved under the Board's 1924 Regulations. Quite simply, the earlier Regulations had failed to meet adequately the needs of liberal adult education in rural areas. The inaccessibility of rural areas, the lack of public transport facilities, the dispersed and sparse population had all contributed to the failure of many courses to enrol students at levels within the prescribed minima for grant-aid and the thresholds for the Board's Regulations were demonstrably too high under such circumstances. As elsewhere, the District recognised that a practicable solution lay in the appointment of resident tutor-organisers in rural areas. The Eastern District had already experienced some success in its early years through the appointment of Sophie Green in the Kettering district and John Newlove in Norfolk as resident tutor-organisers. During the late nineteen twenties and early thirties, the District was to pioneer rural areas schemes in Bedfordshire with Harold Shearman and in East Suffolk through William Whiteley. In seeking to formulate an adequate policy for liberal adult education in rural areas, the demarcation between Chapters II and III over course provision was patently unrealistic. The Board of Education's own Adult Education Committee in their Paper No.9 published in 1927 recognised both the nature of, and solution to, the problems of rural areas:

In the countryside a nucleus of full-time tutors is indispensable for the full development of the work; . . . We think it desirable that the same type of teacher should be employed in these courses (One-

Year, Terminal and less formal) as in University Tutorial Classes and that arrangements should be made whereby staff- tutors appointed for extra-mural work by the Universities should be encouraged to devote part of their time to less formal work, not only in the interests of the work, but also in order to provide a variety of occupation for the tutor and to ensure that he keeps in touch with all phases of the adult education movement.[5]

The 1932 Adult Education Regulations enshrined these principles and permitted the appointment of full-time salaried tutors under Article 11 who were eligible for grant-aid purposes. But such appointments could be made only to the staff of university extra-mural departments and Approved Associations were excluded. As a natural corollary of this initiative, extra-mural departments were permitted to provide courses at standards lower, and of shorter duration, than under the 1924 Regulations. These changes were to lead eventually to competition and dissent between the two main providers, particularly in the Eastern District as it was a predominantly rural area. Another modification intended to assist course provision in rural areas, but also applicable in urban areas, was the inclusion of Short University Extension courses for grant-aid under both Chapters II and III. In the former category, university extension courses of between six and nine meetings, each one of ninety minutes duration, could be grant-aided. Under Chapter III, Short Terminal courses were introduced of between six and eleven meetings. For both types the minimum number of students enrolled qualifying for grant-aid was fixed at nine.

The appointment of Article 11 Tutors and the blurring of distinctions between Chapter II and Chapter III provision in rural areas meant that university extra-mural departments could encroach upon the earlier explicitly legitimate function of the WEA as the main organiser of student demand through its branch structure. Resident Article 11 tutors in rural areas were inevitably involved in the stimulation, promotion, organisation and provision of courses in liberal adult education.[6] Crucially, there was also assured financial support for the permitted grant-aided maximum of two such tutors at each extra-mural department in that the Board of Education grant provided for 75% of the salaries of tutors or a maximum of £300 per annum for each appointment. In sharp contrast, the WEA financed its tutors through student fee income, grant-aid from the Board of Education which was derived only from the number of qualifying classes provided, and from fluctuating, unsecured donations and subscriptions. For its full-time resident tutor-organisers the WEA was almost entirely dependent upon financial support from philanthropic bodies such as Carnegie, Cassell and Thomas Wall.[7] All three bodies provided support during this period for pioneering WEA activity over relatively short periods, usually for three years, although some were renewed to sustain encouraging developments. Perhaps the most enduring of these funded arrangements was the Cassell Fund's support for Miss Green's appointment in the Kettering district, which with Miss Stocks as personal guarantor and additional fund-raiser, support from employers, and modest contributions from the LEA, extended over a period of some twenty years. For the District it was a period of the funded-tutor enterprise which was later to be challenged through the gradual development of a new regional policy by the Cambridge University Extra-Mural Board.

The Kettering District Scheme – II

Further renewals of the Cassell Trustees grant in 1924, 1927 and 1930 were in recognition of the successful work of Sophie Green, and the influence of Helen Stocks with leading figures of the WEA as well as her indefatigable energy in raising monies among her friends to support the scheme. By 1929, ten WEA branches existed in the area – seven more than in 1920. In addition to the original three (Kettering, Northampton and Wellingborough) new centres were established at Corby, Daventry, Desborough, Peterborough, Raunds, Rothwell and Rushden. Although not all had a continuous existence, Miss Green figured in their formation, or revival, often through providing or arranging introductory, short or Terminal courses to arouse interest and create student groups. Much of her success came through her recognition of the importance of social activities. Unlike some of the more academically qualified tutors, Sophie Green believed that if the WEA was to succeed among manual workers it had to be perceived as a social movement striving for a democratic state through its educational purpose. For her, restriction of activities to programmes of formal course provision could not satisfy the wider objectives of the WEA. Her numerous social activities were always linked with the branch, class or study group. For example, for several years she arranged regular Saturday evening social gatherings in Kettering for young people. The average attendance was about a hundred and had particular appeal to young women factory workers and those in domestic service. Similarly, she arranged and encouraged folk dancing groups in the town, monthly reading circles and visits to theatres. Many new members of her classes were enrolled in these ways and if assessed only on numerical growth and continuous class activity, Miss Green's success was impressive in comparison with other more conventional branch activities in the District in the mid- late twenties.

She also regularly accompanied groups of her women students to the Cambridge Summer School. In 1926, eleven of her students attended Newnham College's summer school for working women and a further three joined the summer school at Cheshunt College, where George Pateman and his wife were in charge of the arrangements. A glimpse of her commitment, pride and satisfaction is apparent in her letter to Pateman in August 1926:

> When I saw all my people at the station, I felt completely overwhelmed. I know they are all going to get a great deal out of this experience, I am deeply grateful for all the help that is being given them, they have had such a worrying time, I do not think one of them could have had a holiday this year without help, but I have faith to think it will be a good investment for the WEA.[8]

Later, and in recognition of her own achievements, Sophie Green was awarded a scholarship to attend a summer course at Bryn Mawr College, Pennsylvania in 1928 and in the following year she became a co-opted member of the Kettering Education Committee.

Because she lacked academic qualifications, Miss Green never conducted a Tutorial Class, but she revelled in her Terminal and, less frequently, One-Year courses. Nevertheless, she was unequivocally ambitious for her students, both men and women, and unfailingly encouraged them to proceed to Tutorial Classes. In this ambition, she was unquestionably influenced by the attitude of Helen Stocks who believed Tutorial Classes were the only genuinely worthwhile courses of study. The partnership appeared to work well. For example, at Desborough in 1926–27, Miss Green provided a Terminal course in Industrial History which she believed '. . . was one of the best I have taken . . . and it will almost certainly develop into a Tutorial class under Cambridge next winter'.[9] It did: the subject was European History and the tutor was her mentor, Miss Stocks. A similar pattern occurred at Peterborough. In 1927–28, Miss Green revived the ailing WEA branch there with a Terminal course, followed by a One-Year course in the following year which led to a Tutorial Class from 1929–32.

Under the Kettering Scheme, the sequence of these and other similar developments was remarkable and the combination of the unflagging effort by Miss Green and the guiding influence of Miss Stocks was demonstrably successful over several years. With students, Miss Green had a sure touch and showed great personal sensitivity. Perhaps unsurprisingly, her most valuable asset lay in her own limited educational background. From personal experience she knew and understood the problems of individual study, the difficulty of sustained reading and written work following long hours of manual labour. She gave much of her own time to helping those encountering problems with their studies through individual tuition at her home, frequently during the summer months in preparation for autumn courses.

But she was not uncritical of tutors and students who were perceived by her as failing the wider aims of the WEA. Of one Tutorial Class tutor she complained to Pateman:

> He does not understand the WEA point of view, of desiring to draw out the individual in speech and written work. I am sure no WEA tutor would pass open criticism on the essays . . . this habit lost the class several students this year.[10]

She was equally severe on students from her own branch who withdrew from their Tutorial Class commitment:

> I feel we are *students*, if humble ones . . . The thinning out process has been a great shock to me, I had a higher opinion of working class thought – but it is that where the weakness lies, not in our efforts of propaganda.[11]

Her 1929–30 report on the work of the scheme reflected continuing pleasure in her teaching role when describing her experience of a jointly organised One-Year course by the WEA branch and the local Co-operative education committee in Bedford:

> In many respects this class was quite the best I have taken. It was a mixed class and the students . . . regular in attendance and conscientious about the work for the class. . . . although the amount varied, one student produced some written work every week, two or three others did eight or nine papers . . . enough was produced for me to know that a real interest was being taken in the class.[12]

Of course, there were inevitable disappointments. She worked strenuously to establish the Corby branch and provided courses there in an attempt to sustain a WEA presence in the then new steel town but it became inactive in the early thirties. At Wellingborough, branch existence fluctuated. Its original foundation as an Oxford Delegacy WEA branch pre-dated the formation of the District and in 1919 its membership exceeded seventy-five, but by 1923 it had become dormant. Miss Green revived interest in 1924 and the branch was re-constituted but foundered again in 1927. Ever determined, she helped to re-establish the branch in 1930 and a Tutorial Class in Psychology was launched successfully in 1931.

But a major setback for Miss Green arose in 1931 with the appointment by the Cambridge Board of Extra-Mural Studies of Frank

Lee as its staff tutor in Northamptonshire. As his appointment preceded the 1932 Adult Education Regulations, Lee was not an Article 11 tutor but represented the new regional policy for provision developing at the Cambridge Board, which included the 1930 appointment of Harold Shearman as its tutor in Bedfordshire, and W. P. Baker in Cambridgeshire the following year.

In Northamptonshire, Lee's ostensible role was primarily for the development of Tutorial Classes and for co-operation with voluntary organisations. Although his appointment was officially welcomed by the WEA District Committee, its officers, and WEA branches in Northamptonshire, there was private disquiet. It was not without significance to the WEA (and presumably of similar importance to the Cambridge Board and its secretary, G. F. Hickson) that the Eastern District already had thirteen of its twenty-five Tutorial Classes in that county: several reflecting the combined efforts of Miss Green and Helen Stocks. Thus, it appeared to be a curiously odd appointment to the District as the most active and successful Tutorial Classes already existed in Northamptonshire while there were large tracts of East Anglia where, from the WEA standpoint as a Responsible Body and as joint provider of Tutorial Classes with the Cambridge Board, much valuable work might have been undertaken by a university resident tutor.

For Miss Green, Lee's appointment was perceived as an explicit threat simply because in the previous year, renewal of the Cassell Trust's grant had not been easily secured and had been made on the understanding that the 1930 renewal was to extend only for a further and final two years. The problem had been compounded in 1929 when, in preparing its anticipated difficult bid for further renewal of the Cassell grant, the District had sought to bolster its 'pioneering tutor' case by persuading Miss Green to consider offering her preliminary courses in Huntingdonshire, a county without any adult education provision. For Miss Green her new area was to be along a 'corridor' accessible from railway stations on the Kettering, Huntingdon, Peterborough line, in '. . . a poor county, thinly populated, neglected by all organisations other than Women's Institutes . . .'.[13] The confluence of the difficulties over a further Cassell renewal of funding; the prospect of the focus of her work shifting to Huntingdonshire, and the arrival of Lee in 1931 was perceived by Miss Green as an indication of preparations for her displacement in Northamptonshire and eventual redundancy; for which there appears to be no documentary basis. She and Lee were never close colleagues but as WEA tutor-organiser she continued to play a key role in attracting students to her short courses and from these developed a few Tutorial Classes for which Lee was the tutor.

Eventually, and after considerable discomfiture for the District committee and Pateman, Miss Green accepted the *de facto* position in both counties. She continued to provide courses in her original area around Kettering and pioneered several new ones in West Huntingdonshire and, with Shearman's encouragement, in North Bedfordshire such as at St. Neots and at Wymington. At the end of the supposedly final two-year period, considerable pressure by Helen Stocks and A. S. Firth, then General Secretary of the WEA, led to a further renewal by a somewhat reluctant Cassell Trust for another three years. Although the renewal appeared to secure her position as tutor-organiser into the mid-thirties, Miss Green's personal relationships with the District and Pateman became formal rather than enthusiastic after 1931, but her commitment to her students continued undiminished.

In summary, the developments under the Kettering scheme, especially between 1924 and 1931 were of considerable importance to the provision made in the District. Table 3.1 presents its relative importance in outline statistical form.

The Bedfordshire Scheme

The relative decline in the percentage of the District's courses and classes in Northamptonshire towards the end of the decade was attributable to the introduction of the WEA tutor-organiser scheme in Bedfordshire in 1927.

Perhaps the most important single decision taken by the District during the twenties was to accept the Carnegie Trust's offer to support financially the appointment of a tutor for the development of rural adult education. For a variety of reasons, Bedfordshire presented the most attractive possibilities. The county town had a large, vigorous WEA branch with an impressive record of activity which had extended throughout the previous decade. The District Chairman and a senior member of the Bedford branch was Henry Wash who, as early as 1924, had secured the co-operation of the county LEA. In that year, the LEA had established an Adult Education Sub-Committee and had agreed to provide financial support for WEA courses in Bedford, Luton and Biggleswade where active branches existed. Further, the LEA had agreed to introduce a scheme of 'county scholarships' to enable working adults to attend WEA summer schools, mainly at Cambridge. Several WEA students had benefited from the LEA's support and at least two, E. W. Gurney and Arthur Kempster, were to become prominent figures in the civic life of the county in later years.

Table 3.1 Kettering Scheme and Eastern District Course Provision, 1924–31

		1924–25	1925–26	1926–27	1927–28	1928–29	1929–30	1930–31
a.	Eastern District Preparatory Tutorial and Tutorial	15	18	18	20	21	21	25
	Other Courses and Classes	33	45	36	45	35	65	63
		48	63	54	65	56	86	88
b.	Kettering District Preparatory Tutorial and Tutorial	3	4	5	7	6	7	9
	Other Courses and Classes	8	14	8	7	5	6	5
c.	Northampton Branch Preparatory Tutorial and Tutorial	2	1	2	2	3	4	4
	Other Courses and Classes	3	4	2	3	5	1	2
d. i.	Percentages: Kettering District of District Totals	23%	29%	24%	21%	20%	15%	16%
ii.	All Northamptonshire Classes of District Totals	33%	36%	31%	29%	34%	21%	23%

Most of the early activity was confined to urban areas, but in 1927 the Carnegie Trust offered to finance a National WEA scheme to promote new developments through rural adult education and mid-Devon, the North Riding and Bedfordshire were selected. Ironically, the terms of the appointment of the tutor-organisers were very similar to those later approved exclusively for university resident tutors when the 1932 Adult Education Regulations were introduced.

For the District, perennially in financial difficulties, the £500 annual Carnegie grant over a three-year period was accepted on the understanding that the Bedfordshire Scheme would be financially self-sufficient. The scheme was welcomed by the LEA and the Cambridge Extra-Mural Board and a Cambridge teacher and part-time WEA tutor, Harold Shearman, was appointed. In September 1927, Shearman's work began from his home, initially at Willington and subsequently from Caldecote.

It was given a prestigious launch at a conference arranged by the Bedford WEA branch and attended by many supporters including Messrs. Liddle (Headmaster of Bedford Modern School and Chairman of Bedford's WEA branch), Baines (Director of Education for the LEA), Glazier (County Librarian and a former part-time WEA tutor), Wash (WEA District Chairman) and, of course, Pateman as District Secretary.

An Oxford graudate, Shearman brought skilled professionalism to the role – the first occasion on which the District had enjoyed the benefit of an academically well qualified tutor with experience as a WEA tutor and someone with considerable administrative talents derived from his war service experience. Even more important were his sensitivity, tact and diplomacy in an entirely novel situation. During his first year, Shearman, in his Morris, established contacts in villages throughout east and north Bedfordshire, holding public meetings, giving evening lectures, conducting short courses all with the objective of creating student groups as nucleii of future WEA branches. At Rushden, he also gave a One-Year course in history for Sophie Green and established good, non-threatening working relationships with her.

To publicise his pioneering work Shearman produced an excellent leaflet on the scheme and its potentialities. This leaflet *Towards a Brighter Countryside* (which is reproduced as an appendix in this volume) comprised notes on the objectives and work of the WEA as well as a prospectus of some twenty lectures and short courses. Initially, Shearman provided lectures and courses within the originally planned twenty-mile radius of Bedford. However, it was quickly realised that this area was much too extensive and the southern part of rural Bedfordshire remained largely unvisited during the three-year period.

As shown in Table 3.2 Shearman undertook most of the teaching of the courses. As he had a car he invariably conducted those in the more remote villages such as Carlton, Dean, Millbrook and Riseley. But during the three-year period of the initial scheme he also engaged eighteen part-time tutors, some of whom were also car-owners, who visited the more accessible centres such as Biggleswade and Ampthill. He assumed full personal responsibility for all organisational work, made every initial contact with villages, and constructed a network of social links among the village groups and established WEA centres. By 1930, more than 500 students had enrolled in classes at some twenty-six rural centres. To provide cohesion and identity among them, he encouraged the formation of a county federation of WEA branches, student groups and affiliated societies – the first in the District.

Formed in March 1930, to unite rural student groups with those urban WEA branches not included in the Bedfordshire Scheme, the federation reflected Shearman's experience of the organisation of Baptist chapels in rural Northamptonshire. The son of a Baptist minister, he was familiar with regular district meetings for small chapel groups to provide a sense of unity and broader identity with the larger movement of the Baptist Union, through regular contact and fellowship. He applied these principles in the Bedfordshire rural scheme and held his first meeting of student groups at Bedford Modern School in 1929.

By 1935, the Bedfordshire Federation had developed into the most effective student organisation in the District attracting much attention from other areas within and beyond the District. The Federation stimulated and promoted membership of the WEA - an important consideration in the county as the tenet of every student being also a member of the WEA was not realistic simply because in the initial phase most of Shearman's activity was in rural 'centres' rather than in WEA 'branches'. In 1931, there were only four WEA branches in the county: Bedford, Biggleswade, Dunstable and Luton. By 1935, only one other WEA branch had been established, at Sandy, but by then the Biggleswade branch had disbanded. In 1931, there were twelve Student Groups in villages and by 1935 the number had increased to twenty-one. The importance of the Federation to the District was considerably increased when the Cambridge Board assumed responsibility for the Bedfordshire Rural Scheme and appointed Shearman as its resident tutor in 1930.

Between 1927–30, in the quickening of the slow pace of social change, the WEA rural scheme in Bedfordshire through Shearman's tact, diplomacy, energy and skills as a teacher committed to the role of the WEA in adult education clearly established the credibility and importance of the resident tutor model. It also indicated its potential for meeting the latent demand for adult education which existed in rural areas, at that time handicapped by geographical isolation. Further, during these years the possibilities of the wireless as a teaching medium was being explored through the BBC's 'Listening-in' groups. Although reactions to the role of radio published in *The Highway* were initially dismissive, Shearman responded positively. Using skilled tutors, such as Mary Adams from Cambridge, who shared in the group-listening sessions and then extended the broadcast themes through discussion and supplementary material, the BBC programmes at Harrold and Goldington led directly to longer courses.

Shearman also offered opportunities to existing organisations to join forces with the WEA in the rural scheme. For example, he provided co-ordination and stimulation for the Leighton Buzzard Rover Scouts Troop which affiliated to the District to undertake a course on local government. Three other villages arranged short courses in conjunction with local centres of the League of Nations Union. Other villages linked with Young Farmers' Clubs for joint activities and the social purpose of the WEA was exemplified through course-linked visits to theatres in Cambridge and Oxford while other visits were arranged to Parliament.

Table 3.2 The Bedfordshire Rural Scheme, 1927–1930

Activities	1927–28	1928–29	1929–30
One-Year	–	1	5 (1)
Terminal	–	6 (4)	9 (4)
Short Courses	11	5 (3)	9 (5)
Single Lectures:			
a. Public	38	32 (26)	-
b. Women's Institute	14	16	1
Wireless Listening-in Groups	–	–	14 (1)

Note Other than those columns which show two sets of figures, Shearman gave all lectures and courses. For the two sets of figures, those enclosed in brackets indicate lectures and courses given by Shearman.

Shearman's experience in the county was disseminated through a special National WEA conference on adult education in rural areas held in London in May 1929. Most of the WEA Districts were represented as were the major philanthropic trusts which supported educational enterprise. The District was represented by Wash, Pateman and Sophie Green as well as Shearman who had prepared the main conference document and gave the keynote talk. Shearman's paper provided insight into his experience in Bedfordshire. An important perception was that in villages with fewer than 500 inhabitants interest in adult education had to be generated within the whole community with the intention of creating a social movement, rather than in appeals to sectional interests in such small communities. Therefore, subjects of study required a broad approach which initially in Shearman's view were likely to be local history, central government or local government issues. Further, whatever subjects were chosen, it was the tutor who was the critically important factor in success or failure. For successful work in rural areas, the tutor had to be sensitive to, and well-informed about, both the locality and its people so that a genuine rapport emerged as a basis for mutual confidence and support. Thus, for Shearman, the tutor had pastoral as well as pedagogic responsibilities in villages. The conference was a successful occasion for the WEA and particularly so for Shearman and for the continuation of his work in Bedfordshire.[14]

In 1930, a conference in Bedford reviewed the progress of the District's rural scheme. For the 200 or so who attended, everyone appeared to have been unanimous in believing that the scheme had been wholly beneficial in broadening cultural life in villages. Mansbridge, who was present, caught precisely the collective sense of gratitude and optimism. Apparently, the address was vintage Mansbridge – messianic, inspired and characteristically generous and encouraging. The conference resolved that every effort should be made to retain the services of an outstanding tutor-organiser, the architect and pilot of the rural scheme, to ensure its development on a secure, permanent basis. The possibility of a permanent appointment for Shearman to the LEA's staff as an adult education tutor was immediately explored.

The conference decision arose from an implicit assumption by the Carnegie Trustees that following a three-year funding of successful pilot schemes, subsequent responsibility would be assumed by LEAs. The Trustees made a recommendation to that effect to the Bedfordshire LEA in 1930 which was accepted by the county's Adult Education Sub-committee as the scheme 'had been conducted on sound lines, was distinctly encouraging, that the particular tutor-organiser was exactly the right person required'.[15] However, the county council was reluctant to establish a post for a tutor in adult education and other options had to be considered. Hickson, the Secretary of the Cambridge Board, proposed a shared responsibility for the scheme with the LEA as it offered an opportunity for the Board to extend its role and influence within its region – a new policy stance linked to the Board's gradual withdrawal from its traditional national university extension role. The Board's proposal was received enthusiastically by the District and the LEA. For both organisations, it offered continuation of an outstandingly successful project which had been initiated by the former and supported by the latter – both bodies had continuity as the central imperative. For the LEA, and somewhat untypically of most LEAs at that time, it was not a problem of finance for the scheme which had been difficult but the reluctance to establish a precedent through appointing a tutor for adult education. For the District, although regretting the loss of its major development in a rural area, the main preoccupation was to secure the retention of its outstanding and only full-time tutor who commanded both academic and experiential respect at all levels. In the District, Shearman symbolised academic status and enjoyed enthusiastic acceptability among students and providing agencies in adult education. The District was painfully aware that it could ill-afford his loss, but because of its continuing impecunious position it recognised his services could not be retained. Thus, the Hickson solution resolved the immediate and pressing difficulties for both the LEA and the District.

Under the new arrangements, from the autumn of 1930, the LEA and the Board shared the cost of Shearman's salary. With a revised scale for its deficiency payments, in effect a reduction of 50% grant-aid to WEA classes in the county, the LEA with only marginally increased costs was seen to be acceding to public demand for continuity and simultaneously responding to the recommendation of the Carnegie Trustees. For the District, the assured continuation of the Bedfordshire scheme meant that the Carnegie Trustees would provide a similar three-year grant to finance a WEA appointment in another rural area in the District – identified and launched as the East Suffolk scheme in September 1930.

The outcome of the negotiations appeared to have satisfied the wishes of everyone involved. Nevertheless, a major policy decision had been made, or was forced upon, the District. No record appears to exist of division within, or hesitation by, the District over the surrender of its providing powers in rural Bedfordshire under Chapter III of the 1924 Adult Education Regulations. This appears especially curious as the issue of providing powers was assuming considerable national importance for the WEA which in 1929 was pressing for retention of its Chapter III providing powers during the Board of Education's review of the 1924 Regulations.

Other than the exceptional arrangements approved by the Board of Education for Nottingham University, no other WEA District had conceded this fundamental encroachment on its providing powers. It is possible that in the Eastern District, the committee and officers were not fully aware of the implications of the Bedfordshire arrangement in their natural anxiety over the immediate issue of continuity of the rural scheme. However, as members of the Cambridge Board Committee, both the District Chairman and Secretary were fully apprised of the details of the new arrangements and, presumably, acquiesced in the explicit transfer of providing powers under Chapter III for One-Year and Terminal courses in rural areas so that the complete scheme in Bedfordshire could be maintained as it had developed from 1927. It was only later that the significance of the surrendering of providing powers in 1930 became fully apparent to the District.

Thus, from 1930–31, the District's providing powers in Bedfordshire were limited to urban areas and the Cambridge Board assumed Chapter

III powers in those rural areas which had been included in Shearman's territory between 1927–30. To administer the new arrangement, the Cambridge Board established its own *ad hoc* rural areas committee in February 1930 in conjunction with other developments in Cambridgeshire and which reflected the Board's interest and developing policy for course provision under both Chapters II and III.

The Cambridge Board of Extra-Mural Studies: A Contextual Note

These developments within the Cambridge Board were undoubtedly related to the concurrent measurable, irreversible decline in traditional university extension courses provided by the Board of Extra-Mural Studies on a national scale and which by 1939 had reached the point at which there were only five Cambridge university extension centres beyond East Anglia. Thus, the transfer of initiatives from a national to a regional scale appears to have been a conscious, logical policy decision by the Cambridge Board, using the example of the successful Nottingham University scheme devised by Professor Peers, whom Geoffrey Hickson admired. With Cranage's resignation in 1928, the links with the tradition of university extension on a national scale at Cambridge were gradually replaced by new opportunities for regional development which became available under the 1924 and, later, the 1932 Adult Education Regulations.

Following the recommendations of the Report of the Royal Commission on the Universities of Oxford and Cambridge in 1922, the Board of Extra-Mural Studies was established in 1924 and moved into its new premises at Stuart House in 1928. Another recommendation of the Commission was for increased funding for adult education and with gradual increases in its budgetary provision, the Board in 1931 was able to appoint three full-time lectures: Lee in Northamptonshire, Baker in Cambridgeshire and Hardman for university extension local lectures.[16]

Thus, the Cambridge Board had secured resources to begin the development of its policies for the regional provision of adult education prior to the introduction of the 1932 Regulations. As it sought to serve a predominantly rural region in which the WEA in earlier years had found its own main strength in urban areas, the rural areas were relatively untouched and open to university initiatives when the 1932 Adult Education Regulations were introduced. The Board's role had been afforced through its assumption of providing powers under the Bedfordshire scheme and through its close co-operative relationships with the Rural Community Council (RCC) in Cambridgeshire and for which it provided a series of courses in that county.

From 1927 in Cambridgeshire, the Board, with the assistance of a three-year Cassell Fund grant, had assumed responsibility for the RCC's own programme of village lectures and short courses for which the latter received grant-aid from the LEA. For example, in a dozen or so villages during 1928 and 1929, Pateman and a young teacher, W. P. Baker, provided short courses of the Chapter III type on rural history. When the Cassell Fund's grant ended in 1930, the Cambridge Board and the LEA jointly financed the scheme with Baker becoming a Board tutor for the development of rural adult education in the county.

It should not be assumed that relationships between the Board and the District were adversarial or competitive at that time. Not only did Pateman undertake lectures and courses for the Board, he was also chairman of the RCC's adult education committee. Further, and in acknowledgment of his work as joint secretary of the Tutorial Classes Committee and for his duties in connection with the annual Cambridge Summer School Pateman also received a substantial honorarium which provided him with some security as his salary as District Secretary was not infrequently in arrears. When Stuart House was opened in 1928, Pateman had a room there to undertake Tutorial Class administration and organise arrangements for the annual summer school. It is therefore perhaps unsurprising that the problem over the loss of providing powers in Bedfordshire did not appear to be a major one in the context of such close co-operation and joint endeavour to promote the growth of rural adult education at that time.

However, within the Cambridge Board's committee there was some initial resistance to the extension of its activity into Chapter III work to pioneer courses in rural areas of a lower academic standard than under its Chapter II powers. But the argument which carried the day in favour of providing more elementary studies was that courses of the Chapter III type in rural areas would prove to be attractive and would lead to more demanding studies and higher standards in subsequent years. An indication of the Board's hesitancy and internal division can be gauged from the decision, in February 1930, being agreed only after a vote was taken and that only three of the eight listed recommendations in Hickson's confidential memorandum were approved. As part of the decision-making involved the assumption of responsibility by the Board for the Bedfordshire scheme, it is not surprising that the two WEA members of the Board and Frank Salter, the District Treasurer, who was a University nominated member, cast their votes in favour of the rural areas scheme. However, two other university members voted against the rural areas scheme although one of whom, Professor Ernest Barker, later became chairman of the Board's Rural Areas Committee.[17]

With the appointment of Shearman as the Board's resident tutor in Bedfordshire and Baker's appointment to a similar post for Cambridgeshire for the development of rural adult education, the Board's rural areas sub-committee had emerged as a *de facto* permanent committee of the Board – a position constitutionally confirmed in 1932 through its formal designation as the Board's Rural Areas Committee with Professor Barker as its chairman.

The East Suffolk Rural Scheme

The acknowledged success by all participants in the Bedfordshire scheme led in 1930 to the Carnegie Trust offering to continue the £500 annual grant for a further three-year period to finance a tutor-organiser appointment in another rural area in the District.

The reasons for the decision to appoint a resident tutor-organiser in East Suffolk are not well documented. It is possible a feeling existed that too much attention had been given to development in the western and most populous counties in the District. It is also possible that with the decline in activity in Norfolk, other eastern counties were considered attractive for the next phase in development, perhaps because the ground in the west appeared to have been secured through Shearman and Miss Green. In addition, the appointments of Lee and Baker by the Board and its emerging plans for rural areas development may have prompted the District to consider developing other parts of its region. In East Suffolk it appeared that the Ipswich branch could provide a nucleus around which another successful enterprise might be constructed. It was undeniable that the Ipswich WEA branch was one of the most active, vigorous and successful centres in the District. It had a large membership with several members influential in local civic life and an enviable record of continuous educational activity over several years through its courses and conferences. Further, in earlier years the branch had attempted to extend its WEA social and educational activity into surrounding villages and it is possible that the branch had pressed the District for the appointment of a resident tutor in East Suffolk - although the documentary evidence on this point is somewhat unclear.

However, it is a matter of historical record that in the twenties the Ipswich branch had opposed the development of a district organisation and viewed the period following the introduction of the 1924 Adult Education Regulations as one of increasing centralisation. It was a branch which was highly resistant to any tendency perceived as likely to vitiate the traditional autonomy of WEA branches. Because of these attitudes, there were no established or informally close relationships between officers of the District and the WEA branch. Unlike Bedfordshire, there was no commitment by the LEA to provide financial support for the scheme when it was proposed in 1930.

William Whiteley, a former Tutorial Class student at Rugby and a James Stuart Exhibitioner at Trinity College, Cambridge, in 1929–30, was appointed as WEA resident tutor in East Suffolk and moved to Ipswich in September 1930. With the enthusiastic support of the WEA branch, he followed Shearman's initial policy of making personal contact and establishing his presence through a demanding programme of single lectures and short courses in villages in the county. By the end of his first year, more that sixty village lectures had been provided, about one-third of them at Women's Institutes, and five short courses were arranged in villages near Ipswich.[18] Demand for his services exceeded his capacity to meet the many requests and in the second year of the scheme he acquired a car to provide greater mobility. In the second and third years, he concentrated on more sustained studies through arranging short and Terminal courses under Chapter III arrangements as well as continuing to provide many village lectures. For example, short or Terminal courses were provided at Middleton, Yoxford, Haughley, Hollesley Bay and Stratford St. Mary. At Leiston, Whiteley engaged A. S. Neill to provide a well-attended course in Psychology.

However, notwithstanding his extensive programme, no courses longer than the Terminal type were arranged, possibly because student groups were not formed in the villages of people who would have accepted responsibility to stimulate, organise and sustain local demand. The absence of student groups led to a relatively small growth in WEA activity in most villages during the three-year period and the scheme suffered, perhaps inevitably and unfairly, in comparison with the earlier success achieved in Bedfordshire.

Concurrently with his rural work, Whiteley became a prominent member of the Ipswich branch and his support of some of its antipathetic policies and attitudes towards the District distanced him somewhat from Wash, Pateman and Shearman, who became District Vice-Chairman in 1931. Unfortunately, the East Suffolk scheme also suffered from a reduction in Board of Education grant-aid for courses which occurred in the period 1931–34. This had serious implications for Chapter III courses as the LEA was not prepared to make any substantial financial contribution in support of rural adult education activities, even though the county's Secretary for Education, H. M. Spink, was a part-time WEA tutor. The District was experiencing yet again a deficit on its

84

Chapter III course programme and thus was not in a position to contemplate an expansionist stance in East Suffolk. It was also aware that a further renewal of the Carnegie Trust's grant was extremely unlikely. Nevertheless, Pateman sought a renewal of the grant and received a reduced, conditional offer from the Trust of renewal for one year if the District could secure alternative funding for a further two years. But in 1934, the District managed to obtain only a promise of a mere £70 in grant-aid from the LEA for those courses provided by Whiteley – a wholly inadequate offer. An attempt by Pateman to negotiate a tripartite arrangement for the payment of Whiteley's salary by the LEA, the Cambridge Board and the WEA also failed. The Cambridge Board was fully committed to its existing developments in the other counties, considered earlier in this chapter, and the LEA were averse to contributing to the salary of the tutor until the scheme had become firmly established in the county - a Catch 22 situation – and the scheme petered out in 1934.[19]

The East Suffolk scheme thus ended disappointingly and in 1936 Whiteley left the District on appointment as an adult education tutor in the Manchester area. The collapse of the scheme served to emphasise yet again the dependence of the District's initiatives in rural areas on adequate financial support from philanthropic bodies and LEAs. It was also clear that the creation of a network of village centres for the provision of classes and courses was a necessary but insufficient basis for a well-founded adult education movement. A genuine social conscious-ness, motivated at least to some degree by idealism for the attainment of an educated democracy was an indispensable factor in a self-sustaining, progressive momentum for the growth of the WEA in rural areas. It clearly existed in Bedfordshire, because of Shearman's perception of its importance; it was evident in the Kettering scheme because Miss Green instinctively knew its significance to fellow disadvantaged adults; it appears not to have emerged in East Suffolk possibly because it was not assiduously pursued.

The Norfolk Scheme-II

It will be recalled from the previous chapter, that other than in Norwich the educational activities of the WEA in Norfolk were confined to John Newlove's courses in the north of the county at Dereham, Melton Constable, Wells and King's Lynn. Unfortunately, in 1925, John Newlove became ill once more at the start of the autumn term and hurried, improvised and not entirely satisfactory arrangements were made to provide tutors for his two Tutorial Classes and three One-Year courses. A planned scheme for WEA village lectures, to be provided by some of Newlove's students, foundered with his illness and were abandoned. Although he made a partial recovery in 1926, he could only conduct the One-Year course at Wells, where he lived.

With the continuing uncertainty over Newlove's health and teaching capacity, the LEA withdrew its financial support for Chapter III courses but continued to meet the costs of the existing Tutorial Classes. The LEA decision meant that it was unlikely that any new centre would enter a three-year commitment without a preliminary period of less demanding study and consequently, the Norfolk scheme tapered to its end. Although discussions took place about a possible return to the former scale of activity, Newlove's health did not improve and he was physically limited to Wells where either One-Year or Terminal courses continued until 1934 when the WEA branch became inactive.

A decade of initiative and early success in Norfolk ended somewhat disappointingly, and distressingly for Newlove. It had been of considerable importance to the development of the District's confidence and reputation in East Anglia in the early twenties. Crucially, it had been a notable enterprise in demonstrating the altruistic spirit of co-operative endeavour between a WEA District and a large county LEA which had established the broad principles of role differentiation between voluntary and statutory bodies in the provision of adult education as delineated in the Final Report, 1919. The early success of adult education arrangements in Norfolk, together with the almost contemporaneous Kettering scheme, had unquestionably buttressed the District's early and somewhat insecure position vis a vis some other LEAs in fostering co-operation and in establishing its credibility with philanthropic trusts over grant-aid for subsequent enterprises.

District Development, 1924–35

By 1924, the District had established some twenty branches and more than 1,000 students had attended its classes and courses. They were distributed across nine Tutorial Classes, twenty-five other courses and ten study circles. It was also in a serious financial position but believed the new Regulations would lead to a general amelioration of the deficit position through the ability to earn increased Board of Education grants for its Chapter III work. By 1925, this early optimism had disappeared and the District continued to struggle at a financial subsistence level throughout the whole period, apparently incapable of seriously addressing the resolution of the problem of financial self-sufficiency.

In its educational work the financial deficits were masked by the encouraging developments in Northamptonshire, Bedfordshire, and, initially, in East Suffolk. Undeniably, forward momentum was maintained during a decade characterised by severe political, economic and social problems amongst the majority of those for whom the WEA had an appeal and with whom it had initially prospered. In the District, and in contrast to the national trend, Tutorial Classes virtually doubled between 1925 and 1931 – from thirteen to twenty-five and their membership was composed of about one-third of students from manual occupations. About one-half of these classes were to be found in the footwear and clothing towns in Northamptonshire with other noteworthy Tutorial Class continuities in Bedford, Cambridge, Halstead, Ipswich, Luton and Norwich (see Table 3.3). In all, there was evidence of an active, cohesive social movement typically visible in the programmes members arranged for cultural activities, local winter and summer musical and drama evenings, summer rambles and weekend schools. All these contributed much to a sense of fellowship and corporate social identity as well as providing opportunities for personal development and individual enrichment.

Table 3.3 District-University Tutorial Classes (Cambridge Committee) 1924–31 **

Students: Occupational Groups as Percentages of Total Enrolments

Occupations	1924–25	1925–26	1926–27	1927–28	1928–29	1929-30	1930–31
A.	%	%	%	%	%	%	%
Manual[1].	35	25	31	31	27	36	36
Non-Manual[2].	33	32	34	25	25	23	25
Women at Home	15	19	15	16	18	15	14
Teachers[3].	17	24	20	28	30	26	25
B.							
Total Number of Students Enrolled	423	417	544	486	530	490	607
C.							
Total Number of Tutorial Classes	13	16	16	19	16	18	25

** The percentages shown are for all Cambridge University/WEA Tutorial Classes which included some arranged beyond the Eastern District, e.g. Nuneaton and Rugby. But the majority of classes were arranged at District branches and the statistics are considered representative of the proportion of occupational groups within the District.

1. No classification is entirely satisfactory and was not consistent over the period represented here but the category included: engineers, railway employees, carpenters, building trades and labourers, tailors and dressmakers, boot and shoe operatives, printing trades, postmen, policemen, blacksmiths, farm labourers, textile factory workers, gardeners and caretakers.
2. Non-manual categories included: clerks, typists, shopkeepers and assistants, civil servants, overlookers and foreman, insurance agents and commercial travellers, ministers of religion, nurses and social workers.
3. Teachers, always prominent in Tutorial Classes in the twenties, are given a separate category here to avoid problems of distortion in the percentages of the non-manual category.

Although enrolled student numbers increased during the period in all types of classes, membership of the WEA gradually declined, an indication perhaps that it was more for personal educational value rather than support for a wider social movement that adults attended District classes. Thus, the District gained little direct financial benefit from increased enrolments as the capitation fee which branches paid to District funds was calculated not on student enrolment but on WEA membership. The slogan 'Every Student a Member' was as much a financial appeal as an ideological one and in this respect the District was broadly unsuccessful. In 1926, income from branches received by the District was a mere £49; in the following year it was £46. By 1929, the National WEA reported that ten of its sixteen Districts had lower branch membership totals than in 1924, averaging 59% of all enrolled students, which represented a decline of at least 20% on the 1924 figure. The District was one of the ten mentioned and the national statistics almost exactly reflected its own position.[20]

By 1929 also, the District's educational provision appeared to have reached a plateau for One-Year and Terminal courses but new developments in 1930 and 1931 suggested that expansion beyond the funded tutor-organiser schemes was imminent. The optimism lay in the potential for development in the hitherto largely neglected extra-metropolitan southern fringe of the District. In conjunction with the WEA London District and the London Co-operative Society, six Terminal courses were provided at Southend (three courses), Rayleigh, South Benfleet and

Watford. The success of these courses at centres whose natural affinities lay with the London rather than the Eastern District led to the latter's willing agreement to transfer its expanding, populous southern commuter zone to the former in the summer of 1930. The southern boundary of the District was accordingly modified from the mouth of the Blackwater River in Essex westwards to the Buckinghamshire county boundary. With this re-alignment, Cheshunt, Barnet, Southend and Watford became part of the London District, with Chelmsford in Essex and the rest of Hertfordshire remaining within the District. It was also agreed between the two Districts that if any courses were proposed within a zone extending about three miles on either side of their new, shared boundary the Districts would confer to determine how the demand might best be met.

As in Bedfordshire, interest in the possibilities of broadcasting were explored elsewhere in the District. According to Welch, an approach was made by the BBC to the Cambridge Board in 1926 about the possibility of establishing a local radio station in Cambridge.[21] In 1927–28, the Cambridge and Ipswich Tutorial Classes in Biology participated in a six-talks broadcast on *The Problems of Heredity* given by Mary Adams, then tutor to the Cambridge branch. An illustrated booklet to accompany the series was prepared by a member of the Ipswich Tutorial Class and questions which arose during the post-broadcast class discussion were forwarded to Mrs. Adams who dealt with them during the following week's transmission. In spite of various difficulties over these early broadcasts and the general absence of supplementary printed material for class use, together with some antipathy towards this innovatory form of teaching, the Cambridge branch persisted with radio programmes into 1929. However, this was an exceptional attitude as there was widespread scepticism of radio as a teaching medium and its possibilities did not really materialise for at least another decade.

In other ways, too, the early nineteen thirties marked a period of hesitancy and some pessimism within the District both over its future growth and even its survival. The emergence of the Cambridge Board, well funded and of high status, as a legitimate and major provider of adult education through its new rural areas policies presented problems of overlapping, competitive interests for the District, however well-intentioned the co-operative arrangements might appear to have been. Some LEAs, notably through Henry Morris in Cambridgeshire and Baines in Bedfordshire, were explicitly supportive of the enterprise being developed by a prestigious university body in adult education. For them, linkages with the Cambridge Board represented an attractive partnership between academic altruism of the university and pragmatic local authorities for the development of educational opportunities for adults. Further, the District was perceived by some as an amateur, rudimentary, low status voluntary body whose aims were, at best, quasi-political and, at worst, subversive.

Nevertheless, officers and most members of the Cambridge Board and the District's Executive Committee believed, initially at least, that competition over provision could be avoided during a pioneering phase of development in East Anglia where little adult education provision had been made: in Cambridgeshire, Essex, Huntingdonshire, Norfolk and Suffolk. But the general satisfaction with close and successful co-operation evident through the easy, harmonious transfer of responsibility from the District to the Cambridge Board of the Bedfordshire scheme in 1930 began to evaporate when in the following year, the Cambridge Board asked the District to cede its Chapter III providing powers in rural Cambridgeshire to the Board. In September 1931, Hickson wrote to Wash, then District Chairman:

> Since the Board are entering into a Scheme for adult education in co-operation with the LEA in Cambridgeshire much in the same way (as) had been done in Bedfordshire it seems as if it might be best for the Board to be recognised as the Responsible Body for this type of course.[22]

Although not intransigent, Wash was clearly uneasy about the specific link with Bedfordshire as the precedent to establish a principle. He forwarded the letter to Ernest Green, then Organising Secretary of the National WEA and in the accompanying covering letter wrote:

> Personally, I think that if we can obtain in Cambridgeshire a federation of WEA student groups which will be represented on the Rural Areas Committee of the Extra-Mural Board in the same way as we are represented by a kindred federation in Bedfordshire, there will not be anything lost from the WEA point of view, in the Board being recognised as the responsible body. But it is a development of the work of the Extra-Mural Board which needs thinking out.[23]

In his genuine wish to continue to co-operate with the Board in the cause of the development of liberal adult education, Wash missed the substantive threat to the District's future as the Responsible Body for Chapter III provision. The possibility of a 'domino' effect in all counties in the District could not be ignored and Hickson had also left open the possibilities for further expansion in his original letter to Wash:

> I do not think the situation arises *at the moment outside these two*

counties. Of course, we hope that Baker will undertake pioneer work and organise courses in *neighbouring rural areas* but probably for the moment any courses under Chapter III could be arranged in the usual way.(i.e. through the District as the Responsible Body) (emphasis added)

From Ernest Green's response it is clear that, as Organising Secretary for the National WEA, he had been unaware of the details or significance of the original Bedfordshire transfer agreement and later that month, when writing to Pateman about the Board's proposals for Cambridgeshire, he claimed:

I am afraid I never understood until I saw Hickson's letter to Wash that even in Bedfordshire the Extra-Mural Board had become the recognised body under Chapter III. It may have been my stupidity, but I had not realised it. I think it is unfortunate, and I think the Universities are undertaking a form of work which is going to have the affect (sic) of reducing their reputation for the maintenance of high standards. They are rather too prone to accept the point of view of reactionary educational committees which are afraid of the WEA. If the LEA were to lay down as a condition of grant that we should have nothing to do with the University body, we should refuse the grant, and I do not see why Universities should not show the same loyalty to us.[24]

The last sentence refers to an earlier conversation between Green and Hickson in which the latter had claimed that the Cambridgeshire LEA would not be prepared to support the work of the District, whereas the Board had been offered a grant of £100 for 1931-32 and the prospect of increased grant-aid in subsequent years.

For Green, the proposal of the Cambridge Board had major implications at national level and he sought to arrive at a local compromise to prevent a more widespread set of problems for the WEA. His own proposal, accepted some months later, was that both the Board and District should become Responsible Bodies for Cambridgeshire and that mutually negotiated and harmonious arrangements for local provision be agreed between them, with financial deficits being met from the LEA grant. For Green, the flexibility of the proposal allowed for the meeting of local demand by either or both organisations, it encouraged further co-operative endeavour between them and facilitated the WEA role over the establishment of a county federation of students as an organisational framework to help overcome the perennial difficulty of isolated university extension centres. At a meeting in London in February 1932, which was chaired by Tawney, the membership of the Cambridge Board's

Rural Areas Committee (RAC) was agreed and Green's proposals accepted. The RAC was to comprise: three members nominated by the University, three nominated by the WEA and a further three to represent LEA interests. At that time as only the Bedfordshire and Cambridgeshire LEAs were involved, the third LEA place was allocated to the Bedfordshire WEA Federation to represent the student body. It appears that having agreed on the structure, the meeting did not address the question of functions of the RAC and the development of jointly planned activity, outlined in Green's original proposals, was ignored and led subsequently to competitive activity in Cambridgeshire, Essex and Norfolk.

In the first few years of the informal concordat under the RAC, there appears to have been a tacit agreement that in Cambridgeshire the WEA attempted to provide few courses, largely it is thought because of its financial problems. Equally, it appears that the Cambridge Board also tacitly accepted that although he was its tutor, Shearman's personal commitment to the WEA meant that provision of courses in Bedfordshire was arranged through the WEA county Federation and thus exclusively organised by the District.

This uneasy compromise was not a major difficulty during the first few years as the national economic problems of the early thirties, reductions in public expenditure and depressed employment conditions all led to severe restrictions on the development of adult education. Thus provision in rural areas was concentrated in Bedfordshire and Cambridgeshire with some minor reconnaissance of possibilities and experimental pioneer short courses elsewhere. Until 1936, the other rural counties in the District were regarded as 'open territory' but in that year a partial relaxation over public expenditure restrictions occurred and the issues inherent in the compromise over the rural areas agreement between the Cambridge Board and the District emerged in sharply focussed ways.

The Workers' Educational Trade Union Committee (WETUC)

It was also during the period 1924–35 that a forging of closer relationships between the WEA and the Trade Union movement was attempted. Formed in 1919, the WETUC was represented in each WEA District through divisional committees of affiliated trade unions and WEA members. In the District, Pateman acted as secretary to the WETUC's divisional committee. Although never destined to flourish as an active conduit for combined activity, Pateman linked District students with the WETUC scheme for the remission of fees where appropriate – in aggregate usually never more than £20 a year. The only noteworthy joint activities were weekend schools for trade unionists which the District helped to organise, such as Kingsley Martin's weekend schools on *Public Opinion* in Gorleston in 1924, G. D. H. Cole's on *Trade Unionism* at Norwich in 1925 and Harold Laski's Bedford weekend school on *Economics* in 1926.

In most other respects Pateman's WETUC role was a passive one. There was little demand from local trade unions and the Divisional Committee appears to have been only modestly active, probably because where well-established trade union organisations had members interested in educational opportunities, links between them already existed through the WEA branch organisation and were especially effective in Northamptonshire, Bedford, Luton and Ipswich. Elsewhere, the trade unions appear to have been weakly organised in the District. Even the General Strike of May 1926 had little impact as the five unions represented on the District's divisional committee were not among the major participants at national level.[25] Public support for the General Strike was most evident in Cambridge where students and members of the University were openly supportive and where Pateman arranged a WEA class in public speaking. By 1930, only five or six members of affiliated unions who attended Cambridge summer schools were supported by WETUC funds. Others who attended District courses not infrequently failed to submit claims for the remission of fees – all during a period of high unemployment and short-time working which suggested that in this District at least, the WETUC was of little perceived interest or known value to those it existed to support.

District Finance

Yet again, throughout this chapter there have been repeated references to the precariousness of the financial position of the District, notwithstanding the introduction of grant-aid under the 1924 Adult Education Regulations.

The core of the problem lay in the costs of administering and organising the District's functions. No grant-aid was available for administrative work, of which Pateman's salary represented the largest single item. Further, 25% of tutors' fees were not grant-aided and thus had to be met from other sources principally donations, subscriptions and through appeals to branches, with some assistance from the National WEA when its own difficult financial position allowed, usually about £50 a year.

As already noted, the Cambridge Board from the autumn of 1924, paid Pateman an honorarium of £150 for his services as joint secretary to the Tutorial Classes Committee and in connection with his organising work for the annual Cambridge summer school. By May 1925, the District owed Pateman £115 in salary arrears which amounted to almost one-half of his salary for the year and owed an even larger sum elsewhere.

Arising from this unresolved difficult and unsatisfactory position, Pateman's appointment was renewed for only one further year in 1925–26 and at the reduced annual salary of £200.[26] A further unsuccessful appeal was made to WEA branches in the District in an attempt to secure Pateman's salary for future years and the existing arrears for Pateman were cleared only through the negotiation of a bank overdraft. Pateman naturally sought, and was given, assurances that his reduced salary, which was only one-half of the National WEA's prescribed scale of £400 a year for District Secretaries, would be paid in full and on a regular basis throughout the year. But in spite of the assurances of the District's Executive Committee, his salary was almost continuously in arrears up to 1930. In addition, because of increased opportunities for course provision under the 1924 Regulations the administrative costs of the District almost trebled between 1925 and 1931. In a period when the number of courses increased, WEA membership in the District declined by 150 and in 1931, capitation fees from branches had slumped to a mere £44. Throughout the period, the District appeared to develop a policy of containment of its gradually mounting deficit and became habituated to an existence of permanent indebtedness. In 1929, the position reached its nadir when the District's financial deficit was greater than that of any other WEA District.

Frank Salter, the District Treasurer from 1918, believed that financial appeals for new income in a sparsely populated region with a low wage economy and high unemployment, was an insuperable task and in 1931 he was succeeded by Lionel Elvin, Fellow of Trinity Hall, as the District's honorary treasurer, and who brought much vigour and commitment to resolving the perennial financial problem.

Continuity and Change

In 1934, Henry Wash resigned as District Chairman as a new appointment took him to Kent and was succeeded by Harold Shearman who had been vice-chairman of the District since 1931. At that time, the position in 1934–35 was superficially encouraging and thirteen new WEA centres were established. In addition to the funded schemes, the position in Hertfordshire offered new opportunities. New centres at Harpenden and Old Welwyn were established and Tutorial Classes were arranged at branches in Letchworth and Welwyn Garden City. The WEA branch at St. Albans and a student group at Ashwell also arranged shorter courses.

In Essex, the WEA branches at Harwich and Clacton arranged One-Year courses and, of considerable local interest, the National Institute of Adult Education selected Silver End to stage an art exhibition in a rural area. In Cambridgeshire and the Isle of Ely and arising from initiatives by Bill Baker, new WEA centres were established at Sutton and Stretham and joined others formed a little earlier at Haddenham, Histon, March and Wilburton - most arranging Terminal courses during the year, while Cottenham founded a WEA branch. In Norfolk, the District had only one branch, at Norwich.

However, the real strength of the District lay in its active urban branches: Peterborough, Rushden, Wellingborough, Northampton, Kettering, Cambridge, Bedford, Ipswich and Welwyn Garden City, and two-thirds of the District's Tutorial Class students were concentrated in these branches, a total of some 400. Similarly, more than one-third of the students enrolled in the District's One-Year and Terminal courses were also to be found in these branches. Thus, in spite of the importance of the pioneering work in rural areas, it was apparent even as late as 1935 that the District had made little substantial and quantifiable impact in its rural counties and among its dispersed population.

Tawney, on the occasion of the celebrations of the District's twenty-first anniversary in June 1934, perceptively recognised that the District '. . . was only at the beginning of their task . . .' but was perhaps a little wide of the mark in claiming that the '. . . District has been a pioneer in spreading education among working class students in rural areas . . .'[27] Some 700 delegates attended the anniversary meeting in Cambridge, and following speeches by Firth, Mansbridge and Temple, a tour of the colleges preceded afternoon tea at Trinity College.

The organisation of the celebrations on such a large scale was a major success for Pateman and although he could not have known it at the time he was in the final few months of his long and difficult years of service to the District and the WEA. In the summer of 1935, George Pateman resigned following his appointment as Assistant Secretary to the Cambridge University Board of Extra-Mural Studies – a major surprise to many in the District and which precipitated a major re-casting of the District's policies and priorities.

The precise reasons for this apparently surprising appointment are not entirely clear as there appears to be no detailed documentation, but it is almost certain the initiative came from Harold Shearman, then

District Chairman. Using the example of Cartwright at the Oxford Delegacy, Shearman sought to establish similar arrangements at Cambridge because:

> We were in no position to ensure any security for Pateman . . . he had built up the District but had perhaps nearly exhausted his pioneering drive.[28]

Shearman was also anxious to secure Pateman's future and was conscious of the debt owed to him by the District for many years of difficult, painstaking and often discouraging work. There was also a pressing need to appoint a new District Secretary to re-vitalise and secure the future development of the WEA.

Shearman recalled that, at first, discussion with Hickson was unpromising but eventually the appointment of Pateman to the post, vacant from 1928, was confirmed. For Pateman, the offer, at the age of 46, was understandably irresistible. Apart from the cachet of a university appointment which followed the award of an honorary Cambridge MA the previous year in recognition of his many years of service to adult education, the post offered unprecedented security and an improved, assured salary. Further, his duties were substantially a continuation of those which he had undertaken for several years in connection with Tutorial Classes and the annual summer school arrangements. Significantly, he also became responsible for the development of the Board's Chapter III provision in rural areas. All these duties were administered from a room at Stuart House which he had used from 1928. The District acknowledged that the honorarium Pateman had received as District Secretary could not be continued and, of course, that the hidden subsidy of Pateman's accommodation at Stuart House would not be available to his successor.

Nevertheless, Shearman, as District Chairman, recognised that the District could not continue in its relatively impecunious way 'sustained by a very small number of rather weak branches dispersed over a very wide area . . . most of the branches were struggling'.[29] Further, there was a clear, emerging imperative to establish an explicit and visible distinction between the functions of the District and those of the Cambridge Board as earlier close, co-operative relationships were being eroded through the operation of the 1932 Adult Education Regulations and the ad hoc agreement between both providers in rural Bedfordshire and Cambridgeshire. New initiatives were required by the Chairman, Treasurer and, above all, through the appointment of a new, vigorous District Secretary.

H. C. SHEARMAN, M.A.

Mr. H. C. Shearman, M.A., the Tutor-Organiser, for rural work, was born in an Oxfordshire village and attended the village school at Sulgrave. He obtained a County Council Scholarship to Magdalen College School, Brackley. During the war he served first in the ranks in Mesopotamia and subsequently obtained a commission in the Royal Air Force. Later he went up to Oxford, taking his degree with first class honours in History. He has since been engaged in teaching at Cambridge, and has obtained experience in W.E.A. lecturing there. During most of his life he has been in close touch with village life in different parts of the country.

97

Sophie Green, tutor-organiser, Kettering Scheme, 1919–39

NOTES

1) Op.cit. The Final Report 1919

2) Regulations for Adult Education, Board of Education Grant Regulations, No.33, January 1924

   S. G. Raybould in *The English Universities and Adult Education*, Workers' Educational Association, 1951, provides a detailed analysis of the grant-aid policies of the Board of Education during the inter-war period.

3) However, in the 1926–27 session, the number of Terminal courses in the District fell from twenty-four (1925–26) to fifteen because the Board of Education refused to recognise for grant-aid some classes which had been approved in earlier years, e.g. in Public Speaking, Esperanto and Country Dancing. Thus, the District was required to meet the full costs of deficits incurred on these classes during that year.

4) Regulations for Adult Education, Board of Education Grant Regulations, No.14, 1932

5) Board of Education Adult Education Committee Report No.9 *Pioneer Work and Other Development in Adult Education*. HMSO, 1927, p.49

6) Adult Education Regulations, 1932, Article 11.
   Each tutor was expected to include in his teaching programme '... at least one Three-Year Tutorial class and may include other classes falling within the scope of Chapter II or Chapter III and pioneer work intended to develop adult education'.

7) That the distinction in the appointment and funding of university extra-mural department tutors was significant and had a long-term effect is indicated by Raybould's estimate that by 1948–49, there were 179 full-time, salaried tutors in university extra-mural departments whereas the WEA had a mere twenty-four full-time salaried tutor-organisers. (Source Raybould op.cit. p.32)

8) District Letter File, Botolph House
   3 August 1926

9) District Letter File, Botolph House
   Miss Green's letter to Pateman, 4 April 1927

10) District Letter File, Botolph House
    Miss Green's letter to Pateman, 5 March 1927

11) District Letter File, Botolph House
    Miss Green's letter to Pateman, 12 January 1931

12) Miss Green's draft report on the Kettering Scheme for 1929-30. Archival material, Botolph House

13) Memorandum from Pateman to Ernest Green, undated but late 1931. Archival material, Botolph House

14) See Appendix D
For example, Shearman later wrote articles published in *The Highway* such as: 'What the Villager Wants', February 1934 and in *Adult Education* 'Impressions of the Rural Conference', September 1934

15) Bedfordshire County Council Adult Education Sub-Committee Minutes, Report of the Director of Education, 6 July 1930. County Hall Archives, Bedford

16) See Edwin Welch op.cit., particularly Chapter 9 for a general account of the developments of the work of the University of Cambridge Board of Extra-Mural Studies. The chapter contains much interesting material but also some inaccuracies in relation to the Board's relationships with the District.

17) Pateman's annotations on the confidential memorandum. The two WEA members were Lionel Elvin and Henry Wash. Archival material, Botolph House

18) The courses were at Knodishall, Middleton and Yoxford.

19) Eastern District Minute Book No.3, Botolph House. The matter was discussed at a District Executive Committee Meeting on 28 July 1934

20) WEA Central Office Memorandum on District Reports (Finance), 11 December 1929. Botolph House archives.

21) Edwin Welch op.cit. p.157

22) Board of Extra-Mural Studies File at Botolph House

23) ibid. The letter is undated but was written in mid-late September 1931

24) ibid. The reply is dated 30 September 1931

25) Trade Union representation on the Eastern Divisional Committee came from: The Railway Clerks' Association, General and Municipal Workers, Association of Engineering and Shipbuilding [8C]Draughtsmen, Union of Post Office Workers and the Civil Service Clerical Association.

26) Eastern District Minute Book No.2, Botolph House. District Executive Committee Meeting, 13 May 1925

27) Tawney's contribution printed in the *Coming of Age Celebration Souvenir Programme*, 1934, which was produced by the District to mark its twenty-first anniversary.

28) Shearman in a letter to Williams, September 1976

29) ibid.

CHAPTER 4

FROM CO-OPERATION TO PARTNERSHIP THROUGH CONFLICT: 1935–52

A New Phase

'One of the finest appointments I have ever made'. This was the opinion of Sir Harold Shearman, then Chairman of the Greater London Council, in 1965 when he recalled the selection of Frank Jacques as George Pateman's successor as District Secretary in July 1935.[1] Frank Jacques was appointed from a large and well-qualified field of candidates; one was later to become the General Secretary of the National Association of the WEA and another the Chief Education Officer of a large county LEA. His background was both appropriate and relevant. He was an experienced member of the WEA in the Berkshire, Buckinghamshire and Oxfordshire District as a student, part-time tutor, chairman of that District's Divisional Committee of the WETUC and a member of the Railway Clerks Association. He had contested parliamentary seats in three General Elections and had been a member of Maidenhead Town Council and chairman of its Library Committee. But perhaps above all it was that his candidature was unreservedly supported by Tawney, who knew him well, which convinced the appointing committee that Jacques had the background experience, commitment and personal qualities required by the District at a particularly difficult point in its existence.

Some of the immediate, pressing problems were resolved only on the day of his appointment. For example, it was agreed that the District should have its own office and Jacques quickly negotiated the lease of rooms at Cambridgeshire House in Hills Road; an arrangement which extended over thirty years until the transfer to the existing and more appropriate premises at Botolph House. He furnished much of the office from his own resources although his annual salary of £250 was some 20% below the WEA's nationally recommended minimum for District Secretaries - a reflection yet again of the District's precarious financial position, then in deficit in excess of £100.

Unfortunately, Jacques had the worst possible start to his new appointment. He was involved in two serious motoring accidents in the District's car during his first eighteen months in Cambridge. On both occasions his injuries led to enforced absences during which Pateman generously assumed responsibility for much of the District's administrative work. In spite of these major setbacks, Jacques gave first priority to the setting of new objectives for the District and with Lionel Elvin tackled the problem of financial self-sufficiency. The solution to the financial problem began to emerge with the adoption of a forward-planned annual budget in which each branch and student group was allocated a financial target or 'quota' to be raised each year to eradicate existing deficits and prevent recurrence of indebtedness. The introduction of a financial quota system inevitably placed unprecedented responsibilities on most branches and student groups to make tangible contributions to support their activities, and those of the District, which led to predictable objections from some branches and to genuine difficulty in meeting the allocated quotas in a few instances. But it was a successful scheme and was much more effective than the generalised, unspecified financial appeals of earlier years. By 1938, the District achieved a balanced financial position and thereafter began to accumulate small credit balances.

Initially, the quota system was based on a simple two-element formula. A basic rate was fixed of 1s. 0d. for every thousand population in the area served by a branch. In addition, branch and class members paid annual capitation subscriptions which were earmarked for three purposes: 20% was retained by the branch, 40% was remitted to the District and the other 40% was forwarded to the National Association. For example, Cambridge, the largest branch in the District with a membership of 250, serving a population estimated at 67,000 in 1937 had a quota allocation of a little over £24. The quota system and its responsibilities stimulated a variety of fund-raising social activities and some branches became unprecedentedly active as community foci which, in turn, led to a new sense of social unity through corporate activities and interests.

Additionally, to ease the crisis during his first two years of office when the District's finances depended on 'monthly improvisation', Jacques persuaded some tutors to accept reduced fees while others generously returned their travelling expenses as donations to District funds until the financial position was eased. At the same time, and recognising the importance of building an active membership, Jacques sought to increase the number of branches which had vigour, enthusiasm and commitment to the WEA. He was thus involved in extensive travelling throughout the District, addressing meetings of branches, trade unions and co-operative societies. He also believed that greater financial support for the WEA could be obtained from the LEAs in the region.

With the support of Shearman, District Chairman until 1936 when he was appointed as National Education Officer for the WEA, Jacques turned his attention to seeking co-operative relationships with LEAs who were beginning to expand provision of adult education through the establishment of evening institutes, mostly accommodated in secondary schools. In his view, the presence of WEA classes in evening institutes were valuable indicators of the District's existence, attractive to potential students and demonstrated the contribution made by the WEA to liberal adult education in partnership with LEAs and their own emphasis on vocational courses. Further, on appointment he had realised for the first time that the eastern parts of the District remained largely undeveloped by the WEA. In his early months he sought to stimulate the interest of the Cambridge Board in the appointment of resident tutors to pioneer development in the eastern counties of the District. In that advocacy, he was subsequently to acknowledge he had been unaware of the problems arising from the Cambridge Board's maturing plans for such appointments and the issue of providing powers which were to become particularly difficult and threatening to the District a few years later.[2]

Indications of these future difficulties became apparent as early as October 1935 when, during Jacques' absence through injury, Lionel Elvin and Ernest Green combined to defeat a Cambridge Board proposal to discontinue the long-standing tradition that the new District Secretary should be appointed as Joint Secretary to the Tutorial Classes Committee.

The continued success of the two WEA County Federations in Bedfordshire and Northamptonshire stimulated Jacques to examine other possibilities for similar development. Essex and Norfolk were obvious and attractive areas for development beyond the more urbanised counties and were to become the main foci of his activity until the outbreak of the war in 1939 and throughout its duration, although not in the way he envisaged in 1936.

Jacques was also fortunate in that within a few months of taking up his appointment, the government's public expenditure restrictions imposed in the economic crisis of 1931 were relaxed in 1935- 36 with the restoration of progressive grants and the encouragement of new provision in adult education, outlined in the Board of Education's Circular 1444. The Circular exhorted LEAs to consider new ways of providing opportunities for adult education, including co-operation with universities and voluntary bodies. It also suggested that a mechanism was required to review existing arrangements so that the disparate needs of adults and appropriate types of provision could be met more adequately. The Cambridge Board clearly perceived the Circular's exhortation as an opportunity to provide through its Rural Areas Committee (RAC) both the forum and the mechanism called for and thus to develop its own role and expand its activities within a triumvirate of providers. It began to plan accordingly.

However, in early 1936, the position was apparently discouraging for Jacques. In Norfolk the decline in activity since Newlove's prolonged illness had been considerable. The LEA offered no grant-aid in support of the four WEA Terminal courses Jacques arranged in 1936–37 although a grant of £40 was promised for 1937–38.[3] In 1935–36, the only Tutorial Class in the county was at Norwich, in social philosophy, with a mere seventeen members although another Tutorial Class in psychology commenced in 1936–37. In 1937, the Cambridge Board independently approached the Norfolk LEA to explore the possibilities of an appointment of a resident tutor in the county for adult education in rural areas. In October of that year, Hickson and Jacques joined forces and met the Director of Education over the possibility of a combined approach to the development of adult education which would reflect the recommendations of Circular 1444. Although initially encouraging, the approach proved to be fruitless and both bodies made independent arrangements within separately developed policies which were to lead to disagreement over the Cambridge Board's RAC scheme for liberal adult education throughout the region, and which is considered in the next section of this chapter.

In Essex, Jacques found very little WEA activity in rural areas although there were promising urban branches at Colchester, Harwich and Halstead. Further, he became aware that the District had incurred a financial loss on most of the courses it had arranged in the county: in 1936–37 for example the seven courses provided had led to an aggregated deficit of £92 for the year. The LEA grant-aid for courses of only £45 left the District with a substantial deficit, a position which was to recur in later years up to 1940 when the LEA approved a block grant for the WEA to meet anticipated deficits on courses. The 1940 block grant also helped to support the organisation of the Essex Federation of WEA branches which was formally established in the summer of that year.

The earlier failure of the East Suffolk organising-tutor scheme cast a long shadow over the discussion between Jacques and Martin Wilson, the new Secretary of Education. Although Wilson was undoubtedly sympathetic to the WEA he left East Suffolk on appointment as Secretary for Education in Shropshire and was succeeded by Leslie Missen who, at that time, knew little about the WEA and the discussions with the LEA had to be framed within a longer time-scale than Jacques had originally planned.[4] Other than in Ipswich, where the WEA branch was among the small group of vigorous, active and well-organised centres in the District, there appeared to be little prospect for development without LEA-funded support in the pre-war years and, as in West Suffolk, the development of a substantial WEA presence did not occur until after the 1939–45 war.

Jacques's visits to the LEAs and branches in the rural eastern counties confirmed his belief that without the continuing presence of high quality resident tutor-organisers in rural areas, few people would be prepared to accept responsibility for the organisation and maintenance of self-directing adult student groups in villages. The position in the District was exacerbated by the absence of other cohesive groups such as trade unionists or co-operative societies in rural areas who might have provided cadres of people for active WEA membership.

In the western counties of the District problems of a different order existed. In Northamptonshire, a sense of continuity existed in a WEA tradition from the earliest period of the Association's activities. Many members of the District's branches, classes and courses were also active trade unionists; some of these and many others were linked with the substantial Co-operative movement in the industrial centres. In addition, the considerable influence of Miss Helen Stocks together with the experience and commitment of Sophie Green had given sustained momentum to the District's educational provision and, of course, the Cassell Fund had provided invaluable financial support over many years. The Cambridge Board also had its own resident tutor in the county and thus few opportunities for development were missed in the county even though the LEA's support was limited to specific grant-aid for classes and courses provided by the District and the Cambridge Board.

In February 1935, and unknown to the District, the Cambridge Board had proposed the formation of a joint committee with the LEA to explore and promote new developments in adult education in Northamptonshire on the assumption of increased financial aid from the LEA. A proposed meeting between officers of the Board and the LEA was cancelled as the county council had no clear policy over adult educational provision and the only result of the proposal was confirmation of the LEA's existing policy of specific grant-aid. It was only some years later that Jacques learned of the Board's initiatives and that it had failed because members of the county council had been deeply suspicious of the radicalism associated with liberal adult education in the industrial areas of the county. Apparently, little distinction was made between the providers and the suspicion of some county councillors was linked with the views of other councillors who held antipathetic attitudes over any non-statutory expenditure on educational provision.

In Bedfordshire, the position was complex. Although the most successful county in the District in demonstrating the effectiveness of a resident tutor through the considerable talents of Harold Shearman who had provided the building blocks for co-operative endeavour between the Cambridge Board and the WEA during the early thirties, the position began to change when he was succeeded by Harold Plaskitt as the university's resident tutor in 1936. When Shearman was appointed National Education Officer for the WEA, questions were raised by the LEA over the continued appointment of a full-time resident tutor in the county and agreement was reached only on the understanding that the new resident tutor would concentrate his activities in the undeveloped rural areas in the south of the county. The LEA continued its generous block grant in support of the scheme and Plaskitt established a number of centres in the villages in south Bedfordshire. However, he sought to establish University Extra-Mural Groups or Societies rather than use the County Federation of WEA branches in the promotion of extension classes through gaining support of Women's Institutes and other voluntary organisations. All this activity led to a loosening of the earlier close relationships with the WEA and it was believed within the Federation that the new tutor was pursuing the Cambridge Board's emerging policy for its rural areas programme. It was a policy which led to considerable friction between the Cambridge Board and the District during 1938–39.

A unique set of difficulties existed in Cambridgeshire. With the development of the village colleges, Henry Morris had launched an unparalleled concept of the importance of educational provision as a life-long experience. Perhaps understandably, in view of the problems he encountered and the opposition of some members of the county council, his concern was to establish prestigious links between village colleges and the University of Cambridge in the provision of adult education rather than with the much less regarded WEA. In June 1936, Jacques met Morris in an attempt to explain the ways in which the Cambridge Board and the District were co-operating over the provision of adult education in an attempt to persuade the LEA to increase its annual grant, then a mere £20. As a result, Morris agreed to double the annual grant in 1938–39 and to provide rooms for WEA classes in schools and colleges without charge. Nevertheless, he was not an enthusiast for the work of the WEA and Jacques recalled only one exchange in their discussion with any pleasure:

Morris: Tell me; when is the WEA going to die as a voluntary body?

Jacques: When it ceases to be a voluntary body it is already dead![5]

Other than the later stimulating and substantial growth in Norfolk and Essex, and which is considered in later sections of this chapter, the major encouraging early development for the new District Secretary occurred in Hertfordshire. In the previous decade WEA classes and courses were arranged on an intermittent basis at Hoddesdon, Letchworth, St. Albans, Stevenage and Welwyn Garden City but little had been possible in the organisation of interest or to sustain a social movement in the county. As part of his early strategy to secure the co-operation of the LEAs, Jacques met the Director of Education, John Newsom, and secured agreement for an increase in grant-aid from the £35 in 1935–36 to more than £100 in 1938–39 and, in addition, the promise of a contribution by the LEA towards the District's administrative costs in arranging courses. Expansion of the District's activity in the county began almost immediately although its significant increase had to await the outbreak of the war.

Following Jacques's discussions with LEAs the financial position gradually improved and is summarised below:

Table 4.1 LEA Grant-Aid to District Classes and Courses

County	1937–38 £	1938–39 £
Bedfordshire	45	58
Cambridgeshire	20	40
East Suffolk	–	–
Essex	–	50
Hertfordshire	53	105
Huntingdonshire	–	10
Norfolk	20	80
Northamptonshire	45	68
West Suffolk	15	20
	£198	£351

In addition, Cambridgeshire (£10), Hertfordshire (£45), Norfolk (£40) and Northamptonshire (£30) contributed the sums within brackets exclusively to aid District administration of classes and courses.

Although Jacques was gratified with the response of most of the LEAs he was aware that other LEAs such as Somerset, Dorset, Wiltshire and Staffordshire were contributing annual sums in the order of £200-£300 in support of liberal adult education to their WEA Districts. However, more discouraging from the District's standpoint was the development by the Cambridge Board of its Rural Areas Committee policies for the region.

The Cambridge Board and The Rural Areas Scheme

It will be recalled that following the mutual agreement over the continuation of the Bedfordshire scheme in 1930 and the exceptional arrangements made for Cambridgeshire, the Cambridge Board had established its Rural Areas Committee (RAC) in 1932 to expand its provision of Chapter III courses in both counties through the activities of its university resident tutors, Shearman and Baker.

That these were exceptional arrangements agreed during a period of acute difficulty for the District is revealed in the following table which summarises the provision of Chapter III courses in England and Wales in 1935–36:

Table 4.2 Chapter III Courses, 1935–36[6]

Providing Body	Total	Distribution		
WEA and Others	1,091	(81.6%)	WEA	676
			Other Voluntary	87
			LEA	328
Universities and University Colleges	246	(18.4%)	Cambridge	40
			Other Universities	21
			University Colleges (Exeter, Hull, Reading, Nottingham)	185
Grand Total of all Chapter III courses	1,337			

Within the total for universities, seven were providing no Chapter III courses and of the five which did, most of the twenty-one listed in the table were arranged by Birmingham where this type of course had been offered in the industrial areas prior to the introduction of the 1932 Adult Education Regulations and which had continued under an established precedent. Of the four university colleges, only Nottingham was a substantial provider of Chapter III courses, in the East Midlands, and here again as the provision pre-dated the 1932 Regulations, existing practice was recognised and approved by the Board of Education.

However, in 1933–34, and although the circumstances were quite different, the university college at Hull used the Cambridge Board's exceptional arrangement in Bedfordshire in an attempt to exercise

Chapter III providing powers in East Yorkshire. The bid was vigorously resisted by the Yorkshire North District led by its energetic Secretary, G. H. Thompson, and a compromise solution was reached whereby both the District and the University College offered Chapter III courses under the aegis of a co- ordinating committee to avoid overt competition and unnecessary duplication.

Thus, from a national view, only the University of Cambridge through its Board for Extra-Mural Studies was undertaking a significant volume of new Chapter III activity and it was a matter of concern both to the National WEA and the District that its encroachment into the established and defined sphere of provision should be limited to the two counties in which earlier and exceptional arrangements had been agreed. Nevertheless, following the Board of Education's Circular 1444 in 1936 it was increasingly clear that the provision of adult education was a legitimate responsibility of three providers: the universities, the LEAs and the voluntary bodies, principally the WEA. In this triple partnership the universities could perceive themselves as occupying the middle ground between the LEAs as statutory providers and the voluntary bodies which traditionally existed to articulate and give shape to the aspirations and needs of individuals, groups and communities for liberal adult education.

Further, the universities were the acknowledged custodians of academic standards for Tutorial Classes as well as for other courses of broad intellectual and cultural interest. On the other hand, the LEAs were expanding their provision through a diversified range of courses of 'instruction' in practical skills, many of which were provided for occupational qualifications at 'night schools' or evening institutes. Within the troika of providers, the WEA appeared to occupy an intermediate position through its Chapter III courses. There was, of course, some overlapping of provision. Tutorial Classes were firmly in the university sector and some LEAs were arranging classes which hitherto had been the preserve of the WEA, e.g. civics and esperanto, and even as early as 1936, the number was relatively substantial (see Table 4.2). Thus by the mid-thirties the boundaries of the WEA's sector of provision were becoming somewhat ragged margins as the other two better-funded and organised providers developed their policies and encroached into the territory of earlier voluntary endeavour.

However, and central to its existence, the WEA had originally developed as the organised 'voice' of the needs of working people to secure provision for liberal adult education essential in its view to the emergence of an educated democracy. In the absence of appropriate provision by other bodies, the WEA had grown as a social movement which sought to provide those opportunities for people, denied access to further and higher education, either through its own efforts or co-operatively, but without patronage, in partnership with the universities, LEAs, and other agencies. The prospect of encroachment by some universities without an explicit partnership with the WEA was held by successive General Secretaries of the National Association such as Mactavish, Firth and, later, Green to represent a direct threat to the autonomy of the student, the branch and to the WEA itself. Indeed, as early as 1926 when the Universities Extra-Mural Consultative Committee (UEMCC) issued its first annual report, Pateman had written to Mactavish, then General Secretary of the WEA, expressing concern over the establishment of the inter-university committee:

> If you look at the preamble you will see that it is a self-appointed body with only Executive officers of Extra-Mural Boards and Committees. It has no representation of the demand side and is not representative of the Movement . . . The position re (sic) Rural education in Cambridgeshire will need to be watched.[7]

For the District the establishment of the UEMCC was of particular concern as Cranage was its first Chairman and Hickson a member.

In his reply, Mactavish was characteristically forthright:

> I was not conscious of the existence of such a committee until I received the report . . . No self-respecting working educational body, much as it may desire to retain close and friendly relations with the Board (of Education), Universities, etc., can go on being hampered in its work by the increasing number of organisations concerned either telling it what to do, what it should not do, or advising it in both these directions . . . there is a grave danger of our movement ultimately being strangled by our friends.[8]

This letter from Mactavish reveals the assumption made in 1926 that it was the WEA's exclusive duty and responsibility to provide working class education, but had he read the 1926 UEMCC report more searchingly he would have realised that the universities' role was not merely advisory but intended to promote the development of liberal adult education independently of other providers. The establishment of the Cambridge Board's Rural Areas Committee in 1932 to facilitate its extended role in Bedfordshire and Cambridgeshire may be interpreted as a natural development of the UEMCC's 1926 stance and officially endorsed by the 1932 Adult Education Regulations through the provisions for the appointment of Article 11 resident tutors in rural areas. Following Circular 1444, the UEMCC believed the role of university extra-mural departments should be further developed:

The mere increase in the variety of voluntary interests concerned in the demand for adult education implies new problems of planning and the need for increased participation by the Universities in the tasks of organisation.[9]

This wider context of the developments at university and LEA levels is necessary for an adequate understanding of the difficulties which arose in the years immediately prior to the 1939–45 war between the Cambridge Board and the District as there were serious implications for the National WEA if the District's problems had not been resolved through protracted, patient and complex negotiations.

Involvement in the tasks of organisation in the UEMCC's 1937 memorandum mentioned above, implied, *inter alia*, the appointment of university resident tutors. The Cambridge Board anticipated the publication of the UEMCC memorandum by declaring its intention to extend its rural areas scheme through the appointment of resident tutors in Essex and Norfolk. The announcement led to informal discussion between the Board's officers, District representatives and the National WEA but failed to establish a basis for co-operation of provision in either county. The failure to arrive at an agreement sufficiently alarmed the District to establish its own sub-committee to examine the District's future relationships with the Cambridge Board and LEAs in the region. It appeared that the expedient solution proposed by the District in 1930 for the Bedfordshire scheme had led to a further concession in Cambridgeshire in 1932 and by 1937 had been developed into a strategy for the development of adult education in rural areas for which the Board '. . . visualised the Rural Areas Scheme as an eight counties one'.[10]

The significance of the Board's policy was not confined to the District. Thompson, the Secretary of the Yorkshire North District, and Littlecott, Secretary of the Western District, wrote to Jacques urging that a firm stand be taken on the issue and no further concessions be made. Littlecott believed the District was 'fighting a test case the result of which I feel confident will have far-reaching effects throughout the country'.[11] It was widely recognised within the WEA at least, that the Cambridge Board was seeking to implement the policies outlined in the UEMCC's 1937 memorandum;

whereby provision by extra-mural departments was not to be automatically mediated through expressions of need channelled through voluntary bodies, especially the WEA.

This policy posed a general problem for the National WEA, which lacked a clear view on its partnership with other providers, and was an especially acute one for the District where important concessions had been made in earlier years to the Cambridge Board. For the District a plan for the limitation of encroachment by the Cambridge Board was agreed during late 1937. Three key issues were identified for negotiation between the District and the Cambridge Board. First, there was an unresolved question over the constitutional position of Jacques as District Secretary as a member of the RAC from which he had been excluded. Second, it was necessary to examine and define the ways in which an effective working relationship between both bodies might be agreed for the provision of adult education in rural areas. Third, detailed consideration was required of the reasons which had prompted the Cambridge Board to consider seeking providing powers for courses of a lower academic standard than those traditionally offered by universities in counties beyond those for which exceptional agreements existed.

In the view of the WEA, and unlike the position elsewhere, the Cambridge Board appeared to be in an anomalous position which would create new and reprehensible precedents likely to threaten the traditional and unique role of the WEA as a recognised providing body for liberal adult education. The WEA's attitude was not unreasonable as the practice in other universities was unlike that being proposed by Cambridge. Elsewhere, at Bristol, London and especially at Oxford, for example, the partner WEA Districts were recognised as organising bodies for adult education provision and in these three universities financial support for District work was provided by the extra-mural departments. In contrast, the District's perception of the Cambridge Board's policy was that its own work would be undermined and possibly replaced by expansion of the Board's providing powers for Chapter III courses through the appointment of a cadre of university resident tutors throughout the region.

With the apparent disinclination of the Cambridge Board to consider any major modification to its proposals the District sought to make similar appointments in Essex and Norfolk. In the event, it secured a grant from the Cassell Trust to appoint an Organising Secretary for Norfolk and Norwich but a bid for adequate finance for a similar appointment in Essex foundered.

Through its representation on the RAC, the District engaged with the Cambridge Board in a variety of discursive negotiations during 1938 and 1939 about their fundamental differences. While these were in progress, each body took unilateral action and in Norfolk the Board appointed John Hampden Jackson as its Article 11 university resident tutor in the summer of 1938. In the autumn of 1938 the District appointed Edmund Poole as its Organising Secretary for Norfolk and Norwich. Over the Essex appointment the District objected to the establishment of the post of resident tutor as the terms of the appointment depended on joint funding between the Board and the Essex LEA. Under this kind of joint responsibility the District foresaw that in undertaking the resident tutor's organising and teaching duties in north and mid-Essex some of the courses would fall into the Chapter III category. It therefore refused to cede its authority as the recognised providing body to the Board. Here, the District was in a relatively strong constitutional position as London University already had a resident tutor in south Essex where all Chapter III courses were provided under the control of the WEA London District. In a gesture of goodwill and co-operation, the District having established its official position as the Responsible Body for Chapter III courses with both the Board and the LEA, withdrew its opposition on the understanding that it was not conceding its providing powers in Essex. In September 1938, A. E. Douglas-Smith took up his duties as university resident tutor in the county.

By an extraordinary stroke of good fortune, both resident tutors appointed by the Cambridge Board were supportive of the WEA as a democratic adult educational movement. Equally important, close personal relationships based on mutual regard and trust developed between both tutors and Jacques. The relationship was to be reinforced to a remarkable degree during the following year when the Cambridge Board's expansionist policies in both counties led to frequently acrimonious disagreements between the Board and District officers in Cambridge. Contrastingly, close fraternal relationships existed between Poole, Hampden Jackson and Jacques in the development of District provision in Norfolk.

The period from the autumn of 1938 until the outbreak of the war in September 1939 was characterised by a series of devious stratagems as the Cambridge Board and the District sought to out-manoeuvre each other to gain supremacy in the development of adult education provision under the Board's rural areas scheme. From the surviving documentation, annotations on meeting papers, careful notes made of verbal exchanges and copies of correspondence it is possible to reconstruct the broad sequence of events and the serial proposals and counter-proposals which marked a period of intensive and difficult negotiation with neither side being prepared to risk an open breach in relationships which would have been publicly damaging.

Arising from the resolute opposition by the District to the Board's proposals, a sub-committee was also established by the Cambridge Board to consider its relations with the WEA and met for the first time in May 1938. At a further meeting in July, Green, General Secretary for the National WEA, submitted a memorandum which, in effect, proposed a constitution for a joint University/ WEA Rural Areas Committee. Green's memorandum reflected the WEA's dissatisfaction with its original 1932 representation on the RAC in that although the District was recognised by the Board of Education as the most important providing body for Chapter III courses in the region, it had less than 25% of the committee's membership which thus failed to recognise the WEA's national or regional status. The reason for the imbalance had arisen from the subsequent addition of LEA representatives on the RAC. For example, three representatives from the Isle of Ely sat on the committee although only four short courses had been arranged in that Authority. Green argued that if the principle were extended to all eight counties the RAC would be controlled by the LEAs with a mere three members representing the WEA and only three representing the Cambridge Board with Hickson and Pateman as the committee's servicing officers.

The main thrust of Green's proposals was to modify the 1932 arrangements so that, as originally intended, a balanced committee would be established. He also advocated the addition of Jacques as a committee officer, together with Hickson and Pateman, in recognition of the traditional partnership principle between the University and the WEA, as existed for the Tutorial Classes Committee. The revised Rural Areas Committee would then comprise eighteen members: six from the participating LEAs, six from the Cambridge Board, six from the WEA and, of course, three servicing officers. Further, and using a model in existence elsewhere, Green foresaw the functions of the RAC as an advisory, co-ordinating body with executive powers vested in existing mechanisms such as the Joint Committee for Tutorial Classes, the University Extension Courses committee for Chapter II provision and the Eastern District of the WEA for Chapter III arrangements. Through these committees the RAC would be fully apprised of the demand for, and existing and planned provision of, adult education classes and courses in the eight counties. In addition, an important function of the RAC would be its financial responsibility specifically for rural development for which it would receive and disburse hypothecated funds from LEAs and Trusts and from which it would be empowered to make deficiency payments to the relevant providing body where deficits occurred.

A crucial implication of Green's memorandum was that the District would receive formal recognition as the legitimate providing body for Chapter III courses in rural areas. Further, the promotional functions of the existing RAC policy would be replaced by more limited functions of monitoring and reporting developments in rural areas. Unsurprisingly, the Cambridge Board members were unable to accept Green's proposals as it involved weakening its own *ad hoc* position and strengthening that of the District. The memorandum was remitted to the officers of both bodies for detailed consideration and report at a subsequent meeting.

At officer level, the Cambridge Board through Hickson and Pateman not unreasonably argued that its initiatives in rural areas had been successful; not least because of the financial support received from LEAs who were prepared to grant-aid provision of liberal adult education by the Board more generously than that provided through the District. In addition, and as a result of the work undertaken by its resident tutors in Bedfordshire, Cambridgeshire and Northamptonshire, the Board had developed systematic provision of all types of classes and courses on a scale beyond that imaginable if the District had been the sole provider. From every standpoint, the initiatives taken by the Cambridge Board had been entirely beneficial: to students, LEAs and, not least, to the District which had been relieved of significant administrative and financial burdens. For example, in 1936–37 the costs of providing courses in rural Bedfordshire and Cambridgeshire had amounted to £330 in excess of grant earned under the Board of Education Regulations. For the WEA, Green, Elvin, and Jacques could not adequately counter the authenticity of these claims nor deny the earlier co-operation in developments in all three counties.

The force of the District's argument lay in the clarification and negotiation of future arrangements which would not be dependent on exceptional agreements within the rural areas scheme in the other counties in the region and in subsequent discussion the WEA representatives concentrated on the three main proposals in Green's memorandum of July 1938. First, the equitable representation of the interests in the triple partnership; second, the retention of the District's providing powers for Chapter III courses and, finally, the future role of the RAC as the co-ordinating and financial mechanism for the development of liberal adult education in rural areas.

A period of protracted negotiation followed in late 1938 and early 1939 during which proposals and counter proposals were intensively discussed in and beyond formal meetings in attempts to resolve fundamental differences without arriving at an open breach in formal

115

relationships. During this period Green considered exemplars elsewhere which involved university extra-mural departments and the WEA in co-operative initiatives. But examination of each one at, for example, Oxford, Bristol and Hull revealed their inapplicability to the Cambridge situation and Green was forced to continue to attempt to negotiate a unique arrangement, whereby both bodies might achieve agreement on a co-ordinated scheme for the development of adult education in rural areas.

On behalf of the District, Jacques counselled an unhurried pace and a moderate attitude as the developing rapport with Hampden Jackson and Douglas-Smith was immensely encouraging as were the early initiatives being taken by Poole. The new university resident tutors were convinced of their ability to provide Chapter III courses organised by the District concurrently with their own duties to encourage the growth of Chapter II courses without role conflict or competitive interest. Both were essentially concerned with the expansion of adult educational opportunities irrespective of the providing body, a cause in which both were legitimately involved as their duties were not prescribed in detail.

However, in the autumn of 1938, they informed Jacques that they had been asked not to organise any Chapter III courses in existing, or former, university extension centres, but both had refused to accept such limitation on their activities. Even Poole, the District's own Organising Secretary in Norfolk and Norwich, had been asked by a Cambridge Board officer not to go '. . . into towns or villages where there was or had been Extension work'.[12] He had been given a list of Extension Centres marked 'active' or 'dormant' to ensure there would be no misinterpretation over his activities within the constraints of the document. He reported the matter to Jacques and the problem was quickly resolved in discussion and correspondence between Elvin, Jacques and Hickson.[13]

In Essex, the position was more delicate and less secure for the District. The Board's resident tutor, Douglas-Smith, was also accountable to the LEA which contributed towards his salary. Here, the District had few branches and had failed in its bid to secure funding for its own tutor-organiser. In addition, the LEA was beginning to establish its own network of evening institutes at secondary schools and J. K. Revans, the Assistant Director for Education, wished to learn how the proposals for the rural areas scheme were to operate in the county. At a meeting in Saffron Walden in October 1938, arrangements for Essex were discussed by Revans, Hickson, Douglas-Smith and Jacques. From notes of the meeting and subsequent correspondence it is clear that Jacques was unequivocal in his view that the LEA evening institutes could develop as the 'natural home for adult education activity' and he wished the District's Chapter III courses to be accommodated wherever appropriate within the LEA's existing institutions. In addition, he offered the services of the District's Office in Cambridge as a 'clearing house' for all applications for Essex classes and courses in both urban and rural areas of the county. As the Responsible Body for Chapter III, the District would, after processing applications, pass on those within the rural areas scheme to the Board at Stuart House for the necessary action. By these means there would be immediate recognition of the unity of purpose and co-operation between the Cambridge Board and the District and at the same time the work of the resident tutor would be facilitated. He freely acknowledged that responsibility for the development in rural areas of Essex would lie with the RAC but he invited the resident tutor to expand, if he so wished, his activities into existing WEA centres at Chelmsford, Harwich, Dovercourt and Silver End. In Jacques's view the indivisibility of town and country in liberal adult education might lead naturally to the formation of a county federation of WEA branches as had occurred elsewhere in the District and which had been entirely beneficial to the growth of adult education. Both Revans and Douglas-Smith welcomed the offers made by Jacques, and the latter endorsed the position of the District as the providing body, an important indication of support for the WEA as the attitude of the resident tutor was crucial in the operation of any scheme involving co-operation between the University and the District.

Thus during the autumn of 1938, support for the District by the two new resident tutors in Essex and Norfolk was assured and known to both the Cambridge Board and to the WEA. In Bedfordshire, the earlier agreement over the Board's assumption of providing powers for Chapter III courses in the rural areas was undeviatingly adhered to by Plaskitt, the university's resident tutor. In Cambridgeshire, a middle course was followed by Baker who actively supported Chapter III courses in existing WEA branches and extended Chapter II activity in those villages in which WEA courses had never been provided.

In November 1938, the Cambridge Board produced two new major proposals for the development of its rural areas scheme. The most significant and contentious was a geographical demarcation for each providing body. The proposal centred on a definition of 'rural areas' intended to confer exclusive providing rights for each body. The Board would have exclusive responsibility in those '. . . centres of population less than 6,000 in the counties concerned' with the larger urban centres as the exclusive preserve of the District. To avoid divisiveness the Board also proposed that '. . . it would be of advantage if Resident Tutors were kept informed of the activities of the WEA in the urban districts of their respective counties'.[14]

In effect, this was merely an attempt to generalise the agreement reached in Bedfordshire in 1930, although the criterion adopted then was not based on population size of centres but on local government boundaries, a much more advantageous position for the District, than the 1938 proposal. For the WEA it was an unacceptable proposal and was immediately rejected by the District. Had it been accepted, the District would have been confined to only three centres in Norfolk – Norwich, Great Yarmouth and King's Lynn and would have withdrawn from at least ten other centres at which WEA branches had existed, some from the early twenties.[15] In Essex, the District would have been confined to provision in Colchester, Chelmsford, Clacton, Halstead, Braintree and Maldon. Large tracts of Norfolk and north Essex would have been ceded to the Board and which, perhaps of immediate significance at that time, would have effectively prevented Hampden Jackson and Douglas-Smith from organising their growing number of WEA Chapter III courses and establishing branches in both counties.

Green and Jacques led the considerable opposition to the proposal. In a lengthy commentary on the Board's proposal, Douglas-Smith wrote to Jacques:

I am strongly against this curious division of population at the 6,000 figure. It does not in the least correspond to any difference in the type of population . . . It is important to realise the fact of 'dormitory' villages now so widely spread over England; from any of the Essex towns one can see, as soon as works close down, a long string of bicycles returning to the villages outside . . .

But it is equally important to insist that the WEA is effective among an agricultural population . . .

I should view with great consternation any attempt to exclude Resident Tutors from *any* towns or villages . . . But, indeed, the whole general effect is to divorce Resident Tutors from the WEA; the Resident Tutor would be excluded from urban areas, while on the other hand the WEA would be to say the least of it extremely circumscribed in rural areas. The prospect seems to me unprecedented and highly undesirable.[16]

In more astringent fashion, Hampden Jackson dealt with the realities of his appointment:

J. H. J. is thoroughly satisfied with the existing position which enables him to organise classes under whatever flag he thinks most suitable for the centre concerned. As for confining his work to under 6,000 people areas, he would remind the Board that the terms of his appointment stated 'he will be expected to exercise *general* supervision over the work of the Board in Norfolk and in particular to assist in the development of Adult Education in rural areas'; he would also remind them that the Board decided that his Statutory Tutorial Class should be in Norwich.[17]

The other major new proposal made by the Cambridge Board in November 1938 was equally contentious. It was that the Rural Areas Committee should have executive control over the appointment of tutors for classes and courses and thus, of course, approval of the syllabuses. This was an issue over which neither the National WEA nor the District could afford to compromise. Other than for Tutorial Classes, the WEA as a Responsible Body had not only traditionally provided the organisation for student demand but had also appointed its own tutors and approved syllabuses for courses within its Chapter III provision. Here, Green saw an opportunity to negotiate an arrangement which could have resolved a number of problems. He suggested that if the RAC were to be re-constituted with equality of representation and parity of esteem between the Board and the WEA, an arrangement which already existed in the University/WEA Joint Tutorial Classes Committee, the procedures followed by that committee over the appointment of tutors and approval of syllabuses would clearly offer a satisfactory solution. As for the Tutorial Classes Committee, Jacques would become a Joint Secretary of the RAC, a particularly difficult sticking point for officers of the Cambridge Board.

At this stage in the negotiations, Green was in a relatively confident mood. Through informal contact with civil servants at the Board of Education, he learned that the Cambridge Board had not approached the Board of Education for approval to its plans to provide Chapter III courses in counties beyond its existing recognition in Bedfordshire and Cambridgeshire. He was thus encouraged to believe that the Cambridge Board entertained some doubt over the strength of its case for unilateral action and was therefore anxious to reach a negotiated agreement with the WEA prior to making any application for additional Chapter III providing powers. He was also aware that similar arrangements were being explored between Nottingham and the East Midlands District and that the Cambridge Board/Eastern District solution might set a national precedent.

Sadly, at this stage in the negotiations a degree of acrimony became evident in personal relationships. Hickson and Jacques severed direct contact with each other; Shearman and Pateman had a major disagreement over a question of loyalty to the WEA, and the two new university resident tutors were not informed of the proposed developments nor invited to comment on the proposals which might affect Essex and Norfolk. Thus they viewed all the Board's moves with increasing misgiving and distrust and their personal relationships with Jacques and the WEA were consequentially further strengthened – a position reflected in the majority of their courses being arranged through the Chapter III providing powers of the District. In 1938–39, Hampden Jackson and Poole working in harness established nine new centres of which five were WEA branches at East Dereham, Hingham, Swaffham, Walsingham and Wymondham. The other four were Student Groups at Hockwold, Mattishall, Sheringham, and a revival of interest at Wells. In April 1939, the Norfolk County Federation of WEA Branches was established to provide a sense of unity and cohesion among the scattered clusters of WEA students and members. In Essex in his first year, Douglas-Smith helped to establish three new WEA branches at Dunmow, Maldon and Witham; Terminal courses at three other centres and encouraged the creation of the Essex County Federation of WEA Branches.

But during the autumn of 1938, the distaste that Hampden Jackson felt over the Board's machinations was expressed in a personal note to Jacques:

Every time I go to Cambridge I come back depressed as hell; then as soon as I am back to a Norfolk class spirits soar again.[18]

At Board/WEA level, as neither body wished the impasse with which members found themselves confronted to continue interminably Hickson met Green informally. Both agreed to modifications in the proposals which were then considered from December 1938 until February 1939. These were incorporated into a re-drafted constitution for the Rural Areas Committee and discussed further by Professor Barker, Chairman of the Cambridge Board and the Rural Areas Committee, with Elvin and Green. Agreement to withdraw the proposals for the demarcation of rural areas on the 6,000 population criterion and a compromise over the provision of Chapter III courses was reached. This was that although the District would be explicitly recognised as the Responsible Body for Chapter III courses throughout the rural areas scheme, if any class wished to have a Chapter III category course organised by the Cambridge Board the WEA would agree to the Board assuming providing powers for the purpose of meeting the wishes of the students in the class. In practice this agreement reflected yet again the pattern adopted by

Shearman in Bedfordshire from 1930 onwards, and in effect it gave university resident tutors freedom to arrange both types of Chapter III courses. The other major difficulty over the appointment of tutors and approval of syllabuses for classes and courses in the rural areas scheme was resolved by Professor Barker and Green who agreed that each providing body would submit for the information of the Rural Areas Committee its own approved panel of tutors and syllabuses of approved courses.

However, objections to the Barker-Green agreement were raised by the administrative staff at Stuart House and it appeared that no further progress could be made, when quite fortuitously and coincidentally Jacques received a letter from the Secretary to the Bedfordshire County Federation of WEA Branches.[19] It was a bombshell. The Secretary of the Federation, C. G. A. Watts complained bitterly to Jacques about the recent decline in the provision of, and support for, liberal adult education courses in the county. He presented '. . . a very gloomy picture of adult education in this county . . .': the number of classes had declined from thirty-five in 1937–38 to twenty-five in 1938- 39 and the number of enrolled students had fallen by some 30%, and all at a time when activity in other counties was increasing significantly. Apparently, the formation of University Extra-Mural Groups rather than WEA branches and student groups (on the Shearman model) was perceived by Watts as responsible for undermining the Federation's responsibility to, and involvement with, manual workers:

> One class I proposed to visit, but was warned off as only one member was likely to be interested in a *workers* movement, all the others were retired from professions and it was thought I (a gardener) might offend them. . . One must ask whether the University is aware that such a thing is possible, or do they know that such contacts are sought in order that a class should appear without any justification. Or do they admit that the Rural Scheme is simply a rate-paid organisation to amuse well-educated people in their years of retirement.[20]

Although written with unquestioned partisan commitment to the WEA, the letter reflected some of the fundamental weaknesses redolent of the earlier dissatisfaction which had prompted Mansbridge to write his historic articles in the *University Extension Journal* in 1903. For Jacques and Green the issues raised by Watts were central tenets of belief and commitment and the *raison d'être* for their opposition to much of strategy embodied in the rural areas scheme.

For the District the contribution from Watts was of considerable and immediate significance as Bedfordshire was the only county in the region in which the template for the proposed rural areas scheme had been at least partially developed. It was claimed that the unsolicited letter from Watts revealed the extent to which the partnership principle had failed to secure active, purposeful and genuine co-operation between the Cambridge Board and the WEA. Its disclosures also served to heighten the WEA's apprehension about the problems inherent in the RAC policy and confirmed the worst fears of those WEA members who were involved in the difficult protracted negotiations currently in hand in early 1939. It also reinforced the District's resolve to protect its constitutional autonomy within any approved scheme.

Immediately, Jacques sent a copy of Watts' letter to Green urging him to use its contents in discussion with Professor Barker to demonstrate that '. . . his child is ailing and that seriously'.[21] In his view, the letter should be used to show that the Board's policy in the one county in which it had been implemented for at least two years was a misconceived, divisive one. Further, he believed the Board had no evidence of other successful experience in partnership with the WEA which might offset or counter Watts's trenchant criticism. No documentary evidence exists to indicate that Green acted as Jacques had urged, but a further set of modified proposals were drafted later that month on which agreement was reached by the principals: Barker, Green and Elvin. Green was fulsome in his praise for Barker's determined and generous efforts to reach an equitable settlement and it is possible that Green did acquaint the Chairman of the RAC with the unhappy position in Bedfordshire. Certainly, Jacques passed on Green's approbation of Barker's attitude to Hampden Jackson and Douglas- Smith a few days after the late February meeting:

> There was evident a very strong determination on the part of Prof.
> Barker to remove all obstacles likely to prevent agreement being
> reached and, in the course of a subsequent conversation with Elvin,
> he said that he had recently come to the conclusion that it was of
> primary importance that the WEA should have the full assistance
> of the Extra-Mural Board in all its work throughout the whole of
> this District.[22]

Detailed administrative and procedural arrangements were left with the officers of the Board and the District and, at last, Jacques was invited to attend subsequent meetings of the Cambridge Board pending his nomination as a WEA member. It was an important concession by the Board as Jacques had been excluded since his appointment in 1935 even though his predecessor had attended in the capacity of District Secretary.

However, the concession to Jacques was made on a personal basis and clearly, the matter of his appointment as a joint secretary of the RAC was not to be considered. Nevertheless, in conciliatory spirit, Jacques replied that:

> Some of my colleagues will regard this gesture on the part of the Board with pleasure that will make for whole-hearted co-operation on their part.[23]

Agreement was also quickly reached on earlier difficult constitutional matters such as the reduced representation by the LEAs, the autonomous approval of tutors and syllabuses by the providing bodies and, most importantly, confirmation of the District as the Responsible Body for Chapter III courses throughout the region. It is possible to hypothesise that if the District had surrendered its providing powers under the rural areas scheme, the weakened position of WEA Districts elsewhere in the country might have tilted provision for liberal adult education decisively towards university control in conjunction with LEAs. The conjecture appears to gain substance when one considers the time, energy and determination invested by Green, as the WEA's General Secretary, in the resolution of the District's difficulties with the Cambridge Board's rural areas scheme. Green clearly perceived the protracted negotiations as a major national problem rather than a local skirmish over the retention of Chapter III providing powers by one WEA District. Shortly after the agreement in late February 1939, he wrote to Jacques indicating the importance he had attached to the negotiated agreement with the Cambridge Board:

> ... that after paying at least a dozen visits to Cambridge and engaging in the most unpleasant negotiations I have ever had in my life, we have managed to retain recognition as a body which is normally recognised for Chapter III powers and obtained an agreement which the University people hate like poison.[24]

The reference here to the 'University' is almost certainly exclusive to Cambridge but it is possible that Green had in mind its implications in a wider context. There is little doubt that in his reference to 'people' he was excluding Professor Barker for whom he had a high regard.

But the WEA and District were not entirely clear of their difficulties and in March 1939 objections to the agreement came from an unexpected quarter – the District's own Executive Committee. Under their Chairman, Arthur Allen, the District's committee raised a series of questions about the negotiated settlement and were unbending on the issue of retention of the District's autonomy in all its affairs and highly critical of the failure to secure the appointment of Jacques as a joint secretary of the RAC.

In magisterial style, Green dealt peremptorily with the committee's inflexible attitude, reminding them that on every substantive issue he had fully discussed its possible implications with them. Through Jacques, he reminded the committee that in October 1931 the then District committee had argued:

> ... that it would be unwise to oppose the suggestion of Mr. Hickson in regard to the Board doing Chapter III work. That is eight years ago, and the Board would now be doing Chapter III work, both in Essex and Norfolk, had I not made myself damned unpleasant...[25]

The District committee relented; withdrew their objections and Jacques made it clear to Green it was only through his personal intervention and tenacity as the General Secretary that 'the WEA had been saved from disaster, and that this agreement represented, in fact, the charter which gives us continued and autonomous existence'.[26]

The following month, with the broad constitutional position of the RAC settled, Jacques and Hickson swiftly reached agreement on the outstanding administrative and procedural details. It was agreed that Chapter III course fees arranged by the District would be retained by the WEA and details of the procedures for reporting approval of tutors and syllabuses by each providing body were devised, together with the mechanism for equal tripartite representation.

On the question of representation, an unwelcome flurry of dissent over the proposed reduction in LEA representation came from Bedfordshire and Cambridgeshire. For Bedfordshire, Hickson and Jacques agreed to discuss a variety of difficulties with Baines but the rural areas scheme was not adopted formally by the county council until mid-June 1940 – the last LEA to approve the scheme. In Cambridgeshire, Henry Morris was uneasy that the proposed constitution implied that the WEA had exclusive providing powers for Chapter III courses. With the emerging pattern of village colleges, his LEA was providing its own programmes of liberal adult education and at the April 1939 meeting of the RAC he was successful in adding a clause to the constitution of the Committee to enable other 'approved associations' to provide courses of the Chapter III variety in addition to the WEA.

Somewhat ironically, in view of the detailed, convoluted negotiations of the previous year, the constitutional agreement was not put to the test in the ways intended as the outbreak of war in September 1939 set aside the anticipated position irrevocably. At the beginning of the 1939–40 session, the predominant concern was the capacity and wisdom of continuing to provide adult education in the region irrespective of constitutional proprieties. Energies were devoted to the practicability of maintaining the existing framework of provision, and, not least, the ability to respond to an exceptional anticipated demand from a heavy concentration of military personnel throughout the strategically important counties of East Anglia.

Apart from persistent but unsuccessful applications to re-enlist as an active soldier once more, Jacques, then in his early forties, revelled in organising, improvising and expanding WEA classes and courses throughout the region. In agreement with Hickson, Jacques organised the activities as though the rural areas scheme had been formally introduced and with the enthusiastic commitment of Hampden Jackson, Poole and Douglas-Smith, WEA provision in Norfolk and Essex expanded at an unprecedented pace throughout the war.

As Hickson and Jacques worked together during the war, their mutual regard and close co-operation under adverse wartime conditions grew into a genuine partnership through which the providing bodies came to recognise their inter-dependence. In 1940, Jacques was finally appointed as a joint secretary to the Rural Areas Committee to represent WEA interests for the District's Chapter III courses and through this overdue gesture formal recognition was given to the District's indispensable position in the provision of liberal adult education in the region. That it was also the major provider of adult education in the region was evident through the growth in its classes and courses from 156 in 1938-39 to more that 350 by the end of the war in 1945.

In 1941, the constitution of the Rural Areas Committee was finally approved. It had been further modified to include in its membership all four university resident tutors and six education officers from participating LEAs. The inclusion of the latter group was in recognition that local authority involvement was no longer merely passive through the grant-aiding of classes and courses but was now active in the planning of adult education provision and its shaping in conjunction with developing LEA policies. In this important pointer to the future, the RAC gave substance to the new tripartite partnership in adult education in East Anglia. Through the composition of the Committee it became legitimate for the Board and the District to negotiate with the LEAs jointly or independently over their provision – a new development which Jacques valued highly as it was an explicit, formal recognition of the District as the Responsible Body for the organisation of WEA classes and courses.

But it was not only officers and members of the WEA and the District who were pleased with the final agreement over the rural areas scheme and the conclusion of negotiations of byzantine complexity extending over a period of four difficult years. When introducing the final version of the constitution of the Rural Areas Committee in 1941, Professor Barker as its Chairman confessed:

> I do not remember there having been given such consideration and discussion to the constitution of any other body with which I have been associated.[27]

The full measure of that remark may be gauged when it is recalled that he was a senior member of the University Senate and a Fellow of Peterhouse, Cambridge.

The success of the *ad hoc* collaboration and co-operation between Hickson and Jacques during the war owed little to the elaborate mechanism of the RAC so tortuously constructed and thus led inevitably to its demise. By March 1944 Hickson, as Secretary to the Cambridge Board which was then reviewing its future organisation for the post-war period, was sufficiently assured to write of the Rural Areas Committee:

> The status and functions . . . are rather obscure, and the administrative arrangements are complicated, to say the least. It seems necessary to try to simplify and improve the machinery in the interests of the Board's work, and also in order that the University and voluntary associations may be able to shew to LEAs that their share in adult education will be effectively conducted.[28]

He recommended that:

> the Rural Areas Committee as at present constituted should cease to exist. It has fulfilled a useful purpose, but experience shews that it is better fitted for consultation than for active concern with details of educational provision.

For future joint Board/WEA committees he believed that:

> . . . such an arrangement would be to the advantage of the WEA, provided that the partnership in the Joint Committee is genuine and that the WEA retains and exercises the right of providing its own classes as may seem appropriate. Subject to these provisos, the proposal is no more than a logical development of the original WEA practice of asking the University to provide teaching facilities through Joint Committee procedure.[29]

Thus, in early 1944 the Cambridge Board finally tacitly acknowledged that the central issues over which the WEA and the District had refused to surrender any of their principles during the period 1937–39 had been justified. The Rural Areas Committee formally ceased to exist in December 1945 and its functions were assumed by a new University/WEA Joint Committee with responsibility for all liberal adult educational provision including Tutorial Classes throughout the region. The new committee was composed of equal representation of the University and the WEA. Hickson and Jacques became its Joint Secretaries and Pateman was its administrative officer. The new committee exemplified the intentions of the 1944 Education Act for closer co-operation, joint planning and participation in the organisation and provision of liberal adult education over which there was widespread anticipation of further expansion in the post-war period.

District Development 1935–1945

It is perhaps necessary to set the scene for this remarkable decade in the history of the District to show the ways in which the firm foundation for subsequent growth and consolidation was secured following a period of more than twenty years of uncertainty and improvision.

During 1935–36, the District arranged a total of 114 classes and courses, attended by 2,405 students, distributed among twenty WEA branches and thirty-one Student Groups. The most active counties continued to be Bedfordshire and Northamptonshire which together provided 56% of the total number of classes and students. In contrast, only 3.5% of the District's classes and less than 6% of enrolled students were in Essex and Norfolk. By the end of the 1938–39 session, the number of classes and courses had risen to 156 and the enrolled student total exceeded 3,000. The number of WEA branches had doubled to forty and thirty-six Student Groups existed. The distribution of the District's activities was beginning to reflect the efforts being made in Essex and Norfolk by Hampden Jackson and Douglas-Smith and in that year some 20% of the District's classes and enrolled students were in these two counties. At the end of the war in 1945, the growth in the District's educational activity was very impressive. Some 355 classes and courses had been provided for about 7,000 students in 110 WEA branches and thirty Student Groups.

In every county, except Bedfordshire and the Suffolks, growth occurred in the District's educational activity and was most evident in Essex, Hertfordshire, Norfolk, Northamptonshire and the Soke of Peterborough which in aggregate accounted for 75% of the provision and enrolled students during the years of the 1939–45 war. This remarkable and rapid growth was attributable to a relatively small group of full-time tutors and organising secretaries resident in these counties who demonstrated over several years the importance of their roles, personal qualities and '. . . their intimate association with members of branches and groups, which, in its turn, comes only from . . .

active sympathy with those ends which they seek to achieve through adult education'.[30] But, as earlier sections in this chapter have demonstrated, a decade earlier prospects for the District's future prosperity and work were unpromising and its autonomous existence open to serious doubt on occasions.

That the District not merely survived but flourished is unquestionably attributable to the considerable skilled judgment, shrewd diplomacy and unswerving commitment of Frank Jacques to the principles of the WEA and its social purpose in the best tradition of a disciple of Tawney. He would, of course, be the first to say that the consolidation, development and prospering of the District during the decade owed much more to others such as Harold Shearman, Mrs. Clara Rackham and Arthur Allen who were District Chairmen during the period. He would pay particular tribute to Ernest Green, the General Secretary of the WEA, for his guidance and tenacity on behalf of the District, to Lionel Elvin and David Thomson not only for their unremitting service as District Treasurers but also for their personal support and wise counselling. But above all, he would unreservedly acknowledge his profound indebtedness to the three tutors who were instrumental in the successful achievements in the later years of the decade: Douglas-Smith, Edmund Poole and Hampden Jackson. In Jacques's view, without the considerable talents and skills which Hampden Jackson gave unsparingly to the WEA, the District would not have flourished during the war nor in the twenty-five year period of change and innovation following it and in which Hampden Jackson actively participated in partnership with Frank Jacques.

Development and growth in the District's work was, of course, not found or sustained in every part of the District. Earlier in this chapter, reference has already been made to the decline in WEA activity in Bedfordshire and by the end of the war there were fewer classes in the county than had existed in 1935 and most of these were concentrated in the urban areas such as Bedford, Dunstable, Leighton Buzzard and Luton. In Northamptonshire, Miss Green continued under the Cassell Trust's funding of the Kettering scheme but her relationships with Lee, the university resident tutor, continued to be formal and distant. Her reluctant pioneering activity in Huntingdonshire led to courses at Eaton Socon, St. Neots and the county town. With Miss Stocks's support, the Cassell Trust grant was renewed yet again, but Miss Green appeared to have lost her former enthusiasm for breaking new ground and she concentrated her efforts in established WEA branches with the exception of Corby which she helped to re-establish in 1936. The final period of the Kettering scheme came when in 1938 the Cassell Trustees agreed to renew their grant for a further two years on a reducing scale with a concluding sum of £50 in 1940 to extinguish their support. However, it was not required as Miss Green resigned her appointment as District tutor-organiser in December 1939. Although Miss Stocks and many members of the Kettering and other branches protested at her resignation, it was accepted by the District. In many ways it was a sad ending for a tutor who had given some twenty years to the cause of workers' education in the county and perhaps the most sincere and apposite appreciation of her many qualities came most appropriately from a member of the Kettering branch:

> Miss Green means the WEA to hundreds of people. In her largeness of heart and her sincere desire to help all who needed it, Miss Green has never spared herself.[31]

Nevertheless, the active County Federation of WEA Branches and the collective strength of the members in the established branches such as Northampton, Kettering, Raunds, Rushden and Wellingborough ensured continuity of Tutorial Classes and other WEA courses and about thirty classes were arranged in the county in each year throughout the decade. During the war, the enlistment of many tutors in HM Forces was partly overcome through the appointment of young women graduates as WEA resident tutors to provide a variety of courses. In Northamptonshire, four such tutors were appointed by the District and as a result the number of courses increased from thirty-two in 1942–43 to fifty- two in the following year. (See Appendix B)

As mentioned earlier in this chapter, Jacques had been much encouraged by the attitude of the Hertfordshire LEA and the negotiated increased grant-aid for classes and courses. Between 1936 and 1939, activity in the county expanded from nine to eighteen courses. During the war, the District continued to extend its provision in Hertfordshire through the support of Jack Longland, the Assistant Director of Education. A former WEA tutor, Longland agreed that Hertfordshire would join the rural areas scheme in 1941 on the understanding that the District retained full providing powers throughout the county until an Article 11 university resident tutor was appointed. In the event no university appointment was made during the war, but the District appointed an Organising Tutor, P. N. Molloy, in 1941, and its own resident tutors in each of the following two years: Miss Jolliffe in 1942 and Miss Savage in 1943. In addition, the LEA provided £100 a year towards the administrative costs of the District. The effect of these arrangements was dramatic. Classes and courses in Hertfordshire increased from twenty-six in 1940–41 to more than sixty by the end of the war; yet another reflection of the importance and value of the resident tutor arrangement.

However, the most significant impact of the resident tutor model was seen in Essex and, especially, in Norfolk. The growth in the provision made by Douglas-Smith and Hampden Jackson in the year before the war was endangered by the rapidly diminishing availability of part-time tutors after September 1939. In 1938–39, the District's approved list contained 224 tutors but by 1941–42 the total had fallen to seventy-two. In addition, restrictions on the mobility of available tutors through the combined effects of severe petrol rationing and the withdrawal or serious unpunctuality of public transport services further curtailed the list of those tutors who were available for teaching.

Jacques produced an ingenious and effective solution to the problem. Through established links with a few Oxford Colleges, he visited Oxford annually during the war and offered appointments as WEA full-time tutors to several outstanding young women graduates. No salaries were guaranteed and their income depended almost entirely on a proportion of fees from enrolments in classes and courses at civilian and military centres. This cadre of full-time resident tutors was supplemented by other part-time tutors usually resident within the localities of branches and centres at which courses were arranged. Known as the District's 'Sabine Women' these young graduates not only held together the framework of the District's organisation in the counties throughout the war, but added substantially to the number of courses provided by the District and helped to establish new WEA branches and centres among the civilian population. In addition, their experience in the role of full-time resident tutors provided the basis for post-war appointments of resident tutor-organisers throughout the District.

In Essex, the framework for organisation and provision was in the hands of Douglas-Smith who with the assistance of two young women graduates and various part-time tutors expanded the District's course provision from nineteen classes in 1939–40 to almost fifty by the end of the war.

In Norfolk the scale of expansion was even greater. With the co-operation of Edmund Poole, until his enlistment in the RAF in 1941, Hampden Jackson and seven young graduates augmented by about thirty part-time tutors increased course provision from thirty-five classes in 1939–40 to almost ninety in 1945. For example, in 1942–43, of the sixty-six classes in that year, forty-five (68%) were taken by the then six full-time tutors. The considerable success of these young, enthusiastic and high quality tutors in Norfolk laid the foundation for the District's future activity in the county which, when Jacques was appointed in 1935 had only one class, a Tutorial in Norwich.

Altogether, during the years between 1941 and 1945, the District appointed a total of nineteen women graduate tutors to provide courses and develop the activities of the District in Cambridgeshire, Essex, Hertfordshire, Norfolk, Northamptonshire and Suffolk. (See Appendix B for the complete list.) In aggregated terms, they were responsible for undertaking approximately 40% of the teaching duties in these counties by the end of the war, in addition to a variety of organisational and administrative tasks.

At the end of the war, because of the sustained activities of Jacques and his core of full-time tutors throughout the District, the herculean efforts of both university resident tutors in Essex and Norfolk and the five WEA organising tutors, the District had reached a position in which it occupied the pre-eminent place in the region as the major providing body for adult education provision. Further, during a decade of considerable and protracted difficulty it had secured its autonomous position in co-operative partnership with the Cambridge Board and the LEAs in the region through its own strenuous efforts to expand educational activities in an endeavour to serve the anticipated post-war democratic state.

The Post-War Period to Ashby

For the provision of adult education in the post-war period the way forward had been indicated broadly by the Education Act 1944. It was more closely mapped in the new Regulations for Further Education in 1946, with Local Education Authorities given responsibility for initiatives in conjunction with the universities and voluntary bodies. In addition, the new regulations continued the pre-war advantages for university-provided liberal adult education which further weakened the relative position of the WEA so much so that the Ashby Committee reported that university income for adult education had exceeded £550,000 in 1951–52 in contrast to the WEA's income of little more than £130,000 for that year. Further, under the new Act, LEAs rapidly expanded their own providing roles and Fieldhouse estimates that nationally there were about 5,000 evening institutes in 1947 and by 1950 more than 11,000 existed providing a wide range of social and recreational classes most of which were accommodated through the evening use of school premises.[32]

Thus, in the immediate post-war years the WEA came under

considerable pressure from two more powerful providers and doubts were raised about its future as a recognised Responsible Body – an issue which was closely addressed by the Ashby Committee in 1953, and again raised by the Russell Committee some twenty years later.

In 1947, Tawney in his preface to *The Future in Adult Education*, raised many of the post-war problems facing the WEA in a changing society. He called for responsive adaptation to the new post- war society in which the WEA's 'primary function to cultivate powers and to form intellectual habits which are the necessary basis of good citizenship and social activity . . .' should be pursued.[33] To ensure the achievement of that objective he stressed the importance of informing fully the post-war generation of these basic principles and of securing the co-operation of the universities through their extra-mural departments. Co-operation with the LEAs was equally important and was to be sought on a basis of complementary provision rather than through competitive relationships.

Through an important earlier development, the providers in the Eastern District had already anticipated the trend. Although the 1944 Act did not provide detailed prescription for complementary relationships it was clear from the 1943 Education Bill that the LEAs were to be given the responsibility and duty to secure the development of adult education, in consultation with the universities and voluntary bodies. Similarly, it was intended that the voluntary bodies would have a duty to consult with appropriate LEAs about activities which they planned to undertake.

The implications of the 1943 Education Bill were considered and accepted at a conference at Impington Village College in late January 1944. On the initiative of the Vice-Chancellor of the University, a Regional Consultative Council was established to achieve the purpose of the proposed Act and to represent the legitimate interests of the providers of adult education. All thirteen LEAs in the region served by the District were represented on the Council together with the University, the WEA, the YMCA and the Educational Settlements Association and formed the first consultative body of its kind in the country. The future provision for liberal adult education was to be shared in ways which broadly represented existing arrangements with most, though not all, financial costs being borne by grant-aid from the Ministry of Education and the LEAs. With the new Council established and working effectively, the original University/WEA Joint Tutorial Classes Committee and the Rural Areas Committee were replaced in 1946 by a new University/WEA Joint Committee which assumed responsibility for Tutorial Classes and One-Year Sessional classes extending over twenty to twenty-four meetings. The District became responsible for Terminal and Short courses extending over six to twelve meetings as well as a variety of informal, pioneering courses and discussion groups of fewer than six meetings; the last category attracting grant-aid for the first time. Later, the East Anglian Regional Advisory Council for Further Education (EARAC) was established in 1947, with its secretariat provided by the Norfolk LEA, and the work of the Regional Consultative Council was absorbed into EARAC in 1953 when it became the Adult Education Sub-Committee of the East Anglian body.

Following Tawney's preface in 1947, the National WEA organised a 'programme for action' to stimulate forward planning and new responses to the opportunities provided under the 1944 Education Act. The District responded with characteristic vigour. Many branches and all the County Federations arranged special conferences and functions throughout 1948 leading to a national 'WEA Week' in late Autumn. For the Executive Committee of the District and, especially, for Jacques it was also a fresh opportunity to strive for a rejuvenation of Tawney's basic principle that the WEA was a social movement endeavouring to promote political, social and cultural democracy in post-war England through the processes of liberal adult education. But it was an uphill, unequal task.

The effects of post-war social trends became visible by 1952 when the number of Tutorial Classes and University Sessional classes declined relatively as the number of Terminal courses increased. Fewer students were prepared to undertake the commitment to submit written work on a regular basis, or to study over long periods, and although the number of Article 24(a) Tutorial Classes rose from fourteen in 1947–48 to thirty in 1951–52 as a direct result of the District's programme for action, the totals for Article 24(b) Sessional classes declined from forty- one to thirty-two over the same period. Article 24(c) Terminal courses increased from 235 to 282 between 1947–48 and 1951–52, but the number of students declined from 7,787 to 6,387 – a loss of 1,400. Nevertheless, and a matter of considerable personal pride to Jacques, the District was not becoming a 'middle class' enclave of students. It was still predominantly a rural District and although the numbers of manual workers were slowly declining the full impact of mechanisation in agriculture, workshop and factory lay some years ahead. The characteristic occupational categories, and the relative strength of each of the seven county Federations in the immediate post-war period up to Ashby is shown in summary form in the following tables for the 1949–50 session:

Table 4.3 Occupations of Eastern District Students 1949–50

Occupation	%
Manual Workers	26.5
Clerks, Travellers, Foreman	12.6
Shop Assistants	4.1
Teachers	11.8
Civil Servants, Postal Worker	3.2
Professional and Social Workers	3.0
Home Duties and Nursing	28.0
Miscellaneous	10.8

Student Total = 7,623

Table 4.4 Student Totals by County Federation Areas and Numbers of WEA Branches 1949–50

	Students	%	Branches
Bedfordshire	573	7.5	16
Fenland	1,189	15.6	21
Essex	1,239	16.3	28
Hertfordshire	949	12.4	21
Norfolk	2,364	31.0	49
Suffolk	672	8.8	11
Northamptonshire	637	8.4	12

Geographically, Table 4.4 indicates that the main provision in the District was essentially in rural areas. For example, in 1949–50, nine new branches were formed in villages in Bedfordshire, seven in Essex, five in Norfolk and three in Fenland. In urban areas during that year only three branches were established; two in Hertfordshire and one at Felixstowe in Suffolk. As noted in annual reports in the late forties and again in the early fifties, the main problems in the development of WEA provision lay in the urban areas – a reversal of pre-war conditions when accessibility of rural areas was difficult and prevented significant growth until the appointment of resident tutors. Now, in the post-war years there occurred the onset of new problems through the increased availability of the cinema, radio and, in the 1950s, television. Further, the expanding provision by LEAs of vocational and recreational classes in rural schools and at urban technical colleges siphoned-off potential WEA students, although the long tradition and attractiveness of the WEA programmes in Norwich and Cambridge enabled both cities to withstand the counter-attractions. Elsewhere, urban centres did not experience the anticipated post-war expansion in liberal adult education.

In the winter of 1948–49, a general area survey of studies in Public Affairs was undertaken in Hertfordshire by His Majesty's Inspectorate

(HMI) which included liberal studies offered by the four Responsible Bodies, of which the Eastern District was one, and the LEA. It revealed a relative lack of interest in such studies and that 'the tendency to ignore the problems of everyday life is symptomatic of the general *malaise* of our times ... The reluctance to undertake serious study is equally widespread, but is significant in this area to provide a challenge to all those concerned with promoting adult education'.[34] More encouraging was another survey by HMI in 1950–51 of the adult education provision made by the Responsible Bodies in Norfolk viz. the Board of Extra-Mural Studies and the Eastern District, both grant-aided by the Norwich and Norfolk LEAs.[35] The tutors of both the District and the Cambridge Board were much praised and a particularly handsome tribute was paid to the District's vision in expanding its activities in the county during the war to create a network of classes throughout the area. The value of the Norfolk Federation and its WEA magazine *The Democrat* was also noted. The conclusion of the report was that the resilience and vigour of adult education in the county during the previous twenty years had placed it in a good position to consolidate earlier effort and made HMI confident that further development in the provision of liberal adult education would build on the foundation of the established tradition of co-operative endeavour between the LEAs and the Responsible Bodies.

The grant-aid earned under the new Regulations was adequate but it was not generous and although class programmes were extended to new centres and programmes expanded in existing branches, the costs of provision also increased and the District required overdraft facilities until 1950 when a small surplus was secured. Grants fluctuated in reflection of the provision made and the support it attracted through enrolments. Deficits were offset through membership subscriptions, which declined in the late forties, and through sums remitted to the District which were calculated annually as per capita branch quotas. In addition, the National WEA provided small specific grants such as those towards the salaries of resident tutor-organisers and a few LEAs made grants towards the administrative costs of the District's organisation.

However, in the following year the District experienced two substantial setbacks. The first arose from the government's decision to impose a standstill grant for that year – in effect a reduction in the District's planned programme in the 1952–53 session at a time when much patient work to gain support from trade union branches and members had succeeded particularly in Norwich and Northamptonshire. The success of this liaison could be seen through the arranging of seventeen day schools and six residential WETUC weekend schools. At the same time, closer working relationships with the Co-operative Movement had led to joint classes with branches at Colchester, Ipswich and St. Albans. The other major setback came in the shape of the winter's East Coast floods which had led to the loss of some branch members and severe dislocation of classes in Norfolk, Suffolk and Essex.

In 1953, the National Association celebrated its Jubilee and the District its fortieth anniversary. It also marked the breaking of a link with the past through the death of Miss Helen Stocks who had done much to promote and sustain the work of the District and the WEA in its early years in Northamptonshire. The Jubilee was celebrated by a District Rally held at the Guildhall in Cambridge and reflected the wide support the WEA continued to attract through speeches made by the Chancellor of the Exchequer (R. A. Butler), the Provost of King's College (Sir John Sheppard), the Director of Education for Norfolk (Dr. Lincoln Ralphs), the National Secretary of the WEA (Harry Nutt) and the former Chairman of the District (Arthur Allen, MP for Wellingborough). Nevertheless, and as had occurred on previous celebratory occasions for the National Association and the District, considerable apprehension and anxiety over the future of the movement existed as the achievement of ambitious post-war objectives remained unrealised.

A Biology class at Toddington in 1931–32

A WETUC Weekend School at Heacham early 1950s (District Secretary Jacques extreme left)

NOTES

1) Shearman in discussion with Williams, October 1965

2) Jacques in conversation with Williams, February 1968

3) These courses were held at Methwold, Feltwell, Swaffham and Thetford

4) In later years, Leslie Missen and the LEA became very supportive of the District's activities, especially in the post-war period.

5) Jacques in conversation with Williams, January 1977

6) Board of Education *Annual Report, 1935–36*, HMSO, London

7) The letter is dated 20 October 1926 and refers to the UEMCC's first *Annual Report, 1925–26*, Cambridge University Press. District Letter File, Botolph House

8) Mactavish replied immediately, 21 October 1926. District Letter File, Botolph House

9) UEMCC Memorandum *Problems of Expansion in Adult Education*, October 1937, Cambridge University Press

10) Ernest Green in a letter to Geoffrey Hickson, 15 February 1938, reflecting the views expressed by Professor Barker, Chairman of the Board's Rural Areas Committee. RAC File, Botolph House

11) Littlecott's letter to Jacques of 28 April 1938. RAC File, Botolph House

12) Poole's letter to Jacques, 25 September 1938. RAC File, Botolph House

13) Reported by Jacques in a letter to Ernest Green, 8 November 1938. RAC File, Botolph House

14) Rural Areas Sub-Committee, 9 November 1938: *Memorandum Alternative Proposals for the Rural Areas Committee.* Clauses Nos.2 and 9. RAC File, Botolph House

15) For example, on the population criterion the District would have withdrawn in Norfolk from Cley, Cromer, Dereham, Diss, Downham Market, Fakenham, North Walsham, Thetford, Wells and Wymondham.

16) Douglas-Smith's letter to Jacques, 16 November 1938. RAC File, Botolph House

17) Hampden Jackson's letter to Jacques, 11 November 1938. RAC File, Botolph House

18) The note is undated but was written in late November 1938. RAC File, Botolph House

19) The letter from Watts to Jacques was written on 1 February 1939. RAC File, Botolph House

20) ibid.

21) Jacques in a letter to Green, 2 February 1939, indicating that it was an urgent matter of considerable potential value and importance in the dispute. RAC File, Botolph House

22) The text was identical in both of the letters Jacques wrote to the university resident tutors on 27 February 1939

23) Jacques's letter to Hickson, 27 February 1939. RAC File, Botolph House

24) Green's letter to Jacques, 13 March 1939. RAC File, Botolph House

25) ibid.

26) Jacques in a letter to Green, 16 March 1939. RAC File, Botolph House

27) Extracted from verbatim note made by Jacques of Professor Barker's introductory remarks at the meeting on 30 July 1941. RAC File, Botolph House

28) Confidential Memorandum by the Secretary to the Cambridge Board (Geoffrey Hickson) and considered at the meeting of the RAC on 27 March 1944. RAC File, Botolph House.

29) ibid.

30) H. Edmund Poole (undated but late 1944) wrote an excellent account of the work of the District during the period, 1938–44, and is full of interesting detail. The booklet, *Going Well* was published by the District and the quotation is taken from p.35

31) District Letter File. Mrs. Parish's letter to Jacques is dated 22 December 1939.

32) Roger Fieldhouse, op.cit.

33) R. H. Tawney, *The Future in Adult Education*, published by the Workers' Educational Association, 1947, p.5

34) *General Area Survey of the Study of Public Affairs by Youth and Adult Groups in Hertfordshire, 1948–49*, Ministry of Education, London, 1950, p.8.

35) *A Survey of the Adult Education Provided by Responsible Bodies in Norfolk, 1950–51*, Ministry of Education, London, 1952.

CHAPTER 5

ASHBY AND AFTER
1953–58

In the early 1950s there was lively debate among adult educationists about the future roles of the various agencies in the field. During 1952, for example, *The Highway* carried articles on the subject by the eminent Oxford historian Alan Bullock (who had experience as treasurer of the Berks., Bucks. and Oxon. District), by G. D. H. Cole (elected President of the Fabian Society in the same year), by Richard Hoggart (then a staff tutor at the University of Hull) and by Maurice Bruce (Director of Extra-Mural Studies at Sheffield), all proposing something different for the WEA. Bullock, following suggestions in S. G. Raybould's recent book, *The English Universities and Adult Education*, argued that the universities should stick to Tutorial and preparatory-Tutorial Classes, leaving the WEA as the country's main provider of less advanced courses in liberal studies; for this expanded role, the Association would require increased government aid to finance additional full-time posts and would also need to 'get rid of those characteristics to which its critics have often pointed . . . conservatism, parochialism and class-consciousness'. Cole wanted the WEA to maintain, and where necessary restore, its position as the educational representative of the working-class movement, responding to demands for classes by trade unions and other workers' groups, even if this meant some reduction in the number of courses taught. Hoggart, claiming with some justification that 'in the WEA today . . . we are suffering from an uncertainty of purpose and recurrent feelings of guilt' advocated the raising of academic standards in courses and a readiness to seek working-class students regardless of their commitment to trade unionism or political emancipation: 'as an educational association our business is to educate not to train social reformers', and accordingly courses in literature were as valuable as those in the social sciences. Bruce, defending the expansion of university extra-mural work since the war, saw the future role of the WEA primarily as a student-body rather than as one with a teaching responsibility, 'an organisation of all adult students' with little or no emphasis on the working-class element: 'in the general interest, it would seem best

141

... for the WEA to concentrate its attention upon the stimulation and organisation of demand ... all but the most elementary pioneer work could become the responsibility of Extra-Mural Departments or local authorities' with the WEA left as 'the mouthpiece of lively, conscious student demand'.[1]

Following this came *The Jubilee Highway* of April 1953, commemorating the Association's fiftieth anniversary. Here, R. H. Tawney took a traditional line, asserting that Tutorial Classes and, at the very least, One-Year courses constituted the WEA's real work, that those who had left school at or about fifteen were its most important target and that as a movement it should be largely under the control of its voluntary student members. 'The Association is not a universal provider ... its mission ... is in the first place to the educationally underprivileged ... it must include a substantial body of work sufficiently intensive and prolonged to exercise a permanent influence on students.'[2] This was echoed by J. H. Matthews, recently-retired Southern District Secretary, who called for fresh efforts to recruit manual workers as voluntary branch members and held that, ideally, Tutorials were the courses which should be provided: 'what the WEA has emphasised and needs more thoroughly to practise is the importance of substantial and continuous study, particularly in the social sciences, as the major element in its work' although 'well conceived short courses will have their place'. Both Tawney and Matthews saw education for trade unionists as a growth point of great potential.

The debate about what the WEA was and should be doing had particular point in 1953, the year the government initiated its own enquiry into adult education. Given the Association's fall in membership since the late 1940s, and given the views canvassed by some who worked in the field, exemplified by Bruce in The Highway, there were real fears that the WEA would lose its status as a Responsible Body. The origins of this enquiry lay in an attempt by the Minister of Education, Florence Horsbrugh, to economise on departmental expenditure. In January 1953 the universities and the WEA were told of the Minister's intention to cut grant-aid towards their adult education work by 10% for the educational year beginning the following August.[3] This unleashed such a storm of protest, in which branches in the Eastern District played their full part,[4] that the government quickly backed down. In March the Prime Minister Winston Churchill, replying to a letter from the TUC Education Committee, gave an assurance that nothing had yet been settled and reserved some memorable prose for a concluding tribute to the value of liberal studies in adult education:

There is, perhaps, no branch of our vast educational system which should more attract within its particular sphere the aid and encouragement of the State than adult education . . . I have no doubt myself that a man or woman earnestly seeking in grown-up life to be guided to wide and suggestive knowledge in its largest and most uplifted sphere will make the best of all the pupils in this age of clatter and buzz, of gape and gloat. The appetite of adults to be shown the foundations and processes of thought will never be denied by a British Administration cherishing the continuity of our Island life.

But these are no reasons for not looking through the accounts, and making sure that all we can give is turned to real advantage.[5]

The last sentence was the cue for Miss Horsbrugh to announce to the House of Commons in April that the 10% Cut would be withdrawn and a Committee of Enquiry into adult education established instead.

The composition of this committee was made known in June. Dr. Eric Ashby, vice-chancellor of Queens University, Belfast, was named as chairman; one of his advantages was that he had avoided publicising his personal views on adult education in the past, although he later emerged as a staunch defender of voluntaryism and a critic of those university extra-mural departments which had expanded by lowering standards. The WEA could take some comfort from the presence among the remaining six on the committee of Alan Bullock, who had expressed his sympathies for the movement in the previous year's *Highway*, and of G. B. Thorneycroft of the General Council of the TUC. Although over half the students in Responsible Body classes were women,[6] every member of the Ashby Committee was a man.

The WEA, presented its evidence to the Committee of Enquiry in November 1953. Among the six members of the sub-committee responsible for drafting this submission was the Eastern District's former full-time tutor Harold Shearman, by then Academic Adviser to the Department of Extra-Mural Studies at London and a WEA vice-president. The Eastern District also featured prominently among the appendices to the evidence, where there were several tables of information about selected Districts: the Eastern was a good choice for inclusion here because it embraced almost twice as many branches as any other District,[7] it covered a distinctive part of the country and its relatively-high level of students' and members' financial contributions tended to show the WEA in a good light. Thus, it can be calculated from the figures that in 1951–52 over 72% of all WEA 'centres' in the Eastern District were in places with populations of less than 5,000; only 10%

were in places with over 20,000 people. Comparative figures for the West Lancs. and Cheshire District, for instance, were 39% (under 5,000 population) and 36% (over 20,000). The only national figures quoted on this were for 1939–40 but these showed 48% and 24% respectively. On finances, a table appeared summarising the income and expenditure of branches in the Eastern District for the year ending 31 March 1953. This was impressive, showing considerable commitment on the part of the voluntary members and a high level of financial responsibility among the branches. No less that £3,559 had been raised by the branches in various ways – £2,616 from members' subscriptions and students' fees, £617 from socials, rummage sales and other fund-raising activities, £53 from sales of literature and so on. After £2,067 had been handed over to the District, branches had been left with a net income of £1,492, just one pound less than the £1,493 spent on publicity, room rents and other local organisation and administration. It was estimated that the average sum raised per branch member to finance the work of the Eastern District and its branches as a whole for the year had been £1 3s. 4d.[8]

Figures such as these fuelled the arguments put forward by the WEA in the main body of the text. Voluntary members made more than a fair 'consumer contribution' to the costs of adult education, their unpaid efforts helped to keep those costs down and they were entitled to more grant-aid from public funds. It was in the nation's interest to have a better-educated populace and the WEA had the tradition and the expertise to achieve this, if an expansion of its work could be financed and more full- time staff appointed; in particular, it had a major contribution to make to trade union education. Tutorial Classes continued to be seen as the most important element in the WEA's programme and there had been some increase in their provision in recent years. Although many alternative methods of financing and administering adult education could be envisaged, none would be as efficient or as economical, none would evoke a better response than those already in operation, 'untidy' as these might seem: the Responsible Bodies (primarily the universities and the WEA) and the local education authorities were managing to avoid an overlap in provision and should be left to continue their work.

The Ashby Committee considered this and other evidence and eventually published their report, *The Organisation and Finance of Adult Education in England and Wales*, on 31 August 1954. The WEA received unstinted praise for upholding 'two precious ingredients of education in a free society: objective discussion, free from propaganda or indoctrination, of social and economic problems; and the full

144

participation of the student in organising and conducting classes'. The Report echoed some of the criticism advanced by witnesses that the WEA could not decide on its future and, at least in some Districts, had lost the pioneering spirit, but concluded nonetheless that 'voluntaryism as exemplified by the Workers' Educational Association is essential if the spirit of adult education is to be preserved'. It therefore recommended that the WEA should continue as a teaching as well as an organising body, while suggesting that some increase in financial contributions from voluntary sources 'would materially help to preserve its independence and its status as a voluntary body' – a hint that the WEA could not expect to rely too heavily on government or local authority aid and that its members and friends must continue to dig deep into their pockets.

As with the WEA, so in its treatment of adult education as a whole, the Report was cautious, considered, fairly conservative in tone. It recognised that, with educational provision as a whole in a transitional phase, still recovering from the war and still adjusting to the requirements of the 1944 Act, it was inappropriate to 'set a course for adult education over the rest of this century': 'our recommendations apply to the present transitional period'. It was in favour of retaining the existing partnership in adult education between voluntary bodies (notably the WEA), the universities, the local education authorities and the Ministry of Education; the Ministry should continue to grant-aid the teaching costs of Responsible Bodies, local authorities (if sympathetic) their administrative costs (Recommendations 1, 4, 13). It did suggest, however, some broadening of the concept of 'teaching costs' eligible for Ministry grant, with such ancillary duties as running a library service, guiding junior colleagues and giving pioneer lectures included (Recommendation 14). It advocated increases in payments to tutors, with the removal of maximum salary limits for full-timers and the raising of fees to part-timers (Recommendations 7, 8). More controversially, it proposed greater flexibility in the allocation of Ministry grant-aid to Responsible Bodies. Instead of the present fixed ceilings on grants, Responsible Bodies 'should each be given an allocation representing the maximum amount of grant available for the year, limited to 75% of the teaching costs, after consideration of the quality and standards of work being done by the responsible body, as well as its proposed programme, the needs of the region in which it operates and the activities of other interested bodies in the region' (Recommendations 5, 6). This would mean an amendment of Further Education Grant Regulations 'so as to give less prominence to the length of course as compared with other and equally important criteria' such as the quality of teaching and the amount of written work done by students (Recommendation 10). It suggested that in some places students' fees could be raised and that the Ministry and local authorities should take account of students' contributions when deciding the level of aid (Recommendations 16, 17). Finally, the Report suggested that the Minister might establish 'a small committee to advise her from time to time on the subjects and types of adult education courses which should receive priority in qualifying for grant' (Recommendation 18).

In general, the Ashby Report received modest praise from the press. *The Times Educational Supplement*, for example, called it 'a soothing but useful report in which the evidence is interpreted with good sense' and summarised the conclusions as 'leave well alone'. The leader writer depicted the Minister of Education Florence Horsbrugh as having been 'hoist with her own petard': if she had hoped that her Committee of Enquiry would recommend financial cuts she had been disappointed, for if anything the proposals made some increase in expenditure likely.[9] Within the adult education profession at large, there was gratification that the existing providers had been commended for their work, but some fears lest the proposals for future grant allocation might lead to increased governmental control over courses taught.[10] The WEA shared both the relief and the reservations: duly expressed as a gathering of District Secretaries in September, at the National Conference in October and at meetings of the WEA Central Executive Committee which had the responsibility for formulating an official response. One reservation was that the proposed amendment to grant regulations in Recommendation 10 would be such as to omit all reference to Tutorial Classes. Another was that, while Recommendations 7 and 8 had proposed higher payments to tutors, the Report had seen 75% of teaching costs as the maximum grant available, leaving the prospect of a widening gap to be filled from voluntary sources – 25% of a salary of (say) £700 being greater than 25% of one of £600. Also, under current regulations 75% was the *minimum* grant to Responsible Bodies; although in practice the Ministry had treated this as the standard proportion, not to be exceeded, it was worrying that the Ashby Report gave 75% as the *maximum*. A further cause for concern was Recommendation 6, with its proposal to base grant for the coming year to each Responsible Body not only on the standards of its own work but also on the needs of the area it served and on the provision made by others. Recommendation 18, meanwhile, with its suggestion of a committee to advise on grant priorities, was seen as threatening to introduce a dangerous element of state supervision over what students ought to study. Accordingly, the WEA Central Executive

Committee made a case against Recommendation 18 but in favour of the retention of Tutorial Classes in the grant regulations, in favour of an increase in Ministry grant-aid above 75% of teaching costs (90% was proposed), and in favour of permission steadily to expand provision through further full-time appointments without all the conditions laid down in Recommendation 6.

On Recommendations 6 and 18, the Eastern District found itself out of step with National WEA policy. A memorandum by Frank Jacques to the District Council of 12 March 1955, and an address he gave to that Council, made it clear that he was in favour of both Recommendations. He felt that the Eastern District, serving a widely-scattered, largely-rural population, working generally in co-operation rather than competition with Cambridge University Extra-Mural Board, and always seeking to maintain high standards, had nothing to fear from the amendment of grant regulations proposed in Recommendation 6, an amendment which took into account quality of work, the needs of the region as a whole and the provision made by other interested bodies. In his view, the WEA's Central Executive Committee, by opposing this Recommendation, had been far too defensive. On the proposal in Recommendation 18 to set up a committee to advise on priorities for grant-aid, he argued that this would help to keep the WEA on its toes, true to its traditional concerns for rigorous study of subjects appropriate to understanding contemporary society. 'All of us should be able to withstand investigation and accept advice and correction if we need or deserve it'. The District Council endorsed these opinions and Jacques wrote to National Secretary Harry Nutt the following week to tell him so – adding that the Council had also supported the plea for an increase in Ministry grant-aid to 90% of teaching costs, which was of course in keeping with National WEA policy.

On 28 March 1955 WEA representatives met Sir David Eccles, who had succeeded Miss Horsbrugh as Minister of Education in a government reshuffle the previous October. Eccles told the WEA that he was opposed to the establishment of an advisory committee, preferring to leave discrimination between courses to the Responsible Bodies themselves: that was the end of Recommendation 18. But he also said that, with this exception, he intended to act in the spirit of the Ashby Report. There would be some increase in grant-aid to Responsible Bodies in the next two years; grant regulations would be amended in line with Recommendation 6 and the Ministry would discuss and review work with Responsible Bodies individually before allocating a block grant for the year to each. He shared the Ashby Committee's appreciation of voluntaryism in adult education and did not wish to encourage a substantial increase in the numbers of full-time staff. Needless to say, there was no promise of 90% grant-aid which was not in the Ashby Report anyway, but the Minister did agree to reconsider the proposal to omit Tutorial Classes from the grant regulations. On all this, he was as good as his word. The amended regulations which came into force on 1 August 1955, included two long sentences following the lines of Recommendation 6:

> In determining the amount of grant the Minister will have regard
> to the general standards of the courses maintained by them, the
> needs of the areas, the activities of other bodies providing further
> education in the area and the fees paid by students. In considering
> the standards maintained the Minister will consider, in addition to
> the syllabuses and the quality of the teaching, the length of courses,
> and the arrangements for written work, reading under guidance
> and other forms of private study to be done between meetings.

But they also retained Tutorial Classes as one of the types of course eligible for grant; incidentally they also defined terms long familiar to the WEA – 'Sessional' ('courses lasting for one educational year comprising not less than twenty meetings') and 'Terminal' ('courses comprising not less than ten meetings'), to describe other courses. 75% disappeared from the regulations altogether, whether as a minimum grant-in-aid of teaching costs as in the old regulations or as a maximum as proposed in the Ashby Report: an explanatory memorandum from the Ministry said that the Minister would continue to use this figure as a guide while bearing in mind all the other factors concerned with quality, need, students' fees and so on. The definition of 'teaching costs' was extended as in Recommendation 14 of Ashby to include ancillary duties such as guiding junior colleagues.

However, the operation of these regulations during the rest of the decade kept the WEA on a tight rein. In its evidence to the Ashby Committee, the WEA had asked for more grant-aid to finance 'a considerable increase' in the number of full-time staff. In a letter to the Ministry of Education at the beginning of 1955, in the midst of the negotiations following the publication of the Report, the National Secretary had actually put a figure on this, saying that the various Districts would like thirty more full-time tutors. But the necessary finance was not forthcoming and the appointment of additional full-timers remained exceptional throughout the 1950s. Similarly, those who hoped that the more flexible regulations would qualify them for grant well in excess of the traditional 75% were doomed to disappointment.

Within the Eastern District, Jacques and his voluntary officers felt especially strongly on this point. In their view, the District was meeting the criteria set out in Ashby's Recommendation 6 and in the 1955 regulations quite admirably: was it not entitled to a higher proportion of grant-aid than those whose standards were poorer, whose students' fees were lower and who were meeting the needs of their areas less successfully in relation to other providing bodies? In fact, there was some flexibility and the proportion of grant-in-aid of teaching costs to the Eastern District did rise a little, actually reaching 79% in 1957–58. But what the District continued to seek was the 90% grant which the WEA's national negotiators had raised unsuccessfully with the Ministry in 1954 and early 1955: this goal became a recurrent theme of District meetings and literature through the second half of the decade. In his 1955–56 Annual Report, for example, Jacques wrote that if only this level of grant could be achieved, something could be done to raise part-time tutors' fees and so reduce the glaring disparity between the minima of £1 10s. 0d. for teaching a WEA Terminal class and £3 10s. 0d. for taking a University Sessional class. The Eastern District submitted a motion to the March 1960 National Conference at Brighton, calling on the government 'forthwith to increase its normal rate of grant-in-aid of voluntary Providing Bodies from 75% to 90%'. The District's Annual Report for 1959–60 said that, although the WEA's national officers were still trying to achieve this increased grant, the Eastern had exceptionally-strong claims and accordingly 'we are now pressing for special consideration': in other words, Jacques was arguing with the Ministry that, even if it could not afford 90% grant to the WEA as a whole, could this not be allowed to the Eastern District individually? In June 1960 he went so far as to write to Ashby himself – by then Sir Eric and the Master of Clare College, Cambridge – setting out the case and asking whether he would make personal representations to the Minister to secure unilateral treatment for the Eastern District. Statistics were enclosed showing that the average student fee per class meeting (12.45d.) was higher and the teaching costs at least 50% greater in the Eastern than in any other District. Ashby sent a sympathetic but non-committal reply. The campaign was to no avail: the 90% grant was never received and the District's Annual Report for 1960–61 was the last to mention the issue.

The Ashby Report did not make a dramatic impact upon the Eastern District, but it was important nonetheless. After all, it did help to save the WEA as a Responsible Body at a time of serious threat. It also contributed to a shift in opinion at the Ministry of Education away from the curtailment or freezing of grant towards modest and flexible expansion – and the Eastern District was able to take advantage of the new grant regulations which followed the Report in 1955 to achieve a level of aid a few percentage points higher than the 75% hitherto regarded as standard. It was disappointing, given the stress in these new regulations on quality of courses, the needs of the area and the amount of students' contributions, that an even higher proportion of grant-aid could not be given: but the Ashby Report itself had talked of only 75% and that as a maximum, so any advance on this was an achievement, and a tribute to the District's work. Equally important, one may argue, was the boost which the Report gave to the District's morale through its praise for the WEA's voluntary and democratic traditions. Although the Minister could use this as a reason not to finance the appointment of additional full-time staff, the success of the Eastern District in serving far-flung rural communities, too numerous and too widespread for full-timers to cover efficiently, has always depended primarily upon the strength and zeal of the voluntary members. As it happened, it was in the years immediately following the Ashby Report that the implications of voluntaryism, and the role which professionals should play as part of a voluntary movement, became matters of major concern within the District. Decisions taken on these issues were to have a lasting effect on the geographical deployment of full-time staff.

The Voluntary-Professional Dilemma

> In a world noisy with the organs of mass communication and riddled with propaganda, modern man is hard put to it to preserve his status as an individual. To help to preserve this status is (in my view) the contemporary task for adult education . . . [But] . . . any system which weakens the small voluntary group will in the end defeat its purpose . . . I believe it is vitally important to preserve voluntaryism in Britain. I believe this cannot be done by local authorities, however well meaning they are, nor by universities, however efficient, but only by voluntary bodies. Many people believe that voluntary bodies as they are today cannot be entrusted with this national responsibility. My thesis is that the remedy is not to discard voluntary bodies but to infuse them with a new purpose and to make new demands upon them; and I have suggested that the new purpose is nothing less than to preserve the individuality of man.

This might have come from a WEA rally. In fact the words are those of Eric Ashby: while others were digesting his Committee's carefully-worded Report, he gave vent to his personal opinions in the Will Harvey Memorial Lecture, delivered at Fircroft College, Birmingham on 24 March 1955 under the title *The Pathology of Adult Education*.[11] He criticised the WEA for allowing some branches to be 'swallowed up by the vortex of gentility', failing to engage in serious study and neglecting their mission to manual workers: he wanted such branches closed. But he criticised at greater length those university extra-mural departments which had expanded since the war through bypassing the WEA and putting on their own programmes of courses, courses with popular appeal to the already well-educated and .of a quality below that traditionally associated with universities. He was obviously very impressed by the WEA at its best, where courses mounted were those the voluntary members themselves had chosen and where high standards were sustained by tutors and students alike; he saw the growth of university extra-mural work as a threat to all this.

If we are not careful adult education may become a social service like national insurance, 'laid on' by the university in a spirit if efficient paternalism. I have a vision of resident tutors beating up classes with the cheerful persistence of a sports organiser on a trans-Atlantic liner; of extra-mural directors deploying their forces through the English countryside, themselves deciding what classes are suitable for the people of Swindon and Banbury and Slough; of district organisers calling on mill hands in the remotest dales of Yorkshire with the regularity of the man who collects the rent . . . Imperceptibly the voluntary spirit would distil away from adult education . . . The mainspring of voluntaryism is that initiative lies with the volunteers. They are free to be energetic and enterprising; they are equally free to be lethargic and dilatory; the self-respect of the voluntary group depends on the fact that any success it has is due to its own efforts. Now the wise extra-mural department would doubtless maintain a facade of what appear to be voluntary committees. But if the extra-mural department has a budget of the order of £50,000 a year, and a salary bill of the order of £40,000 a year, adult education has got to go on whether so-called voluntary committees want it or not; and since a good deal of the teaching is done by full-time tutors, even the subjects taught will inevitably be dictated to some extent by the department and not by the voluntary groups. A clever organiser with a history tutor on his hands may *persuade* the citizens of Chipping Camden that they do not really want a class in biology, they want one on Queen Victoria: but (make no mistake) that very persuasion will to some extent have injured the mainspring of voluntaryism in adult education in Chipping Camden.

Frank Jacques quoted the Harvey Memorial Lecture extensively and approvingly in his 1954–55 District Annual Report. He added his own comments that Ashby's tributes to voluntaryism present us with a very serious challenge – to the professional to be patient in service, to aid and abet but not to take over from the voluntary worker any of the tasks or decisions which he should do and make: to the voluntary worker to recognise that the only sure safeguard against injury to the mainstream of voluntaryism is that that mainstream, which is himself, shall never slacken.

This went to the heart of a question which the WEA is never able to ignore and which the Eastern District had particular cause to ponder in this period: how should the full-time professional tutor-organiser fit into a voluntary movement? Ashby's warnings of the dangers of professionals, although apparently directed against those in extra-mural departments, could also be applied to the staff of the WEA. This implication was not lost on some members of the Eastern District, notably several in Essex where the views of leading WEA activists were such that the District eventually decided to do without a tutor-organiser for the county altogether.

By the early 1950s, the Essex Federation had become one of the strongest in the District, in terms of the enthusiasm and sense of purpose of its Executive Committee, composed of members elected from constituent branches at the annual general meetings. To quote the Federation's annual report for 1948–49, 'one purpose of the Federation' is 'that of bringing together in a friendly atmosphere the members of different Branches and Groups and thereby strengthening the unity and spirit of the WEA in Essex'. Another purpose, as expressed in the 1949–50 report, was 'to act as a link between the Essex branches and the Eastern District'. It was to further these aims that the Federation launched a newsletter, E.F. and mounted a varied programme of weekend and one-day schools. The county tutor-organiser from 1948 to 1951, Arthur Brown, remained in Essex as a committed voluntary member and notable part-time tutor and, as Federation chairman from 1953 onwards, also encouraged the Executive to develop as a forum for lively debate on matters of WEA policy. The opinion gained ground – an opinion with which Eric Ashby would evidently have had some sympathy – that the employment of a full-time tutor for the county, whether by the WEA or by the University Extra-Mural Board, placed constraints on branches' freedom to choose subjects of study because of pressure to find a viable programme for the full-timer to teach. It was also thought that the presence of a WEA officer such as the tutor-organiser at branch AGMs and committee meetings was liable to bring improper influence to bear on behalf of the District Secretary. Beyond these specific issues, there was an acute sense within the Essex Federation of the general threat posed by professionalism to the WEA's essential character: and several leading voluntary members came to feel that through their own initiative they could advance the movement more effectively than any tutor-organiser.

Elsewhere in the District around this time, a gap between the resignation of one full-time officer and the appointment of another provoked distress and urgent resolutions to the District Council. This was so in Bedfordshire, for example: in 1952 the District Council carried a motion deploring 'the withdrawal of the services of a full-time officer of the WEA from Bedfordshire when so large a proportion of branches in the area are so recently formed and still in need of assistance and encouragement that only a full-time organiser or tutor-organiser can give'. There was a similar reaction in Hertfordshire when the resignation of the University's resident tutor in the county, Vivian Ramsbottom, to become Administrative Officer of the Joint Committee, led the District AGM of 1955 to carry a motion expressing 'belief that the presence of a Resident Tutor in the County is vital to the growth of the educational work which the WEA and the University do together'. But no similar resolutions came from Essex. The views of prominent members here are best expressed in a motion originating from Wickham Bishops branch, passed at the Essex Federation AGM in May 1957, considered by the District Executive in the following month but eventually withdrawn from the agenda of the subsequent District Council:

> That it is in the interest of the Workers' Educational Association that the organisation of its activities and its expansion, and the direction of its policy, should continue in the hands of its members; that the work of the professional officers in the field should be supplementary to that of the Branch and Federation members and not a substitute for it, and that all constitutional impediments to the holding of any Branch or Federation office by voluntary members of the WEA should be removed.

Although not every member of the Essex Federation Executive shared these views, Brown's successors as tutor-organiser for the county understandably found the context a difficult one to work in. Janet Walters, an Oxford history graduate who had previously served as a full-time tutor in Northamptonshire in 1943–45, arrived in August 1952 but resigned two years later: she went on to a successful career in adult education, eventually retiring as Principal of Hillcroft College, Surbiton, in 1982. Kate Collingwood, who had read Modern Greats at Oxford and was well-known as a luminary of the Kelvedon Players, gave up her seat as a Labour county councillor, was appointed in November 1954 but eventually resigned in December 1957. Both left with warm appreciations from the District Executive and District Council, both managed to win the friendship and confidence of many voluntary members in Essex: but it is clear from their correspondence with the District Office that they came to feel frustrated at having less freedom to use their initiative than tutor-organisers in other counties. The District's response was not to appoint a successor to Mrs. Collingwood but to give the Essex Federation Executive the opportunity to take on the tutor-organiser's work, leaving all teaching to part-time tutors: an arrangement which was still in force at the District's seventy- fifth anniversary in 1988.

The controversy which surrounded these events, and which periodically exercised the District Executive and enlivened the District Council, took place at a time when tutor-organisers were less established figures than they were to be in the 1960s and 1970s. For example, in March 1955 at the time of Ashby's Will Harvey Lecture, there were only five tutor-organisers employed by the Eastern District, those in Essex, Fenland, Norfolk, Northamptonshire and Suffolk: the posts in Bedfordshire and Hertfordshire were vacant and there were as yet no tutor-organisers with special responsibilities over several counties. In June 1956 the number was temporarily down to four, with Norfolk also being without. Restrictions by the Ministry on grant made available for new appointments also meant that vacancies between the resignation of one tutor-organiser and the arrival of a successor could be prolonged. Bedfordshire lost the services of its professional officer (actually a non-teaching organiser) Gwen Rawlings late in 1952 and did not receive a tutor-organiser to replace her, Evan Richards, until August 1956. The Fenland (covering Cambridgeshire, Isle of Ely, Huntingdonshire and the Soke of Peterborough) was without a tutor-organiser from the time Frank Cossey resigned in July 1956 until the appointment of Robert Darby in July 1959: here it was the decision not to reappoint in Essex following Collingwood's departure at the end of 1957 which allowed the District to negotiate with the Ministry for a new tutor-organiser to be assigned to the Fenland instead. In these circumstances, voluntary WEA members such as Rachael Evans in Bedfordshire and (successively) Barbara Brenchley and Margaret Bland in the Fenland took on the task of Federation secretary and, along with other enthusiasts, did their best to fulfil the non-teaching duties of a tutor-organiser. This left the way open for those prominent in the Essex Federation to argue that if such arrangements were acceptable during a temporary absence of tutor-organiser, there was no reason why they should not apply on a more permanent basis if the voluntary members wanted to give their 'voluntaryism' full rein. Accordingly, since the beginning of 1958, a succession of volunteers from Leslie Tilbury onwards have served as secretary to the Essex Federation, a post which would otherwise have been held *ex officio* by the tutor-organiser. Even the District Secretary was not averse to reminding his tutor-organisers that they were dispensable. In his 1955–56 Annual Report, at the end of a year when insufficient Terminal courses had been provided to use up all available Ministry grant, he commented that 'we may find it increasingly difficult to resist a reduction in the number of tutor-organisers we now employ, let alone claim a further appointment, if additional Terminal courses are not successfully organised in both established and new centres'.

A complicating factor in all this was that despite the opposition of the Eastern District Council, expressed both before and after the decision had been taken, Cambridge University Extra-Mural Board resolved in December 1955 to withdraw its resident tutors from some of the counties it served. Those in Norfolk, Northamptonshire and Suffolk were to remain but the tutors in Bedfordshire and the Cambridgeshire area were to be withdrawn and there was to be no replacement for the one in Essex who had resigned in the previous year. The post in Hertfordshire, also vacant, was left for further consideration and was eventually filled in 1959. There were advantages for the Board in deploying all but a few of its full-time teachers as subject-specialist staff tutors based in Cambridge – notably the fact that there would be little problem in constructing a viable programme for each one, with the whole of the Board's area to cover. But resident tutors were much appreciated by the WEA: they were admirable colleagues for the tutor-organisers, doing what they could to help and advise the branches in their counties, and they had a particular responsibility for promoting Tutorial Classes. Coming on the heels of the Ashby Report, which had lacked conviction in Tutorials and had recommended that the reference to them in grant regulations be dropped, the Board's decision seemed to be another blow to what had traditionally been regarded as the apex of WEA work. Syd Robinson, a vice-chairman of the Eastern District, was so incensed by this move that he resigned as one of the District's three representatives on the Extra-Mural Board forthwith. But the new policy went ahead from the following autumn, 1956, with the former resident tutors for Bedfordshire and Cambridgeshire being redeployed as staff tutors and with Vivian Ramsbottom as Administrative Officer of the Joint Committee given a roving commission to encourage WEA branches in those counties now deprived of resident tutors. So here was another demonstration to WEA members that the resident professional officer, whether Extra-Mural Board tutor or WEA tutor-organiser, need not be regarded as essential. If anything, however, these developments had an opposite effect, for the Eastern District was able to argue with the Ministry of Education that the withdrawal of resident tutors, far from calling tutor-organisers into question, made their appointment even more necessary than before.

Of course, the tutor-organisers of this (as of any) period were well aware that in trying to serve the voluntary movement they were walking a tightrope between doing too much, so depriving branch members of their rightful participation in and control of affairs, and doing too little, so appearing idle and inefficient. In January 1956 Jacques requested from each tutor-organiser a summary of the previous six months' work, in order to prepare a general report for the Ministry of Education. Among the questions to which he invited replies was one on whether tutor-organisers had done anything (other than teaching) which voluntary members could not have done. Some of the responses to this, although informally phrased because never intended for publication, are worth quoting.

Bruce Cooper, tutor-organiser for Suffolk, made some very honest and perceptive remarks on his organising work:

> Technically all could be done by voluntary workers with the possible exception of (arranging) Weekend Schools. But one has greater resources of time . . . and contact with more people of all walks of life and those in the movement too. Mark you it's a very bad thing if Federation or branch officials merely rubber stamp the efforts of an enterprising TO. It's a very difficult position. As a TO one wants to do as well as one can, and the paradox is that the better one does in a sense the worse it is for the *voluntary* movement, who should be persuaded to do the maximum rather than the minimum. And so they become willing aiders rather than initiators. And I, instead of following and recording, tying up, smoothing, lubricating, find myself providing a great deal of the steam and piston work.

Kate Collingwood, writing as tutor-organiser for Essex with a Federation Executive highly committed to voluntary participation, felt that 'any of my organising work could be done by voluntary branch members if they had the time. A considerable amount of such work is done by officers of the Federation area'. As Federation secretary she was much involved in arranging Saturday lectures, concerts, jumble sales, theatre visits and suchlike for the branches: 'these would probably be arranged by the Federation officials without me, but perhaps not on so large a scale'. Henry Parris, tutor-organiser for Northamptonshire who had previously served in a similar capacity in Yorkshire North District, also acknowledged that most of his organising work could have been done by voluntary members, given the time and opportunity to travel around the county. But he also considered it important that a full-time professional should represent the WEA when dealing with other professional organisers such as local authority officers, representatives of management and trade unions, and the warden of the county's residential college Knuston Hall. 'The tutor-organiser is on a par with them; the voluntary officer feels – and is sometimes made to feel – inferior.' Similarly, he felt that part-time tutors were more likely to respond to advice from a professional tutor than from someone not involved on the teaching side. The tutor-organiser was also best-placed to counsel WEA students considering full-time higher education on adult state scholarships (of which there were two in Northamptonshire at the time); he was also in a position to attend daytime meetings of local bodies, on behalf of the WEA.

The issues raised by these comments are as relevant today as they were at the time. As Cooper implied, a tutor-organiser's success in encouraging rather than destroying the voluntary movement is largely a matter of degree – of knowing how much to do to advance the WEA here and there, while leaving as much as possible to the voluntary members. Over the years, sensitive tutor-organisers, with the personality to work harmoniously with Federation and branch officers, have consistently been able to promote rather than to threaten voluntaryism. But as the replies from Collingwood and Parris make clear, there is more to a tutor-organiser's success than this: for success has to be measured by different criteria according to the context of the work. Whereas in Northamptonshire the tutor-organiser saw himself as a professional liaising with other professionals in areas where voluntary participation was barely appropriate, his colleague in Essex was apparently expected to spend a lot of time in routine organising work which voluntary members could readily take over when she eventually resigned. What the WEA's voluntary membership really wants from its tutor-organisers remains a profitable subject for debate – as does the basic question of whether such appointments should be made at all. Having been without a tutor-organiser since 1958, Essex Federation representatives on the District Council have suggested from time to time that other counties might benefit from following their example. The strong points in their argument have been that they exhibit voluntaryism in its purest form, that they are free of any obligation to find a programme for the tutor-organiser to teach and that, in managing on voluntary effort alone, they are saving the District that portion of a full-time salary which would not be covered by government or local authority grant-aid. The principal counter-argument has been that Essex has enjoyed the benefit of a former tutor-organiser as Federation chairman and that, in the absence of an equivalent person to give a lead elsewhere, tutor-organisers have continued to be essential. Apart from that, a more general argument may be advanced in favour of tutor-organisers – or any other professional field officers such as non-teaching organisers for that matter. It is this. In reality, despite its justifiable pride in its voluntary and democratic principles, the WEA cannot simply allow its members to decide policy and to act however they like. The WEA has obligations which at all costs it must strive to fulfil. Some of these relate to its heritage – its traditional concern for rigorous academic study of socially-relevant subjects and its traditional mission to the educationally-underprivileged. Others relate to its receipt of government and local authority funds, which are granted in the expectation that the WEA is providing a public educational service in the liberal studies: that courses will be run not merely for the benefit of existing members but will be widely canvassed and advertised to attract as many of the adult population as wish to take part. A tutor-organiser (or equivalent) who as a professional employee is susceptible to discipline if he or she proves negligent or misguided, can help to ensure that the voluntary movement lives up to its obligations – through advice and encouragement as far as possible, through seizing the initiative himself if there is no alternative. Equally, voluntary members of branch and Federation committees, many with far longer service to the Association than their tutor- organiser, can see that he remains true to the traditions of the WEA. So in normal circumstances the WEA is a voluntary movement up to a point, but also a partnership between voluntary and professional members – and a partnership which usually achieves the best results in a context of mutual respect.

Grassroots

Against the background of national and local tensions, the more routine work of the District carried on. 1953 brought not only the Ashby

Committee of Enquiry but (as already mentioned) the WEA's fiftieth anniversary: the celebrations to mark the Jubilee provided welcome relief from the anxiety of awaiting the Report. Within the Eastern District, Berkhamsted branch (Hertfordshire) hung a banner proclaiming '1903-WEA-1953' in the High Street for a week, using the hoardings protecting the new site of Woolworths, and also sold literature and distributed publicity from a stall in the marketplace; Sprowston branch (Norfolk) arranged an exhibition of Victoriana in the village school, with local firms and libraries as well as members themselves lending material; Peterborough branch held a garden party at the Bishop's House, featuring addresses by Lady Simon, one of the WEA's vice-presidents, and by Dr. Charles Morris, chairman of the National Foundation for Adult Education. The climax came with a Jubilee Rally in the Guildhall, Cambridge, organised by the District Office and attended by over six hundred people: 'universally agreed to be one of the finest meetings that the District has ever seen', according to the *Bulletin* of the Fenland Federation. The main speaker, the Chancellor of the Exchequer R. A. Butler, was warm in his tribute to the WEA:

The idea of siphoning the matured learning of the Universities to the industrial and agricultural areas is as fresh and germane as if it had first been thought of last night. In the Eastern District of the Association, I know, you are behaving as though the idea were a brand-new one; and with something of the enthusiasm of your founder-members you are carrying it into the countryside.[12]

The praise was well-deserved, but this was no time to be resting on laurels. Taken as a whole, the 1950s can be seen as a decade in which everyone had to work very hard just to keep the District on an even keel: it reflects great credit on all concerned that, in statistical terms, the decline of the early fifties was halted so that ultimately an expansionist phase could begin. One major worry was finance: in the years when deficits were avoided, it was as a result of stringent economies, such as unpaid overtime in the District Office and restrictions on the course programme. The financial year ending 31 July 1956 showed an alarming excess of expenditure over income in the general account of £2,238. Although this looked worse than it might have done since it covered fourteen months instead of twelve – the result of an adjustment to a different financial year – such figures demanded a response. Peter Laslett, who had succeeded his fellow-historian Edward Miller as District treasurer three years before, made a further point to the District Executive when it considered the financial position early in September: the local education authorities had recently received a circular from the

Ministry asking that students' fees for courses be raised to 10s. 0d. per term. So a special meeting of the District Council was summoned for 22 September and – on the very eve of the new academic year – agreed to some swingeing increases in course fees. For Terminal courses, the fee for a non-branch member (covering course and registration) went up from 7s. 0d. to 10s. 0d.; for a branch member (whose subscription was added to the fee) it rose from 10s. 0d. to 12s. 0d. For Long Terminals, Sessionals and Tutorials, non-branch members who had previously paid 11s. 0d. now had to pay £1; instead of 12s. 6d. branch members had to find £1 4s. 0d. The District Council also agreed to a 50% increase in the Quota, the extra sum paid by branches to the District on a sliding scale according to the populations of the communities they served: branches in places with a population under 1,000, for instance, were now expected to pay £3 per annum, those where the population was between 5,000 and 7,000 £5 5s. 0d., those in places of between 50,000 and 75,000 £9 and so on.

The introduction of higher fees in 1956 did not solve the District's financial problems, only make them manageable. In January 1958 the District Executive agreed to further increases for 1958- 59 to 12s. 0d. for a Terminal (branch members 13s. 0d.) and £1 2s. 0d. for long courses (branch members £1 5s. 0d.). This time the District Council was less amenable: the March meeting rejected the new fees, while promising to meet the higher remittances required by the District. In other words, branches agreed to retain less than before of what they had collected from students, and if necessary raise extra funds through special events. It was understandable that branch members should be reluctant to risk a fall in recruitment through another increase in fees: yet the rises of 1956 had had no discernible effect. Student numbers within the District as a whole remained remarkably steady through the middle years of the decade: totals of 5,241 in 1953–54, 5,433 in 1954–55, 5,295 in 1955–56, 5,298 in 1956- 57 (the first year of higher fees) and 5,539 in 1957–58. More relevant to the figures in 1956–57 than any increase in fees was the introduction of petrol rationing in December 1956 as a result of the Suez crisis: this severely hit the following spring term's programme. The District Office obtained some extra coupons to keep tutor-organisers mobile and part-time tutors showed splendid generosity in using up their own allowances to fulfil their commitments: indeed, not one course in the whole of the District had to be abandoned part-way through the spring term because the tutor could not travel. But student attendances after Christmas were appreciably lower, as cars stayed at home and public transport was withdrawn, and several branches

160

decided not to start a spring course at all, or to restrict them in length. The petrol shortage even caused that rarest of events, the cancellation of the March District Council. But for this problem, the encouraging increase in student numbers in 1957- 58 – which was maintained in subsequent years and so marked the beginning of an upward trend – would probably have been apparent one year earlier.

Branch membership also remained steady, following a period of decline since the immediate post-war years. In 1953–54 the figure of 2,982, down from 3,151 in the previous year, dismayed the District Secretary, especially since branches had been asked to make a drive to recruit new members in Jubilee Year, 1953. His calls in the District's Annual Report for renewed efforts to encourage students to become members were echoed in the *Norfolk Democrat*, the magazine of the Norfolk Federation among whose branches there had been a particularly serious loss of membership. For the Autumn 1955 issue, Mary Short of Norwich wrote an article entitled 'Compel them to Come in' predicting that the WEA would die a natural death unless more young members were recruited and advocating adventurous experiment: 'it may mean holding afternoon classes, or running a baby-sitter service so that young couples with children can come . . . has any Branch tried to recruit new members by advertising courses on child psychology at ante-natal clinics and infant welfare centres?'. Happily, the trend was reversed: 2,926 members in 1955–56, 2,984 in 1956–57, 3,197 in 1957–58, with further growth thereafter. This was attributable mainly to an increase in the number of branches, from 158 in 1953–54 to 189 in 1957–58; losses in Bedfordshire (15 branches down to 11) and the Fenland (23 down to 15), both of which had been without a tutor-organiser for much of the period, were more than offset by gains everywhere else, notably in Essex (27 branches up to 40) and Suffolk (14 up to 32).

A few more statistics will suffice to show the trends of the time. Advanced courses held up very well indeed: in 1953–54 there were 33 Tutorials and 34 Sessionals in the Eastern District, in 1957–58 there were 35 and 29. But taking all courses together there was a steady decline in the proportion of manual workers attending and a gradual drift away from subjects regarded as 'Social Studies'. In 1953–54 nearly 40% of all male students were classified as manual workers; men as a whole made up 45% of the total number of students. By 1957–58 only a quarter of male students were manual workers and men were down to 42% of the total student body. Against this, the attendance of 'house-wives' increased: by 1957–58 53% of women students and 31% of all students were placed in this category. On subjects, whereas 'Social

Studies' made up 67%, 'Arts' 26% and 'Natural Sciences' 7% of the course programme in 1953–54, by 1957–58 the proportions were 64%, 26% and 10% respectively. Broad classifications of this sort are rarely satisfactory, but the trend away from social studies in favour of science (with arts remaining steady) was a consistent one in the intervening years, despite violent fluctuations in demand for individual subjects within all three categories. The clearest pattern was that for local history and archaeology (both counted among 'Social Studies') which were rapidly gaining in popularity, with 58 courses between them in 1957–58 compared to only 26 four years earlier.

To those with a commitment to the WEA's traditional mission, there was cause for concern in some of these statistics, but certainly not for dismay. Nearly 2,000 students in 1957–58 – approaching two-fifths of the total – were in the category of either 'manual workers' or 'non-manual, technical and supervisory workers'. In the same year, there were 91 courses on international affairs, international history, current social or economic problems, political theory or machinery of government – well over a quarter of the District's total programme. With figures like these the WEA, here as elsewhere, was a long way from being the body of 'middle-class' students pursuing 'soft options' which its critics liked to allege. If the Eastern District was less successful in some respects than it would have liked to be, it was not for want of trying. With its finances balanced precariously, with Ministry restrictions on the appointment of tutor-organisers and the withdrawal of some of the university's resident tutors, it had to rely heavily on voluntary effort – and no-one who reads the branch or Federation literature of this period can fail to be moved by the zealous commitment of ordinary WEA members, a commitment based upon the sheer love of learning and an earnest desire to offer something worthwhile to society. During the 1950s, most of the Federations managed to publish magazines two or three times a year, composed of articles by both professional and voluntary members. Of these the *Norfolk Democrat* and *Suffolk Punch*, both printed and carrying advertisements, were particularly impressive. In spring 1957, for example, the *Norfolk Democrat*, edited by Grace Thicknesse of Diss, herself a specialist on the Middle East, ran an 'international affairs' number. This included articles on Nigeria by former tutor-organiser Robin Hallett, on Kenya by current tutor-organiser John Smith, on West Germany by Anna Multhampt of Cambridge branch and on Russia by Irene Baczkowske of Long Stratton; publication coincided with a series of single lectures arranged by the Federation on trouble-spots around the world, such as Cyprus, Jordan and Algeria. For its part, the *Suffolk*

Punch of March 1956, under the editorship of tutor-organiser Bruce Cooper, included contributions on the Aldeburgh Festival by Ronald Blythe (*Akenfield* was still thirteen years in the future) and on oral history by George Ewart Evans, then coming to be recognised as a leading authority on the subject. Beyond this, the Federation magazines served to publicise forthcoming meetings and courses, to inform branch secretaries of one another's addresses and to provide a forum for members to exchange ideas: for instance an article by George Tweed of Cambridge branch in the *Fenland Bulletin* of spring 1956 and another by 'Cesnoh' in the *Hertfordshire Parcel* of autumn 1957 both stressed the importance of personal canvassing as a means of recruiting students to courses. But the publication of these magazines was of course very demanding both in time and money and several faded away in the following decade, to be revived from time to time in spasmodic bouts of enthusiasm.

As for the branches, it is perhaps invidious to focus upon a chosen few since in some places merely to carry on unheralded was a considerable triumph. But among those with special achievements to their credit were the branches at Knebworth (Hertfordshire), Kelvedon, Manningtree and Wivenhoe (Essex), all of which published village histories during 1953–54; at Hemel Hempstead which duplicated and sold *Welfare and the State*, the log-book of weekly discussions in a Long Terminal on 'Economic and Social Problems' held in 1956–57; at Linton (Cambridgeshire) which followed up a music course by helping to launch the Linton Music Festival in July 1957, destined to become an annual event; and at Colchester where a Tutorial on archaeology from 1955 to 1958 led to the formation of the Colchester Archaeological Group. Otherwise, two detailed reports of the mid-1950s allow us a glimpse of more usual branch activity.

The first of these, an HMI Report on local history classes throughout the Cambridge Extra-Mural Board's area in 1954, commented very favourably upon the general standard of teaching in both university and WEA courses and was also complimentary about the quality of students' work.

> Of the classes visited, it can certainly be said that those in which the teaching and the interest of the students revealed vitality, enthusiasm and the promise of sustained interest in the subject far outnumbered those in which a short and superficial survey . . . seemed all that the tutor was prepared to offer or the class prepared to accept.

Norfolk had a particularly strong tradition in the subject and the university's resident tutor, Rachel Young, was given due credit for this, albeit anonymously: 'her work is outstanding and has influenced not only many students, but also some part-time tutors.'[13]

The second report was one composed by Suffolk tutor-organiser Bruce Cooper, for the benefit of HM Inspectors, on the eve of his departure for a new post in July 1956. This was a remarkably-thorough and penetrative survey of the WEA's work in a predominantly-rural area; worth citing at some length because it encapsulates much of the spirit of the Eastern District at this time. Cooper outlined the work of the twenty-two branches in East Suffolk and six in West Suffolk, all but three of which (Ipswich, Southwold and Sudbury) ran only one course at a time. Eight branches (Bungay, Burgh Castle, Hollesley, Ilketshall St. Lawrence, Kersey, Leiston, Walberswick and Wrentham) had been founded since the New Year, although the first of these had previously been a Student Group. Most of the courses planned for the forthcoming autumn term of 1956 were 12-week Terminals, although there were also two 21-week Long Terminals and five 24-week Sessionals; local history, literature and art were the most popular subjects. Among the tutors who would be taking courses were three employed full-time by Cambridge University Extra-Mural Board, plus a fourth full-timer in the person of the newly-appointed tutor-organiser Robert Johnson. Of the part-time tutors, about a quarter were local schoolmasters, and there were also a number of parish clergy, local government officers and retired professional people; only two of those so far booked for courses were women, although when the programme was finalised there were three.

The recruitment of part-time tutors was a matter of concern:

The area is small in population and particularly academic population. This (combined with the fact that in the great majority of branches one has to find tutors who possess cars on account of the very poor public services) multiplies the difficulty of providing the Branch with the class they desire . . . Increased tutorial fees would not, I think, attract a great deal more people to our work. Either one likes the work or doesn't.

He went on to reflect on the foundation of new branches. These usually arose through personal contact:

Picking a village which seems suitable or where someone lives who has been recommended, and talking to as many people as possible: later sending a letter to these people and others calling a meeting to form, one hopes, a WEA branch. Occasionally the initiative comes from local sources, an enquiry or request for information about WEA provision and sometimes a keen local person will take upon himself the responsibility of calling a meeting.

On branches' publicity for their courses and other events, he commented:

> With some branches this is by word of mouth, with others personal letters by the secretary to members and those who might be interested. Some branches go in for quite lavish posters, some make do with local draughtsmanship. Some advertise in the local papers – to my mind quite the most profitless form of contact or recruitment. The only worthwhile way is by personal contact. Occasionally some Branches open the year with a One-Day School by a celebrity or an opening talk. Lowestoft started their Music course by a lecture from Imogen Holst.

Then he came to the difficulties faced by the WEA in a large town:

> One of the reasons why it is harder to run classes in Ipswich is not so much the diversity of entertainment provided but the overlapping of cultural activity. The WEA offers a broad cultural front, and a Branch in a village is the fount of all learning, but in a large town the musicians . . . artists and dramatists . . . historians and archaeologists have respective organisations catering for their taste, even the natural scientists do . . . Also [WEA branch members] have the reputation in official circles of being so 'dreadfully earnest' – more an indication of the frivolous attitude that all education must be made palatable to be consumable than a valid criticism of their activities.

He ended by trying to convey the essence of the WEA in Suffolk, offering a description which reads as an affectionate tribute:

> The WEA takes its pattern partly from the history of the movement but quite largely I think from the county in which it is implanted. I think you would draw a different picture of it here than you would in Manchester or the Derby area. It is not so demonstrative or assertive. Socially it is mixed and unreforming. So very many of its members are foremost parish councillors, chairmen of the British Legions, WIs, village hall committees, Football Clubs. But they benefit much from the subjects they study. If it does nothing more than act as an educational lubricant or leaven, it serves its purpose well, by enriching minds, broadening outlooks, removing prejudice and opening vistas.

Pointers to the Future

One of the WEA's abiding characteristics is that it dare not become complacent, can never afford to stand still. Even as this portrait of the work in Suffolk was being painted, the Eastern District stood on the threshold of a major new development, which was to become a source of considerable pride. This was the launching of courses of twelve 1 hour meetings in liberal studies for young workers (mostly craft and commercial apprentices) employed by different firms within the District. The first of these, under the title 'In Search of Democracy', ran in the autumn term 1956 for seventeen apprentices with the Marconi Company in Chelmsford, and the experiment was repeated on a regular basis thereafter, usually with one course in each of the autumn and spring terms. Later titles included 'Behind the Headlines' (autumn 1957), 'International Affairs' (spring 1959) and 'English Social History Since 1900' (autumn 1960). Similar courses were provided for Hoffman Manufacturing Company, Chelmsford, from spring 1957 and for English Electric at Stevenage from autumn 1958; by the end of 1961 no less than eight firms were on the list, among them De Havilland, Imperial Chemical Industries and International Computers and Tabulators. A 22- meeting course on 'The Making of Modern England' was also run for Police Cadets in 1957–58. Although arrangements differed in detail from one place to another the usual practice was for the management to allow a preliminary meeting in works time at which the aims of the WEA could be explained and for those apprentices interested to stay behind to plan a course. Normally, classes were held on works premises but at least partly out of works time, with the apprentices themselves paying some or all of the fees, electing their own voluntary officers and choosing their own subjects of study. This work was of course in addition to, and quite separate from, the long-established provision for trade unionists run in conjunction with the WETUC, which also enjoyed some expansion during the 1950s: in 1953–54, for example, there were five residential weekend schools for trade unionists, in 1958–59 there were eight. Particularly close links were forged with the National Union of Boot and Shoe Operatives, whose head office was in Northampton and whose Assistant Secretary in these years, Syd Robinson, was chairman of the regional WETUC, chairman of the Northamptonshire Federation and vice-chairman of the District. Most of the students in a Tutorial Class in Northampton on Political Theory, launched successfully in 1955- 56, were members of this union.

For the promotion of this work, with apprentices and with trade unionists generally, a new tutor-organiser was needed. Jacques had already put in a plea to this effect in December 1954, when asked by the National WEA officers to state his ideal requirements at the time of negotiations with the Ministry following the Ashby Report. On that occasion he had made a case both for a tutor-organiser to increase provision for trade unionist students and also for one to develop work in the New Towns of Harlow, Stevenage, Hemel Hempstead and Hatfield. The eventual appointment, in June 1957, was a compromise between the two: a tutor-organiser to work with trade unionists and industrial personnel over the District as a whole, but with emphasis on the New Towns in one of which he would live. The man chosen was Russell Butler, a research student in social history at the University of London, who as a part-time tutor had taken the first course for apprentices at Marconi and had greatly impressed both here and in other courses for the branches in Hemel Hempstead and St. Albans. The Development Corporation of Harlow New Town made a flat available, but unfortunately he had little opportunity to make his mark because of recurrent illness and eventually resigned his post in September 1958. He subsequently came briefly into the national spotlight when, fighting Bexley for Labour in the 1966 General Election, he gained only 2,333 votes fewer than Conservative leader Edward Heath in a 54,826 poll.[14] His successor, John Carthew, was able to make a bigger impact within the District.

The advent of work with apprentices gave a new dimension to the Eastern District's overall programme: alongside the expansion in trade union provision and the increase in branches and branch membership, they contributed to the growing self-assurance of the District by the later 1950s. That assurance, derived from the conviction that the WEA had a major role to play in society and that the Eastern District was successful in fulfilling it, was apparent in the paper, 'A Consideration of Aims and Purposes', written by former treasurer Edward Miller in 1956. This started from the premiss that fundamental changes in the nature of government and politics since the foundation of the WEA over fifty years earlier fully justified the Association in redefining its aims. The increased range and penetration of government activity, the tendency for specialised administrative departments to function with little political control, the growing complexity in the affairs of trade unions and other voluntary organisations which led to greater dependence upon professional experts – all these made it imperative that the general public should be better informed than ever before.

> A democracy . . . demands a dissemination of political understanding wide enough to make the people's will in government an effective thing . . . the uninformed citizen . . . can be misled by the easy halftruth and the persuasive slogan; or he can feel that understanding will always be beyond him and fall into that apathy

which leaves everything to authority.

So the true task of adult education these days ought to be first and foremost to equip a sufficient body of ordinary citizens so that they are capable of forming rationally grounded opinions upon matters of public importance.

This was best fulfilled by a voluntary association independent of all authority so free to criticise it, and prepared to conduct a mission against apathy and escapism aware that there would be small returns for great effort. Because of its traditions and expertise, the WEA was best equipped of the voluntary bodies to play this part.

There was an acceptance here that the WEA was not necessarily educating for political and *social* action: its task was to create a better-informed citizen democracy, whether or not its students went on to join pressure groups or assume civic office. There was also an acceptance, as the implications were worked out later in the paper, that Terminal courses with 'a good deal of teaching at quite an elementary level' were 'a most important part' of the WEA's work; that university graduates, who usually had a narrow academic education, could benefit from the breadth of learning offered by the WEA quite as much as manual workers; that courses in literature and the arts were clearly a valid part of the WEA's total provision because they attracted new members, taught the processes of serious study and by enriching lives helped 'in raising the quality of the public which has the power of judgement upon those set in authority over it'.

Of course the paper was not totally iconoclastic. Although Terminal courses would probably remain as the bulk of provision – 'the breadth of the base of the movement amongst ordinary folk' – 'the Tutorial Class must be the demonstration that real understanding, whatever the purpose, requires sustained effort; and a significant expansion of activity at this level is the true index of a significant expansion of a genuinely informed public.'. Again, courses in politics, society and economics retained priority in the task of educating for citizenship; for the WEA 'it must be the acid test of the extent to which it is doing its job that the primacy should lie in these fields'. But Miller's achievement was to liberate the District from feelings of guilt that the bulk of its provision really ought to be Tutorial Classes for manual workers in political and social studies. He boldly asserted that while courses with these characteristics remained goals to be aimed for, there was genuine value in shorter courses for people of all backgrounds in a wide range of subjects – and that in offering such courses the WEA was furthering the spread of an educated democracy.

The paper was discussed by branches and Federations during the academic year 1956–57 and at the District Council of July 1957. Out of all this came a resolution passed at the District AGM the following November. The original motion was proposed by Frank Jacques as an Individual Member but the various amendments from the floor were sufficiently substantial to make the final version a fair representation of majority opinion among the voluntary members. The motion as carried read as follows:

That the Workers' Educational Association recognises its particular responsibility for the furtherance of liberal studies, at a time when stress is increasingly laid on the need to encourage and aid the development of technical education. It sees no antithesis between the liberal and the technical and contends for the wider acceptance of the truth that the latter will be of no lasting value to the community unless the people of this country are adequately equipped to participate actively in its government and culture.

It declares that

a) it seeks as students in its classes all who feel, and can be caused to feel, the need to understand the way our society works, to assess its values and to comprehend the problems which confront it now, in order to discharge more effectively their duties and responsibilities as citizens;

b) it considers such an education to be the greatest safeguard against the dangerous growth of State power, to be indispensable for the preservation of an effective democracy and to be the one, moreover, which can only be the province of a voluntary independent movement;

c) it therefore determines to provide increasing opportunities for the study of the social sciences and the arts in courses of such type and standard as will demand of students the effort essential to understanding;

d) it will carry its campaign with increasing vigour among all classes of people, whatever their professions and occupations, but particularly among members of trade unions, seeking their interest in and active association with the achievement of its aims.

In one sense, this can be read as the Eastern District's response to the Ashby Committee's vote of confidence in the WEA little more than three years before. In another sense, it was a manifesto for the 1960s.

Botolph House: Eastern District Office since 1966.
The original house dates from 1812 and is a Grade II listed building.

NOTES

1) A. Bullock, 'The Universities and Adult Education', *Summer Highway*, 1952, pp.1–7; G. D. H. Cole, 'What Workers' Education Means', *Highway*, October 1952, pp.2–11; R. Hoggart, 'What Shall the WEA Do?', ibid., pp.46–53; M. Bruce, 'The Universities and Adult Education', *Highway*, November 1952, pp.54–61. For a bibliography on the debate in general, see R. D. Waller, 'The Great Debate', *Adult Education*, XXV (1952–53), pp.250- 63, reprinted in E. M. Hutchinson, ed., *Aims and Action in Adult Education, 1921–1971* (1971), pp.66–78.

2) Tawney proclaimed a very similar message in his lecture, 'The Workers' Educational Association and Adult Education' to the University of London in May 1953, reprinted in his collection of essays, *The Radical Tradition* (1964), chapter 7.

3) Opening a new primary school at Waterbeach (Cambridgeshire) in April 1953, Miss Horsbrugh was reported to have said on the subject of adult education: 'I am not in the least in favour of trying to press these classes. I do not believe it will do a bit of good . . . Let the people pay for them rather than pay out of the rates and taxes.' (*Cambridge Daily News*, 20 April 1953)

4) Typical of many letters were one from Bedford branch to the local MP Christopher Soames ('it is against the national interest to restrict provisions for enabling people . . . to learn more about the economic, industrial and social well-being of the country'), one by Earls Colne branch (Essex) to the Chancellor of the Exchequer R. A. Butler ('the damage done by curtailment will be out of all proportion to the financial gain to the Exchequer') and one by Martham branch (Norfolk) to the Minister of Education herself ('as we are a small branch it appears we are threatened with extermination . . . the amount saved by such an economy represents a direct threat to adult education in our village').

5) Ministry of Education: *The Organisation and Finance of Adult Education in England and Wales* (1954), pp.66–67.

6) In 1953 the figures for all Responsible Body classes in England and Wales were: men students 62,756, women students 74,447 (Ministry of Education: *Report and statistics for England and Wales for 1953*, PP. 1953–54 XI, p.714).

7) In 1952–53 the Eastern District had 161 branches; the next highest totals were London District (88) and Northern District (85): *WEA Annual Report for 1954*, p.107. The WEA's evidence [8C]to the Ashby Committee is contained in *The Workers' Educational Association Memorandum on matters within the scope of the terms of reference of the Committee*, etc., published in January 1955.

8) Ibid., p.48.

9) *Times Educational Supplement* (hereafter *TES*), 3 September 1954.

10) H. C. Wiltshire, 'The Organisation and Finance of Adult Education', *Adult Education*, XXVII (1954–55), pp.199–204; S. G. Raybould, 'The Ashby Report and Afterwards' in his *Trends in English Adult Education* (1959), pp.222–47.

11) The William F. Harvey Memorial Lecture, inaugurated in 1947, commemorated the warden of Fircroft College between 1919 and 1923.

12) *Cambridge Daily News*, 28 September 1953.

13) Ministry of Education: *Report of HM Inspectors on Classes on Local History provided by Responsible Bodies in the Cambridge University Extra-Mural Area during Michaelmas Term 1954* (1955).

14) *Whitaker's Almanack 1967*, p.325.

CHAPTER 6

UNFINISHED BUSINESS
1959–72

The policy statement adopted at the 1958 National Conference, *Education for a Changing Society: the Role of the WEA*, earned for itself the nickname of the WEA's 'White Paper'. In framing the statement, the newly-elected President, Asa Briggs, then Professor of Modern History at the University of Leeds, drew heavily on the views of Districts, such as those enshrined in Edward Miller's 'Aims and Purposes' and in the resolution passed by the Eastern District in 1957. Briggs declared that the future success of the WEA rested on the twin pillars of social relevance and active membership: 'they are old WEA themes but they need to be restated in new forms'. Social relevance was seen as embracing the traditional WEA concern with the socially and educationally underprivileged, but also meant addressing in particular 'four danger points' in contemporary society. These were identified as the mass apathy which rendered democracy unreal, the growing gulf between experts and ordinary citizens, the tendency for occupational and professional groups to think and act in isolation from the community at large, and the uncritical acceptance of mass culture. Under the third of these, special mention was made of the importance of trade union education and of 'the necessity for relating initial training in trade union procedure to the whole range of the social studies'. The WEA was seen as being in a most advantageous position from which to tackle these issues: 'a broadly based voluntary movement' which 'works in close association with universities and local authorities . . . teaching subjects which inevitably involve controversy and differences of opinion, organising disciplined liberal and social studies . . . educating co-operatively without the spur of tests, examinations and diplomas'. Alongside this the WEA's second pillar, active membership, was characterised by lively voluntaryism. Branches were exhorted to organise balanced programmes attractive to new students as well as challenging to old ones, to use initiative in administration and fundraising, and to give members a sense that they were part of a movement. In the last resort the WEA's strength lay in voluntary participation: 'members of the Association are not merely well-wishers but doers' and (as a reminder to professional staff) 'the officers are the servants of the movement'.

This was a skilfully-drafted document because while remaining true to the WEA's traditions as a voluntary movement promoting adult education with a social purpose, it was an invitation to branches and Districts to express those traditions in novel ways. The message, above all, was that the WEA must extend its horizons and attract new students. Although much of this echoed Miller's 'Aims and Purposes' – in deploring professional isolationism, for instance, in encouraging trade union education and in asserting the values of voluntaryism – Briggs's statement marked a more radical break with tradition insofar as it never once mentioned Tutorial Classes. Although branches were to offer 'a sound programme, one which maintains the high standards of work the WEA has always set' and although 'there is no substitute for prolonged and systematic study based on reading as well as discussion', these standards were not precisely defined nor were they linked to courses of a particular duration. Less advanced courses were also very important: 'the WEA must develop classes which provide stimulating introductions to subjects which require further study . . . an effort must be made also to develop residential weekend schools for young workers'. Apart from trade union education, 'there are special opportunities in the rural areas and classes should be encouraged there as much as possible'. And in some industrial towns and villages, Districts 'should carry out pilot schemes in problem areas'. There was little sense of elitism in all this: educational pioneering was the order of the day.

Did the Eastern District fulfil these objectives? Certainly, there was a great deal in the Briggs 'White Paper' which found a place in the District's programme in subsequent years. Of the immense contribution to adult education in rural areas there can be no doubt. In towns as well as villages, branches run by voluntary members with minimal professional help could fairly claim to be doing their bit to combat the apathy, philistinism and occupational isolationism pointed to by Briggs. If one counts mothers tied by the necessity to bring up pre-school children among the educationally underprivileged, this was one disadvantaged group catered for by a rapid expansion in daytime courses. Provision for trade unionists also showed a significant increase; the tutor-organisers responsible were very aware of the importance of relating their studies to wider social issues and of integrating such courses into the work of the voluntary movement at large, even if not always successful in doing so. Other pioneering ventures included courses for prisoners, handicapped people, and workers preparing for retirement.

With so much new work undertaken, alongside an appreciable increase in numbers of students and courses generally, the 1960s and early 1970s were exciting years for those in the Eastern District with a deep commitment to the WEA. Here, as throughout the country, there was an optimism within the movement, as demand for adult education blossomed and repeated assaults were made on different aspects of educational disadvantage. This confidence was apparent in yet another policy statement, *Unfinished Business*, drafted by Yorkshire North District Secretary, Fred Sedgwick, and presented to the National Conference in November 1969 as a commentary upon work in progress during these years. Developments within other agencies – the growing provision of liberal studies by local authorities and their introduction of student associations to some of their centres, the increasing tendency of extramural departments to mount programmes independent of the WEA, the arrival of the Open University whose first undergraduates entered in 1971 – all of which might in the past have been seen as competitive threats, were welcomed for the opportunities they offered for constructive partnership.

> Post-war experience has shown ... that the student population grows with the increase of facilities. The only limiting factor of any consequence is lack of money to provide the facilities. The WEA, if it ever was really worried about competition, need now only think in terms of co-operation.

But *Unfinished Business* also drew attention to some of the problems, tensions and disappointments which accompanied innovative work: the deterrence of potential students through disillusionment with education in the past; the unsuitability of traditional branch organisation as a means to involve some new groups of students; the tendency for professionals rather than voluntary members to direct affairs; and the impossibility of achieving uniform practice in a diverse and democratic body. As the policy statement put it:

> [the WEA's] aims seem as varied as the people who compose it and any policy declaration it produces must be a statement of intent, a guide to action for its democratic leadership and not a creed. Because of this there will be differences between what the Association states as its aims and what it actually achieves in particular situations.

The Eastern District had its fair share of difficulties in this period but also many notable achievements, as it rose to the challenge of new work on several different fronts. To quote Frank Jacques in his 1961–62

175

Annual Report, 'the field, thank God, is never quiet'.[1]

Advances in Industry

Courses for industrial personnel witnessed both a dramatic increase and significant change of emphasis in this period. John Carthew, appointed to succeed Russell Butler as tutor-organiser for Industry in August 1958, was a Cambridge graduate in English Literature who during National Service prior to university had taught in the army education corps. As a student he had edited *Cambridge Forward*, the journal of the University Labour Club, and had been President of the University English Club. He devoted much of his time to the development of courses for young workers along the lines pioneered by Butler, and the expansion outlined in the previous chapter was essentially his achievement. By autumn 1964 ten of these courses were running on the premises of seven different firms, with another supported by various companies at Letchworth College of Technology. A further innovation came in 1962 with the introduction of two week-long courses for apprentices as part of the WEA Summer School at King's College Cambridge, a successful experiment which became an annual feature. Fourteen apprentices resident in the first week of the 1962 Summer School studied 'Africa, Its People and Their Problems' with Robin Hallett, who had resigned as tutor-organiser for Norfolk seven years earlier to become an extra-mural tutor in Nigeria. Ten in the second week tackled 'Trade Unions, the Government and the Public' with Carthew and Michael Posner, University lecturer in Economics and fellow of Pembroke College, Cambridge, who contributed to many of the courses for apprentices and others in Industry as a part-time tutor during the early 1960s. Carthew's own teaching focussed on literature and current affairs – 'Introduction to Modern Poetry' for the apprentices at Marconi in summer 1960, for example, or 'Literature and Society' at W. H. Allen and Sons, Bedford in spring 1962. Part-time tutors helped to meet the growing demand for courses and to provide variety of subject-matter: from psychology to international affairs to philosophy. Carthew spent the academic year 1963- 64 teaching in the USA, based on Elmira College, New York State University, during which his temporary replacement, Gordon Crosse, encouraged an interest in Music: one of his compositions around this time, 'Meet My Folks', performed at the Aldeburgh Festival in 1964, was the prelude to an illustrious career as a composer of a wide range of orchestral, chamber and vocal music, including operas, ballets and works for children. For his part, Carthew became in 1965 the first recipient of the R. H. Tawney Memorial Tutorship, an award introduced by the National WEA in memory of that great pioneer who had died in 1962 and which was intended to be granted at three-year intervals to a full-time tutor employed by a WEA District.

Industrial classes conducted by Responsible Bodies in Greater London, Hertfordshire and Essex were visited by Her Majesty's Inspectors during 1963 and 1964. Their subsequent report, although not of course concerned solely with the Eastern District, gave a very favourable impression of all aspects of this work.

> Quality was generally good and in some cases remarkably vigorous and searching work was achieved ... This work is a genuine and welcome advance because it brings into classes students who would not otherwise come into contact with a form of adult education which has much to offer them ... The responsible bodies concerned all believe that there is a growing demand for this type of provision and that they are best fitted to meet it. The evidence of this survey would appear to lend strong support to their contention.[2]

In his turn, the District Secretary set great store by the courses for apprentices and in his 1963–64 Annual Report mentioned three former students who had recently gained scholarships to higher education. On the other hand, Carthew, in his Tawney Memorial Lecture, delivered immediately after the Eastern District Council of 14 May 1966, seemed less convinced of what had really been achieved. Under the title 'Education, Social Class and the WEA' he bemoaned the fact that many of the apprentices and other young workers he had taught felt that a liberal education was pointless when major decisions which shaped their lives remained out of their hands.

> 'What', as one student put it during a discussion on the balance of payments, 'are you telling us all this for? You ought to be telling it to the people who make the decisions'. Everyone knows that political and economic decisions affect the way we live, but they will do as they will: what difference does it make what we think or know? One hears a good deal about working class apathy but, if my analysis is accurate, apathy is quite the wrong word. It is, rather, a fundamental contracting-out from public affairs; given the bias of our system of education and decision-making processes it should not surprise us.

He found more grounds for hope in the joy in education that many of his students had found at a personal level – not because it led to a better job or enabled them to control decisions but because it contributed to a more subtle enrichment of their lives. He also paid tribute to the 'outstanding success' of the courses for apprentices held as part of the WEA Summer School in Cambridge: 'almost without exception the students leave the schools determined to revive, establish or develop in their own firms WEA courses on a weekly basis'. These were the aspects of his work on which he evidently looked back with most satisfaction when he left the District's service later in the year to take up a lectureship at the University of Dar-es-Salaam.

By then, however, a major shift in priorities was under way. The Workers' Educational Trade Union Committee was dissolved on 31 December 1964. This was the body in co-operation with which the District had hitherto run one-day and weekend courses for trade unionists, such as a residential weekend on the European Economic Community at King's College Cambridge in March 1961 attended by forty-one students on WETUC scholarships. The Trades Union Congress introduced a new educational scheme in 1965 to replace the provision previously made by both the WETUC and the National Council of Labour Colleges. TUC Regional Advisory Committees, through educational sub-committees, were to arrange and approve courses suitable for trade unionists, and Regional Education Officers were appointed with responsibility for this. WEA Districts, who were represented on the educational sub-committees, were envisaged as making a substantial contribution in the provision of courses, for which the TUC would meet all students' fees. The scheme gave the opportunity for more sustained study than had been possible in the old one-day and weekend schools: courses equivalent to Terminals or Long Terminals were to be arranged, the students meeting once a week either in the evening or in works time wherever this could be negotiated with employers. Accordingly several 1-2 hour evening courses were arranged to begin in September 1965 in various technical and further education colleges around the District. These made a mixed start. One at Luton Technical College on 'Economic Problems of Industry' taken by Bedfordshire tutor-organiser, Ted Evans, had only three students for the first two weeks but then attracted seven more and ran for eleven weeks. Another on 'Trade Unionism in the Sixties' at Harlow had twenty students for ten weeks. On the other hand, a proposed course in March recruited none at all and one on 'Communications' in Chelmsford with Carthew as tutor closed after three meetings with only two students on the roll. But where there were failures, much could be laid at the door of organisational teething troubles in the early stages of the scheme. More evening courses followed in 1966- 67, and from October 1967 half-day release courses as well, as at the London Brick Company, Stewartby

(Bedfordshire) where a course on 'Industrial Relations' for shop stewards consisted of ten weekly sessions each of three hours with a break in the middle. By the early 1970s an increasing number of these TUC-sponsored courses were being held on a full-day release basis, leaving the evening courses as no more than an occasional expedient for those who could not obtain release from their firms. In 1971–72 the District ran twenty-five full-day release courses on 'Industrial Relations' (or a closely-related subject), over half its total provision for Industry.

With the expansion of this TUC-related work, the District appointed two new tutor-organisers for Industry, Reg Carnell in June 1966 and Mike Friesner in January 1967. Both were Economics graduates, Carnell from Cambridge after Ruskin, Friesner from Manchester, and both had had previous experience as trade union representatives. Partly because of the buoyant demand from the TUC for courses to train shop stewards, and partly because of their own trade union backgrounds, these tutor-organisers achieved a most impressive expansion in courses on 'Industrial Relations' and the like, tailored to the needs of trade union representatives. The District's commitment to trade union education was such that in July 1968 a third tutor-organiser was appointed to meet the growing demand. Out of this a rough geographical pattern emerged. Carnell took the west of the District (focussing on Northampton, Peterborough and Cambridge) while Friesner, succeeded in 1970 by Bert Torrison, was responsible for the south (Bedfordshire and Hertfordshire). The new appointment, successively Bill Kaye in 1968–69, Paddy Kitson 1969–71, Peter Sherriff 1971–72, was based in the east (Suffolk and Essex). With three tutor-organisers the District was able to rely far more heavily on its own full-time staff: important because, with the advance of full-day release courses, it became increasingly difficult to find qualified part-time tutors available for the whole of a day. Thus, in the forty-six courses of one sort or another provided for Industry in 1971–72, only four part-time tutors were employed, other than as 'guest speakers' on specialist topics in single sessions. But meanwhile the more general courses for apprentices and other young workers declined in number – a reflection both of changes in firms' training priorities and of the competing demands upon the tutor-organisers' time. As Carnell explained in his annual report for 1967–68:

> the year under review has been one of overall expansion, but it has been a distorted expansion. I feel however that such a pattern is inevitable, given our limited resources . . . At the outset, it can be said that it was the District's policy to expand our provision for trade union education. Having this commitment we then devoted

the major part of our organisational time to the ground work for this specific expansion . . . Other work, in particular the apprentice classes, has tended to suffer some decline.

Indeed by 1972–73 only one course for apprentices remained in the programme – a twelve week Terminal on 'Youth and Its Problems in Society' at Lucas Aerospace, Hemel Hempstead taken by Hertfordshire tutor-organiser Simon Maddison – and none were to be held thereafter. Selected apprentices from several firms within the District did, however, continue to attend the annual Summer School in Cambridge until 1978.

In developing the work with trade unionists, the Eastern District was certainly living up to one of the calls in *Education for a Changing Society*. But was it doing anything to broaden the horizons of those who were taught? Were trade union representatives losing some of their occupational isolation and were they learning anything of social studies in general, beyond their initial training in industrial relations? These were fundamental objectives which Briggs had laid down. There is no easy answer to this. Superficially, one can look at the lists of courses for industrial personnel in District Annual Reports and observe that the breadth of liberal studies offered to apprentices in the early sixties was replaced by a much narrower concentration on the practicalities of trade unionism. As late as 1965–66, the year the TUC scheme began, about a third of the District's total provision for Industry was still in courses which had little or no link with the students' daily work: 'Hamlet' and 'Macbeth' for the apprentices of Hoffmann Engineering, Chelmsford, for example, 'Philosophy' at the British Aircraft Corporation, Stevenage, or 'The Sociology of Sex' at Davey Paxman, Colchester. By 1967–68, however, 'Industrial Relations' had come to dominate the list: of some forty-five courses for Industry in that year, two-thirds carried that or a very similar title, leaving topics such as 'Jazz Today' at ICT Letchworth and 'Social Psychology' at Marconi's Chelmsford in a tiny minority. But to draw unfavourable conclusions from all this would be too simplistic. For a start, courses in industrial relations and the like for shop stewards and other trade union representatives reached many people who would never otherwise have come to a WEA class, whether as apprentices or as members of the general public. The training they received enabled these men and women to play an active role in shaping their working lives – to participate in the decision-making process, something Carthew had regretted that his apprentices had seen as beyond them. Moreover, tutors had considerable freedom to frame their own syllabuses and create their own teaching materials, and in the hands of the skilled practitioners whom the District employed in this field courses could touch a broad range of topics which the mere title might not imply. For instance, the syllabus for a half-day release course on 'Industrial Relations' for shop stewards and other workshop representatives, taught by Reg Carnell at Lowestoft in autumn 1967, included sessions on the history of trade unions, the law and trade unions, communication problems, and trade unions and the economy. Similarly two evening courses for trade union representatives, one at Cambridge the other at Northampton in autumn 1969, went under the title 'The Economics of Productivity Bargaining'; the syllabuses explained that 'collective bargaining never takes place in a vacuum, it is influenced by the economic and social policies of the government', clearly the cue for wide-ranging discussion.

Nor would it be true to suggest that TUC-related courses were the only significant new developments in industrial provision during the 1960s. An important venture was the introduction of a day-release course, 'Men in Steel', at Stewart and Lloyd's steelworks, Corby in 1964–65. The students were not necessarily trade union activists: they were hourly-paid workers who during the two terms of the course tackled a range of subjects under a variety of tutors, including economics, communications and human relations, all with special reference to the steel industry. The firm met the fees. The success of the first course led to its annual repetition until 1970–71, with several of the students ultimately leaving the industry to pursue some form of further or higher education. By 1967–68 they were being given the opportunity of individual tutorials on communication skills, both in essay-writing and in the spoken word, with one of the part-time tutors, Barbara Brenchley. And in 1968–69 Northamptonshire tutor-organiser, John Lowerson, who contributed a session on social history, was so impressed by his visit that he wrote in his annual report: 'this was one of the best groups I have taught both in the WEA and outside it. The critical quality of their involvement was much greater than many of our traditional groups'.

Another innovation was the provision of Pre-Retirement courses. The first of these came in autumn 1969, six afternoon sessions for employees of Baker Perkins, Peterborough under the title 'Problems and Opportunities for Retirement' led by Fenland tutor-organiser, Nick Harden. This successful experiment led to similar courses on the premises of Baker Perkins annually for the next ten years. The idea was taken up in autumn 1970 at the University Centre, Northampton, this time with eight afternoon sessions for people either released from their firms or coming on their own initiative, and quickly spread throughout the District. By 1975–76 such courses were being held on the premises of two firms in Peterborough (Baker Perkins and Peter Brotherhood), for civil servants in Cambridge, Northampton, Norwich, Stevenage and Mildenhall, and for Area Health Authority employees in Northampton. The basic pattern was for workers within a few years of retirement to attend sessions some of which were of a practical nature – on pensions, taxation and social services provision – others more philosophical, concerned with attitudes towards an unfamiliar future. These courses have continued to be a comparatively-small but nonetheless important part of the District's total programme, especially in Northamptonshire.

The District's overall record in advancing its work in the industrial field was highly impressive. There was, however, one genuine cause for regret, namely that the branches themselves were largely divorced from the process. This was an issue which certainly exercised the tutor-organisers concerned. In his annual report for 1967–68, Mike Friesner wrote that:

> The problem still remains of integrating the students who have taken part in the type of course we have arranged in industry into the life of the voluntary movement . . . The voluntary principle must underlie every aspect of our work and it must be our prime objective to extend this into every area of our activity. The present dichotomy in the life of the movement imposes considerable strains on the organisation and the atmosphere in which we work. In eventually drawing into the democratic life of the WEA the present 'passive' industrially-based student, we shall I believe activate a potential source of energy which can only be of benefit to the movement.

In the *Suffolk Federation Newsletter* of spring 1970, Paddy Kitson pursued a similar theme:

> It is part of our purpose, in all this industrial work, to achieve some kind of carry-over from the industrial courses to the more traditional WEA branches. Perhaps we will do this by means of the 'conversion' of individuals, or by the establishment of official and meaningful affiliation links between workers' organisations and the WEA branches, but try we must! One is forever hearing resolutions moved at AGMs that we should drop the 'W' from our title because it is no longer relevant – I say that it can, and must, be made completely relevant by our bringing of the industrial worker back into the mainstream of our movement.

For their part, most voluntary branch members were keen on closer links with the industrial work. St Albans complained at the 1967 District AGM that the branch had apparently received no notification of a course for trade unionists in their town; in October 1968 the District Executive reaffirmed that branches should be kept informed of any such courses in their areas; in March 1971 the District Council carried *nem.con.* a motion from the Fenland Federation applauding developments in industrial work but calling for various initiatives which would improve liaison, including invitations to branch members to all industrial courses to talk about local WEA affairs.

Yet despite the concern about the apparent gulf between the industrial and more traditional work, and despite many efforts to bridge that gulf, on the whole these two aspects of WEA provision remained separate. It was unfortunate, for example, that whereas in 1966–67 both tutor-organisers for Industry had done some teaching for ordinary WEA branches – Carnell at Hemel Hempstead on 'Problems of Modern Society', Friesner at Hertford on 'Current Economic Problems' – this became a rarity in subsequent years owing to pressures of other work. But the division was by no means total. Many individual students in industrial courses did indeed enrol with WEA branches; some went on to become branch officers, notably at Corby where the 'Men in Steel' course instilled a lasting enthusiasm for study. Corby branch also put on a twenty-four week Long Terminal on 'The History of Trade Unions' in 1969–70, with the intention of attracting trade unionists as students. And Eastern District Councils, like National Conferences, continued to be places where people from contrasting backgrounds, with widely differing perceptions of society in general and of the WEA in particular, could meet on equal terms as members of the same Association.

Other Pioneering Work

Apart from the developments in Industry, the District also broke new ground during the 1960s with the introduction of daytime courses with creches provided, so that the mothers of young children could take part. Afternoon classes, attended largely by retired people, were already well-established in a few urban branches, but courses with creches usually took place in the mornings and tended to attract female students in their twenties and early thirties. Courses of this type first appeared in Hertfordshire in the early years of the decade. In autumn 1963, for example, Hatfield branch launched a twenty-one week Long Terminal, with creche available, on 'Modern Trends in Education', which ran on Wednesdays from 10.00 to 11.30 a.m.; all twenty students were entered in the register as 'housewives' (a term to which many have objected over the years) and in her end-of- course report the tutor, Patricia d'Arcy, commented very favourably on the liveliness of discussion, having herself been forced to reconsider her ideas. Some three years later, a group of ladies from a council estate in Hertford approached the District for daytime courses of a rather different sort: six meetings in the late mornings on 'Ancient Chinese Civilisation' alongside six in the early afternoons on 'China Now', with a short break between and children looked after while classes were in session. Both courses enrolled the same twenty-one students and similar linked morning-and-afternoon courses were run in Hertford for the next three years.[3] Courses with creches soon appeared in Bedfordshire and Suffolk, and by 1968–69 were to be found in Essex and Norfolk as well. Indeed by 1970–71 there were over sixty daytime courses run by different branches in the District (although not all with creche), of which no less than twelve were held in Bishop's Stortford and another nine elsewhere in Hertfordshire. Three years later over 50% of WEA students in this county (and 46% of the total class programme here) was accounted for by daytime classes.

The appeal of such courses is not hard to understand. One of those much involved in the early years, the Extra-Mural Board's resident tutor in Hertfordshire, Ray Pahl, wrote in 1962 of the 'numbing effect of unrelieved domestic work' on the minds of women who resented staying at home all day and looked for intellectual opportunities. He suggested that:

> The mother and not the father will in the future be the cultural growing point of the family. She has more time at home in which to do general reading and more desire to leave home in her leisure time.[4]

But accommodation for students and their children in the day could prove very expensive: Bishop's Stortford branch was having to find £100 in rent for its twelve courses in 1970–71, meeting this from special moneyraising efforts and higher-than-normal fees. It was for this reason that the Hertfordshire Federation set up a special fund in the following year to offer financial help to branches which provided creches. From 1980 onwards the District also gave a subsidy to those branches which requested help in financing creches.

One very gratifying feature of this daytime provision over the years has been the challenging subjects frequently requested by the students. The programme for 1970–71, for instance, included a range of literature and history topics but also such titles as 'The Morality of Society' at Langford (Bedfordshire), 'The Family' at St. Ives (Fenland), 'The Sociology of Education' at both Danbury and Saffron Walden (Essex) and 'World Poverty' and 'Poverty in Britain' at Bishop's Stortford: all successful Terminal courses which (although not deliberately excluding men) were in fact attended only by women. All these courses were clear examples of the 'social relevance' for which Asa Briggs had been pleading twelve years before.

It was to encourage the further development of these courses that in August 1970 the District appointed a tutor-organiser with special responsibility for the promotion of daytime work. This was John McDonald, an Oxford graduate in English Literature who over the next five years, working from his home first in Luton then in Stevenage, concentrated on initiating such courses in Bedfordshire, Hertfordshire and Cambridgeshire; he also taught those which came within his subject-range. In spring 1971, for example, he helped Bedfordshire tutor-organiser, Derek Tatton, to re-found the branch at Leighton Buzzard and he taught the first daytime course here on 'Contemporary Social Problems in Literature': this was one of many cases, as at Godmanchester and Linton (Cambridgeshire) in 1974–75, where the launch of a daytime course was the occasion of the foundation or re-foundation of a branch. His own assessment of his contribution to the District came in his final annual report in 1975. He pointed out some of the difficulties attendant upon daytime courses with creches, such as the high cost of accommodation and more-than-usual organisational problems: but he also stressed some of the benefits both to the students – for whom courses provided much-needed intellectual stimulus – and to the WEA, which recruited people new to the movement, a fresh source of energy, ideas and enthusiasm. It is some measure of his achievement that the three counties in which he worked were long to continue (along with Essex) to host nearly all the District's daytime courses with creches. Thus by 1979–80 there were twenty-six such courses in Hertfordshire, fourteen in both Bedfordshire and Cambridgeshire and ten in Essex, out of sixty-six in the District altogether.

Of course there were many other pioneer ventures during the 1960s. Some of these related to broadcasting, for throughout the decade there were high hopes of what could be done by linking courses to radio and television programmes. Norwich branch, for instance, ran Terminal courses in 1963–64 on 'The Instruments of the Orchestra' and 'Molecular Biology', both in conjunction with television series of the same names. In the spring of 1962, two BBC education officers visited a Long Terminal in Wisbech taught by Fenland tutor-organiser, Doris Wheatley, which carried the same title, 'Growing Up in the Sixties', as a radio series which the class listened to and discussed. But these courses never became more than a minor part of the District's provision. Among successful experiments elsewhere were a language course of ten meetings for immigrants, 'Everyday English', run by Bedford branch in autumn 1968, and several enterprises in Northamptonshire in 1970–71: a course of six meetings on 'The Rights of Unemployed Men and Women' at Corby, one of four meetings for the parents of handicapped children in Northampton and another of three meetings, also in Northampton, on aspects of local history for blind students.

Particular mention should be made of courses provided by the District at Blundeston Prison, Lowestoft, which began in March 1965. The first course on 'Social Problems of the Sixties' attracted ten students, all serving prison sentences; their general enthusiasm was such that the number of meetings was extended from ten to twelve. All but three of the students attended at least two-thirds of the course; one who did not lost the privilege of attendance through attempting to escape in early May. In his report at the end, the tutor, Jack Nobbs, said that:

> This was the most worthwhile course I have taken in about twelve years' WEA work. The prisoners were most appreciative of all efforts made on their behalf and they had more time to follow up the studies. Their only disappointment was that we often did not have time to go into subjects fully enough. Many of the men stressed the value of the course because of the deterioration that one faces after years of being institutionalised.

An earlier progress report had referred to the students' diligence in reading, essay-writing and note-taking 'and the discussion is red-hot'. The prison tutor-organiser was also most impressed, writing to say that 'this has been one of the most successful groups run here under my control'. Not surprisingly a follow- up course was arranged for the autumn and a regular series of twelve-week courses ensued on subjects such as 'The Common Market', 'Economics', 'Sociology' and 'Mass Media', almost invariably with Nobbs as tutor. The last course was held in autumn 1977. Nobbs reflected upon his experience in the *Eastern District Bulletin* a year and a half later, explaining that subjects had been chosen by the prisoners on the same democratic principles as in normal WEA classes, and commending the remarkable freedom of discussion, with the majority of his students expressing right-wing views. Clearly this was a most valuable contribution to the District's many-fronted attack on educational disadvantage, one in which both tutor and students found considerable fulfilment. As Nobbs wrote:

> If the WEA, through me, has been able to help one prisoner to find prison less irksome, or to impart to one prisoner a deeper knowledge and understanding, then the association has indeed fulfilled the function envisaged for it by its founders.

Measures of Achievement

The focus, so far in this chapter, upon new courses of one sort or another in no way detracts from the importance of more traditional WEA branch provision. This continued to prosper: although the actual number of branches fluctuated, student recruitment showed steady increase. 5,395 students, 314 courses and 156 branches in 1958–59 had become 6,162 students, 349 courses and 185 branches in 1964–65 and 8,348 students, 443 courses and 163 branches by 1971–72. The only negative trend of any significance was the steady decline in three-year university Tutorials: thirty in 1958–59, twenty in 1964–65, eleven in 1971–72. The overall expansion would undoubtedly have been greater but for restrictions on the level of government grant in the early and middle 1960s. A Ministry of Education standstill on grant for 1963–64 was repeated for 1964–65, evoking a protest similar to that which had responded to the threatened 10% Cut in 1953. District vice-chairman, Edward Miller (as warden of the Extra-Mural Board's residential centre, Madingley Hall) wrote to *The Guardian* in March 1964 asking 'whether there is a deliberate policy to weaken the voluntary movements engaged in adult education'.[5] In an adjournment debate in the House of Commons on 24 April 1964, James Boyden, Labour MP for Bishop Auckland, asked how the standstill squared with paragraph 518 of the Robbins Report on Higher Education, published in the previous October and accepted in principle by the government: this had praised, and advocated further support for, the adult education offered by the WEA, local authorities and university extra-mural departments.[6] *The Eastern Daily Press* was one local newspaper to give its backing to the WEA, publishing letters of protest from Eastern District Chairman, Jessie Roberts (urging all concerned to write to MPs and to the Ministry) and from Norwich branch committee member, Shirley Holman ('I first discovered the WEA in 1946, since when my real education has begun'). It also offered a favourable editorial on 29 March: 'we in East Anglia whose towns and villages have so long benefited from the services of [WEA] tutors have the best of reasons to appreciate its lasting value'. But the Ministry did not budge and an expanded provision without any increase in grant to accompany it meant that government aid for 1964-65 amounted to only 69% of educational expenditure compared to the 75% or so hitherto regarded as normal. Even more disappointing was the fact that the Department of Education and Science, established by the 1964 Labour government to replace the Ministry of Education, continued the restrictions, forcing the District to cut its programme to make ends meet: more than fifty courses had to be closed in the autumn term of 1965 through the rigorous application of the rules on low enrolment, and many courses planned for spring 1966 could not be sanctioned. It is a reflection of the imbalance between supply and demand that although the District had thus to reduce the number of courses offered, more students actually enrolled in these courses than the total of the previous year! Fortunately, an expansion in course provision once again became possible from 1966–67 onwards.

The upward trend in both student numbers and courses provided was against a background of escalating fees. These had stood at around 1s. 0d. per meeting since 1956–57 but were raised 50% to a minimum 1s. 6d. per meeting for 1965–66, to 1s. 9d. for 1967–68, to 2s. 3d. for 1969–70 and (after decimalisation) to 16p. for 1971–72. So in 1959–60 3,555 students on WEA Terminals and Long Terminals had paid minima of 10s. 0d. and £1 respectively (including 1s. 0d. registration fee) plus a little more to become branch members; in 1971–72 5,668 students on the same types of course paid £1.92 and £3.36 (with a further 10p. added for registration). This represented a rise in fees at a rate appreciably faster than inflation: in broad terms, prices did not quite double between 1959 and 1972, while Eastern District fees more than trebled.[7] It is true that all the agencies of adult education were substantially increasing their fees during this period. Between 1963–64 and 1971–72, when the Retail Price Index showed an increase of 50%, local authority fees in England and Wales as a whole rose by 146%; in East Anglia the increase was 149%. In the same period, the average fees charged by university extra-mural boards increased by 107% and those by WEA Districts by 137%. Even so, the increase in the Eastern District from 1963- 64 to 1971–72 was of the order of 220% and at 16p. per meeting WEA fees here became once again the highest in the country.[8]

The rising cost of WEA courses naturally provoked some resentment. Faced with a refusal by two branches to implement the new scale of 1s. 6d. per meeting, the District Executive decided in February 1966 that all branch chairmen and secretaries must sign an undertaking to levy the agreed fees when applying for courses. There was particular grievance against the increase in fees in 1971, especially from members who lived close to neighbouring Districts which charged lower sums. An Essex Federation motion opposing the increase 'as being socially divisive, likely to discourage choice of difficult but valuable subjects and harmful to weaker branches' was noted by the District Executive in October 1971; this motion also pointed to the fact that 'Essex branches in London District charge what they wish, some of them situated a few miles from our own branches will charge only 10p. a meeting this year'.

A similar motion from King's Langley branch (Hertfordshire) was fully debated but ultimately defeated at the 1971 District AGM; this said that

the decision to impose a minimum student fee of 16p. per evening was ill-advised, an unwarranted infringement of the autonomy of the Branch, an unrealistic economic mistake and contrary to the best traditions of the movement

and called for each branch to have the freedom to set its own fees. Against this it could be argued that the bodies which grant-aided the WEA expected certain minimal fees to be paid: local authorities had no wish to see glaring disparities between their own fees and those charged for WEA courses, while the Department of Education and Science in awarding grant also expected WEA fees to be broadly in line with those of other providers. It could further be pointed out that, despite the rising fees, student recruitment and course provision continued to grow. Nevertheless, in recognition of the escalating cost to students, some concessions were made. From 1971, branches were allowed to charge lower sums to those dependant on the state retirement pension; in 1972, following a motion from Great Waltham branch (Essex), a reduced fee for married couples was also introduced.

Two other important changes affecting branch finances occurred in this period. One was a significant alteration in the method whereby a share of students' fees was remitted to the District. Hitherto the practice had been for branches to pay over a fixed proportion of the fee collected from each student. For the academic year 1959–60, this was replaced by a new 'class contribution' scheme: the class contribution varied according to the length and type of course, so that for a Long Terminal a branch would pay the District £17, for a Terminal £9, but the sum remained the same regardless of the number of students enrolling. This innovation helped to insulate the District's finances from unpredictable fluctuations in student numbers, while also giving branches the opportunity to accumulate healthy balances if they enrolled students well above the minimum required. It was also agreed in 1959 that the registration fee of 1s. 0d. from every student attending for the first time, which had been collected along with the course fee in previous years, was to be levied and remitted to the District Office as a separate item. The Quota system, whereby branches paid dues to the District based on local population figures, survived these reforms but only for one more year: it was widely regarded as unfair, branches in large towns often finding it no easier to recruit students than those in small villages, and with many branches falling short of their allotted sums it was decided to abolish the Quota at the District Council of May 1960.

The other major change in financial matters was the end of the requirement that WEA students should pay extra to become members of their branch. In the country as a whole less than 40% of students did so by the middle-1960s. A special National Conference, summoned in December 1966 to consider the Report, *Working Party on Structure, Organisation, Finance and Staffing*, decided that henceforth almost everyone who enrolled for a course run by a WEA branch would enjoy automatic membership and so be entitled to vote at branch AGMs, to hold office and to serve as a delegate to councils and conferences. The new constitution, approved in December 1966, described the position thus:

> The Association in each branch shall consist of (i) persons who are students in the courses it promotes (excluding one day and weekend courses and courses provided for other bodies); (ii) persons who while not being students in courses it promotes subscribe to its funds; (iii) representatives appointed by local organisations affiliated to the branch, the minimum affiliation fee to be determined by the districts.

As a response to falling branch membership, this measure has been described as 'analogous to solving the problems of sin by abolishing the commandments'[9] but in fact it made little difference in the Eastern District. By the middle-1960s almost two-thirds of students already chose to join their branch, appreciably more than the national average and the third highest proportion in the United Kingdom.[10] And under the class contribution arrangements introduced in 1959 branches paid the same amounts to the District no matter how many students were members, so no adjustments were necessary to the scheme.

One of the requirements imposed upon Districts as a result of the 1966 National Conference was that of establishing development committees to recommend priorities for future expansion. In response to this the District Executive agreed in February 1967 that each Federation should set up a committee which would produce a development plan for its own area. These plans led in turn to a District Development Plan, considered at meetings of the Executive and Council during the first half of 1970 before being submitted to the WEA National Office and to the Department of Education and Science. The Eastern District Plan was expansionist in tone, calling for substantial increases in full-time teaching and organising staff – six more tutor-organisers immediately and a further five in the long-term, six new developments officers and ultimately another three. These included both tutor-organisers and development officers for Luton and Ipswich, development officers in Norwich,

Peterborough and Northampton and two more tutor-organisers for Industry; stress was laid on the expected rapid increase in daytime courses for which only a limited number of part-time tutors were available, although none of the projected appointments were specifically linked to this. Beyond these recommendations, there was even mention of the long-term possibility of a tutor-organiser in Colchester, a development officer in Chelmsford and another tutor-organiser in Bishop's Stortford who could cross into the western part of Essex: but motions opposing such appointments were submitted to the District Executive and Council from the Essex Federation and from several branches in the county. Firmer and more immediate proposals were for the employment of a senior tutor-organiser with responsibility for the supervision of teaching as an academic adviser throughout the District, and for the establishment of a Federation office with part-time clerical help in each county. The District Secretary projected that if all these recommendations were implemented, the level of class activity in 1968–69 (502 courses in all) would be all but doubled to 996 by 1980–81. But the sheer cost, including an extra £22,000 for tutor-organisers (assuming a starting-salary of £1,400 but not taking account of grant-aid), £14,700 for development officers and £3,000 for Federation offices, was sufficient to ensure that very little of it ever came to pass. By 1980–81, despite a rise and fall in the meantime, there were in fact eight tutor-organisers in the District, one less than in 1968–69, and the actual number of courses in that year was 521.

The District Development Plan was deliberately ambitious, framed at a time when another Committee of Enquiry was considering future patterns and priorities in adult education, and clearly designed to show what could be achieved if only more funding was allowed. Yet not all of the proposals came to naught. As we have seen, a tutor-organiser was duly appointed in 1970 to meet the growing demand for daytime courses. A tutor-organiser for Luton, Tony Dennis, eventually arrived in 1974 to supplement the work of the tutor-organiser for Bedfordshire. The number of tutor-organisers for Industry stood at five for a brief period in the later 1970s. Reg Carnell held the post of tutor-organiser for development, with responsibilities not unlike those envisaged for a senior tutor-organiser, between 1980 and 1983. But whether the appointment of *all* the extra staff proposed in the Plan would have fundamentally changed the character of the Eastern District must remain a matter of opinion.

The individual Federation Development Plans, on which the District's Plan was based, make interesting reading as surveys of the WEA in each county at the time they were compiled during 1968. The Plans did not follow a standard formula and varied in the type of information given, but nevertheless some significant conclusions emerge. The importance in the Eastern District of the one-class branch in the small village comes through very clearly indeed. Of thirty-two branches in Norfolk, for example, all but Norwich was running only one course at a time. Eleven of the branches here, ten of the twenty-nine branches in Suffolk and thirteen of the nineteen branches in Northamptonshire were in places with less than 1,000 population. The exception to this pattern was Hertfordshire, where all fifteen active branches served places of at least 2,500 people and most offered two or more courses together. The Hertfordshire Plan commented on the comparatively-young, well-educated and mobile population in the county, leading to a diminished sense of identity with a particular local community: rather than support the nearest WEA branch 'the inhabitants of Hertfordshire were prepared to travel several miles to a WEA class if they were at all interested'. But elsewhere, localism remained very important. The Fenland Plan, summarising answers to questionnaires distributed to branches, quoted one which said of its students: 'about half attend because of interest in the subject, the other half are committed to keeping their own branch going, in whatever subject'. The Norfolk Plan pointed to the inadequate public transport system which obliged anyone without a car to rely on local provision:

> Very small branches have no bus services at all, and even market towns on major roads have few or no buses in the evening. It is possible to go by bus to courses in Watton, for example, but not to get home again. There is no evening transport late in the evening from either Wymondham or Dereham to large and growing housing estates on their outskirts.

There were also some eloquent tributes to the value of rural one-class branches. From Northamptonshire, a county notable for experimental courses in the towns of Corby and Northampton, came a reminder of the importance of adult education in the countryside:

> Rural areas in an urban society are in danger of becoming a new depository of underprivilege as many of the facilities for community participation are to be found only in towns.

In Suffolk, opinion was that, apart from developments in industrial work, it is undoubtedly in the smaller settlements that the future of the WEA lies. In fact the one class- per-week branch is a remarkably efficient and suitable way of bringing advanced adult education to isolated settlements. The ideal of 'An Athens in every village' is a distinct possibility.

On the other hand, despite praise for the work of one-class branches, there was some difference of view about their viability as course-providing agencies. The Norfolk, Suffolk and Essex Plans suggested complete confidence in them, but in other counties there were worries about their frailty and impermanence. Of fourteen branches in Bedfordshire, no less than six had been founded in the past three years so were not yet firmly established. The Fenland Plan reported that, although there had been sixty- five different WEA centres in the area since 1945, twenty of them had never run a course for more than two years at a stretch and nearly forty never for more than six consecutive years: 'traditionally the problem in the Fenland has not been developing new centres of activity so much as maintaining interest and voluntary effort in those centres already in existence'. Cambridge, Haddenham and Peterborough were singled out as the only branches founded before the Second World War which had been continuously active since. The Northamptonshire Plan called for a reduction in the minimum enrolment figure for rural branches from fifteen to ten or twelve to help them to keep going, for the treatment of new foundations as 'probationary branches' for three years until they became established, and for a 'federal structure' in which one branch served several neighbouring rural communities and perhaps offered classes in more than one of them.[11]

But if there were scores of small villages which had a WEA branch, there were also places with five-figure populations which did not. Most of the Plans drew attention to these. Examples included Lowestoft in Suffolk (population 52,267), Great Yarmouth in Norfolk (50,236), Kempston in Bedfordshire (12,862) and Whittlesey in the Fenland (10,456).[12] Some of these were highlighted as priorities in a programme for the foundation of new branches, although here again the Hertfordshire Federation was the exception. Notwithstanding that there were three towns in its area with populations over 10,000 but no WEA branch, Letchworth, Ware and Abbots Langley, the Plan recommended that WEA expansion should be concentrated elsewhere, largely because the residents of these towns already had access to WEA branches in smaller places nearby.[13] In another aspect of branch distribution, some of the plans demonstrated major disparities between the more-favoured east and the less-favoured west: this was true of Norfolk, where there were only two branches (Heacham and King's Lynn) north-west of a line from Feltwell to Wells, and also of Suffolk, where only a quarter of all branches were in the West Suffolk local authority area.[14] It was also the case in Essex, the Plan for which acknowledged that of the sixty WEA centres which had existed in the area since 1948, forty-six had been in the east. Both the Norfolk and Essex Plans made development in the west a priority for the future.

But what education were the branches actually providing? For analysis of subjects studied during the 1960s and early 1970s we must turn from the development plans to more routine District Annual Reports. Broad classification of subjects was not attempted in these reports after 1963–64 but in this final year the figures showed a revived interest in Social Studies (68% from a nadir of 56% in 1959–60), a consistent demand for Arts (28%, although it had reached 33% in 1962–63), and a steady decline in Natural Sciences (only 4% from a peak of 12% in 1959–60). On the other hand, growing interest in conservation reversed this decline in the second half of the decade: there were only 15 courses in the biological sciences in 1965–66 but 44 in 1969–70 and a similar number in the two following years. Perhaps the most significant long-term trends were the decline in courses on international affairs but the increase in those dealing with current social and economic issues. If we compare two years at the end of the fifties, 1958–59 and 1959–60 with two years in the early seventies, 1970–71 and 1971–72, we find a total of 670 courses offered by branches in the earlier period and 863 in the later. Of the 670, 69 were in international affairs and 37 on social and economic issues; of the 863 a decade or so later, only 19 covered international affairs but there were 69 in sociology and economics.

In 1965–66 the District Secretary also stopped publishing analyses of students' occupations. The proportions in this last year were little changed from those in the late fifties, with men making up 41% of all students (29% of men being manual workers) and 'housewives' accounting for 33% of the total. Had figures been published in the early 1970s these figures would certainly have been higher, given the increase in the meantime in daytime courses with creches and in industrial provision. It is of interest to note that teachers, who represented 37% of the initial intake to the Open University in 1971, composed only 11% of Eastern District students in both 1964–65 and 1965–66. By contrast, only 9% of the Open University's original students were 'housewives' and 26% various types of non-professional worker; some 35% of the District's students were in the latter category in the middle 1960s. These differences in student personnel, plus the fact that a high percentage of the Open University's initial intake gave reasons related to work or higher qualifications as their motivation for study, made that institution less of a competitor to the WEA than some might have forecast.[15]

Away from the surveys and statistics, several branches had notable achievements to their names in a variety of spheres. Between 1959 and 1966 Hatfield branch (Hertfordshire) produced a twelve- volume history of *Hatfield and Its People* with an additional volume of pictures to round off the series. Among others which published local histories based of students' work were King's Langley (Hertfordshire) in 1963 and Westleton (Suffolk) in 1968, both hardbacks, and Sawbridgeworth (Hertfordshire) between 1966 and 1970. All the Hertfordshire publications were the result of Tutorials taken by Cambridge University Extra-Mural Board's staff tutor in local history, Lionel Munby, while that at Westleton followed a course by the Board's resident tutor in Suffolk, David Dymond. Another Tutorial on local history taught by Christopher Taylor at Cambridge led to his discovery of 'polyfocal villages', and the resulting publication on Great Shelford, *Domesday to Dormitory* (1971), long continued to be cited in learned works on medieval settlement.[16] Elsewhere, Sessional courses at Long Buckby (Northamptonshire) taken by Ronald Greenall of the University of Leicester led to published studies based on parish registers and the 1851 census, both in 1971,[17] and to the foundation of a local history society in the village. In another field altogether, branches in Hertfordshire consistently showed an interest in World Poverty which had an impact beyond their immediate membership. Hoddesdon branch submitted a motion to the 1962 National Conference 'that the WEA should actively support the educational work of the Freedom from Hunger campaign at National, District and Branch levels'; in 1970–71 the branches at Stevenage and Ware ran courses in response to requests by local World Poverty Action Groups; a similar course a year later in Hatfield led on to a Lent Study series in the town organised by Christian Aid, to a Federation One-Day School on the subject and ultimately to the foundation of a Hatfield World Development Group with WEA committee members as active participants. In the meantime, the publication of the Newsom and Robbins Reports in October 1963, the former recommending the raising of the school-leaving-age to sixteen, the latter advocating a major expansion of higher education to cater for all who were qualified, also prompted widespread interest around the District, particularly in the Fenland where nine branches held single meetings or one-day schools on the Reports and two, Linton and Sawston, ran courses specifically devoted to them. The Hertfordshire Federation even had the District's former full-time tutor, Harold Shearman, to speak at a one-day school on Robbins, held in St. Albans in January 1964: as a member of that committee he had been responsible for the Report's only departure from unanimity, having objected to placing higher education under a Ministry of Arts and Science. And at a more routine level, as weekly study was faithfully pursued in all parts of the District, such well-known figures as the author and playwright, Jeremy Seabrook, the Norfolk 'television naturalist', Dick Bagnall-Oakeley, and the future England cricket captain, Mike Brearley, were happy to give service as part-time tutors.[18]

Among the Federations, the Executives of Norfolk, Suffolk and Essex were particularly active during these years. The Norfolk Federation produced in July 1959 a very well researched and coherently presented analysis of 'Some Problems of a New University', which reviewed the reasons for founding a new university in Norwich on the basis of national need and local advantage: this was a year before the University Grants Committee gave its approval to the project. The Suffolk Federation became increasingly involved from the middle-1960s in the promotion of lectures, courses and social events which would bring members of different branches together. In November 1964, for example, the Federation sponsored the first Harry Clement Memorial Lecture to commemorate the University's resident tutor in the county who had died some months earlier after eighteen years' service. The initial lecture, on 'Population and Planning', was given by J. R. James, chief planner for the Ministry of Housing and Local Government, and set the high standard which it has always been the intention to follow. From 1967 it became customary for the Federation to organise a theatre visit on the first Saturday in December, and in April 1972 it ran its first residential course in practical archaeology on a threatened Roman site at Scole in Norfolk, subsequently publishing the results of the excavation. Meanwhile in Essex, voluntary members of the Federation Executive fulfilled the non-teaching tasks which a tutor-organiser might have undertaken elsewhere, and a glance at statistics serves to measure progress in the county. In 1956–57, the last full year when there was a tutor-organiser in Essex, the area already had more WEA courses (62) than any other county in the District, barring Norfolk which ran an identical number. In subsequent years Essex remained to the fore, so that by 1971–72 there were 79 WEA courses here, a number exceeded only by Hertfordshire's 89.

It is most appropriate, however, to pay tribute to the unspectacular work of innumerable WEA branches which, in the face of increasing fees and occasional disappointments, determinedly kept going: in the villages usually as the only adult education presence, in the towns often struggling for an identity and making considerable demands upon voluntary officers, especially where more than one course was being attempted. On the whole the Eastern District and its branches benefited from good relations with local authorities, through the provision of grant-aid and of free accommodation and through the personal help given by LEA principals and adult tutors. A survey of branches' difficulties, conducted by the District Secretary in 1970, revealed very little problem on this score: Bedfordshire branches, for instance, whether in the town of Bedford or in villages such as Cranfield and Riseley, consistently reported a spirit of goodwill and co-operation on the part of local authority officers. Elsewhere, Norwich branch was given the use of rooms and secretarial help in the local authority's new Adult Education Centre at Ivory House 1971, and also began about this time to hold more classes at Wensum Lodge, the Norfolk residential college; from 1979, a change of local authority policy meant that most of the branch's activity came to focus on Wensum Lodge. But in the end, however much support was forthcoming from professionals inside and outside the WEA, success in any particular place depended on the voluntary members: on their willingness to learn and to bring that learning to others. And as a reminder that in the midst of all the organising, administering and pioneering, the WEA is essentially about hard but enjoyable study, let this extract from the annual report of Northamptonshire tutor-organiser, John Lowerson, for 1969- 70 suffice. It concerned his local history students in Brackley.

> I have noticed an increased willingness to do hard extra class work on the part of a substantial number of students . . . One man, a busy headmaster, spent a considerable part of his free time tracing the distribution of cottage commons among the parish registers and the documents of the National School Society. Another, a fitter, had spent a considerable time field walking, to identify pre-enclosure field boundaries in the present landscape. A teacher and mother of three young children spent three weeks at Christmas tracking down the ownership and distribution of over 1,000 strips of land in 1830. Another proposes to survey the age of buildings in Brackley systematically. Another, a history master, became so interested in local history that he left the class to teach it as one of our part-time tutors!

The experience highlighted in the final sentence is by no means uncommon. The WEA teaches all who participate that they have much to learn from one another and many individuals, in the Eastern District as elsewhere, have served in their time as both students and tutors.

Administrative Change

In the administration of the Eastern District during the 1960s, two significant developments stand out. One was the transfer of extra-mural provision in Northamptonshire from the University of Cambridge to that of Leicester in 1962: this meant that WEA branches in the county now looked to a different university for their joint committee courses. The other was the opening of a new District Office at Botolph House, 17 Botolph Lane, Cambridge, in 1966. Neither change was straightforward.

The origins of the transfer of Northamptonshire can be traced back to 1954 when Geoffrey Hickson, secretary of Cambridge University Board of Extra-Mural Studies, received a proposal from the University College at Leicester that at least part of the county should become its responsibility. Hickson told Frank Jacques, who in turn acquainted both John Rhodes, secretary of the WEA East Midland District, and Syd Robinson, chairman of the Northamptonshire Federation, linking the proposal with the possible transfer of Northamptonshire branches from the Eastern to the East Midland District. But although there were some preliminary discussions during 1955, nothing further came of the idea until the early 1960s, by which time Leicester was a university in its own right.

In 1960 the Council of the Senate of Cambridge University established a committee to consider extra-mural work. This committee recommended the growth of residential courses and also – of more immediate concern to the WEA – the divesting of at least some of the Extra-Mural Board's teaching in the field to other universities. This was at a time when new universities were contemplated for Norwich, Stamford, Essex and Hertfordshire: if all of them had come into being and had become involved in extra-mural provision, Cambridge might have been left with a residual area composed of Cambridgeshire, the Isle of Ely, Huntingdonshire and Bedfordshire only. The Extra-Mural Board responded to these proposals with equanimity, partly because the suggested increase in residential courses was a vote of confidence in its future and partly because the prospect of losing work to new universities was a distance one, not envisaged before the 1970s. Nevertheless, the Board recognised that Northamptonshire was a special case, already having a university at Leicester (and another at Oxford) which could conveniently provide extra-mural courses, and promised to enter into the necessary consultations for transfer without delay.

The Board's discussions with the WEA were conducted at meetings of the District Executive in May 1961, District Council in June and

Northamptonshire Federation in October: there was no substantial opposition to the proposals at any of them. Indeed, the Board encountered more hostility from its own local centres at Kettering, Towcester and Wellingborough than it did from the WEA or the two local authorities involved. Accordingly at a meeting on 31 October 1961 the Board decided to go ahead with the transfer of extra-mural provision in the county to the University of Leicester as from the start of the academic year 1962–63, but with the proviso that its three local centres could remain with Cambridge for up to five more years; there was also a special arrangement whereby two Tutorial Classes being run for the WEA branches at Corby and Northampton would complete their three years with Cambridge.

The university representatives concerned in these negotiations clearly regarded the issues as one between their respective institutions: a matter on which it was right to consult interested parties such as the WEA but one which affected those parties only marginally. However Jacques, having mentioned the possibility of moving Northamptonshire to the East Midland District when the whole topic was first mooted in 1954, consistently kept the prospective change of District boundaries as an item in the discussions. It was raised at the District Executive in May 1961, at a meeting with Rhodes, of the East Midland District, and Professor A. J. Allaway, Head of Leicester University's Department of Adult Education, in June, and at the Northamptonshire Federation meeting in October. However, Rhodes told Jacques that he had no wish to add another county to his District: 'my own feelings are that Northamptonshire should stay in the Eastern District', he wrote in November. Meanwhile the Northamptonshire branches became increasingly alarmed about their position. Once university provision switched to Leicester, would they still be fully a part of the Eastern District? Would they really have a say in any decision to move to East Midland? This concern surfaced at the District Council in March 1962 when Northamptonshire Federation chairman, Lillian Norman, protested that the branches 'are in a kind of no-man's land – we don't know what is going to happen to us, where we should go or whom we should write to'.[19]

One of Jacques's major worries was that work with the university in Northamptonshire would be in an anomalous position, as terminology, procedures and expectations would differ. The Eastern District, accustomed to the ways of Cambridge University, would have to accommodate to those of Leicester; in its turn, Leicester University, familiar with the East Midland District, would have to adjust to the Eastern. This certainly led to initial difficulties, for example over Leicester University's readiness to offer the WEA courses of only one term's duration when those of Cambridge had always lasted two terms or more. It is also true that Leicester, regarding Northamptonshire as a county under-served with adult education in the liberal studies, eagerly and successfully expanded its provision over the next few years, inevitably in some competition with the WEA. But on the WEA side, the appointment in July 1962 of a new tutor-organiser, Terry Jackson, himself a former branch secretary in Rotherham before proceeding to Ruskin and Oriel College, Oxford, was followed by an impressive increase in activity: the fourteen branches of 1961–62 had risen to twenty-six by 1963–64. Not all of these survived for long (his successor Lowerson reported nineteen branches in 1968) but at least such expansion reassured WEA members in the county of their own potential for growth. Alongside the rise in WEA provision came increasing familiarity with the practices and personnel of Leicester University, all of which meant that concern about a transfer to another District receded. The District Executive agreed in February 1963 that Jacques should write to Rhodes saying that 'no move towards a transference of the membership of the Northamptonshire branches to the East Midland District should be made until a request for consideration of such action was received from the Federation'. No such request was ever made. The officers of the District settled down to build a sound working relationship with Leicester University and succeeded in maintaining the principle that university courses for branches in Northamptonshire must run for more than one term. For their part, the county's branches and Federation have remained an integral part of the Eastern District.

It was also during 1963 that the District celebrated its Golden Jubilee with a rally for over five hundred people, held at the University Chemical Laboratory, Lensfield Road, on 5 October. The University vice-chancellor and Master of St. John's College, Canon John Boys Smith, chaired the meeting, which was addressed by both Christopher Chataway, MP, parliamentary secretary to the Minister of Education, and Professor Asa Briggs as National WEA president. Chataway, deputising for his Minister, Sir Edward Boyle, who was ill, spoke of the need to cater both for those who were already well-educated and wanted more, and for those 'who had never had their imaginations stirred by the possibilities of improving the quality of their lives'. Briggs forecast increasing leisure time and problems over how this would be used: 'those who are interested in adult education must show that it is exciting and interesting in its own right. They must show that it can enable one to do things one would not otherwise be able to do.'[20] Everyone who attended received a four-page commemorative leaflet, *Growing Up and Going Ahead*: this summarised the Eastern District's expansion from eight branches in 1913 to its current figure of 175 and quoted Ashby's Harvey Memorial Lecture of 1955 in promising continued commitment 'to preserve the individuality of man'.

But the Jubilee was more than an occasion for boosting morale: it also gave the opportunity to appeal for funds to finance a new District Office. Gonville and Caius College, landlords of Cambridgeshire House, 7 Hills Road, where the District Office was located, wanted to redevelop the site and decided not to renew the lease from September 1964. This affected not only the WEA but also the other tenants, Cambridgeshire Huntingdonshire and Isle of Ely Community Council, the National Council of Social Service, Cambridgeshire Federation of Women's Institutes and Toc H; of these, the WEA and the Community Council occupied most space, both using four rooms in addition to the shared committee room. As it happened, the District was already considering moving its headquarters to new premises, since those at 7 Hills Road were really too limited for current requirements: at the District Council of May 1962, treasurer Benny Farmer had suggested a Jubilee appeal for funds with this in view. However the matter became much more urgent on receipt of the notice to quit and at meetings of the District Executive in February and October 1963 it was decided to set up a trust to handle such an appeal, the target originally being set at £15,000, then increased to £25,000. Accordingly, the Friends of the Eastern District came into being under the chairmanship of a Fellow of St. John's College, Claude Guillebaud, and with Edward Miller and the Master of Sidney Sussex, David Thomson, as vice-chairmen. The Friends produced a special leaflet, *WEA: the Eastern District make a Jubilee* Appeal, requesting donations, and officially launched their appeal at the District AGM of November 1963.

During the following year the District Secretary anxiously searched for new premises near the centre of Cambridge, convenient for University members and prospective part-time tutors. 7 Regent Street was rejected because of the surveyor's report on its condition; 25 and 25A Hills Road fetched too high a price at auction; negotiations to buy 4 Glisson Road ended when planning permission to convert to office accommodation was refused; 4 Trumpington Street and 22 Maids Causeway were other properties given serious consideration. In the end, Michael Posner of Pembroke, who was still an occasional contributor to industrial courses, arranged for Jacques to meet the President (and subsequent Master) of Gonville and Caius, Joseph Needham. As a result of this, the College not only extended the lease to allow the District more time to raise funds but also agreed to sell (at a price below valuation) one of its own properties, Botolph House, a late Georgian building of four storeys plus basement sited over the medieval King's Ditch.[21] The purchase of this House, with its neighbour 13 Pembroke Street, was completed in May 1965 and was followed by several months' renovation and alteration, during which all the paint both inside and out was supplied free-of-charge by ICI. The total cost of purchase, repair and refurbishment came to about £30,000.

An outlay of this magnitude was rather more that the Friends' appeal had previously envisaged, but the appointment in November 1964 of Major Ian Higginbotham, recently-retired from Stewart and Lloyd's Corby, as professional director of the fund-raising campaign, produced excellent results. Generous donations were received from local authorities, Cambridge colleges, the Extra-Mural Board, trade unions and local firms, as well as from WEA members and branches, and over £16,000 had been found by the time contracts were exchanged. This figure had risen to £19,000 by 14 May 1966, the day when the University vice-chancellor (by then Arthur Armitage of Queens') officially declared the new office open in a ceremony conducted from the Cavendish Laboratories in Free School Lane. But there was still a large overdraft at the bank and it was decided in 1967 to take out a mortgage for £9,000 with the Co-operative Permanent Building Society. The task of paying this off was to prove a long haul. A proposal from some branches to organise a Football Pool was considered by the Friends but dropped when a referendum in the spring of 1967 showed a large majority of branches against it. Silver and paper collections were regularly taken at District Councils from March 1967 to May 1970, when the more discreet method of leaving a box for donations on one of the tables was introduced. A fresh appeal for £4,000 in two years was directed to the branches at the District Council of June 1967, but was less than halfway towards that figure by November 1969: as late as March 1972 the branches in only one Federation area, Hertfordshire, had met their individual target, with those in Norfolk 98% of the way towards their goal. A separate appeal launched in January 1967 to help meet the £700 spent on furnishing Botolph House suffered to some extent from the fact that most of the items which branches were invited to purchase had already been paid for and installed; even so, £332 was raised in this way, with Blisworth branch (Northamptonshire), for example, sending £4 13s. 0d. as the cost of two committee room chairs, Pulhams branch

(Norfolk) £14 14s. 0d. for a typist's desk and Harpenden branch (Hertfordshire) £4 1s. 0d. for an easel. Quite apart from this, other gifts were received during 1967 in memory of former District chairmen Clara Rackham and John Chear.

By the time the mortgage was fully paid off in 1979, the District was in possession of a considerable asset. Policy over the years has been to lease 13 Pembroke Street, usually as a shop, but to preserve Botolph House itself as office accommodation, plus a warden's flat on the top floor. However in 1986 individual rooms in Botolph House began to be leased to Cambridge University Unit of Mongolian Studies and also (as a temporary measure) to the Extra-Mural Board, which needed a base near the city centre to supplement its out-of-town headquarters at Madingley Hall: a striking demonstration of partnership between the two Responsible Bodies!

On the opening of Botolph House, Megan Mothersole became resident warden, a position she retained until her sudden and untimely death in December 1987. By then, she had given the Eastern District over thirty years' service, having been appointed as a shorthand typist in 1955, been promoted to Administrative Assistant in 1957, and then succeeded Deborah Jackson (herself with ten years in the post) as the District's Assistant Secretary in 1965. All who visited the District Office were impressed by the unfailing patience, courtesy and quiet command which Megan Mothersole brought to her work, and her exemplary record of loyalty to the WEA and selfless devotion to its cause deserves to be placed on record. Her contribution to the success of the Eastern District, particularly in her twenty-two years as Assistant Secretary, is incalculable. One of her major responsibilities was the arrangement of the class programme, and branch officers and students all over the District have much cause to be grateful for the tireless efficiency and resourcefulness with which, year after year, some four hundred or more courses were provided with tutors. Her death shocked everyone connected with the WEA in eastern England and deprived the District not only of a most able, conscientious and experienced administrator but also of a warm and generous spirit.

Others who became employees of the District during the 1960s have also given long and devoted service. Moira Smith was appointed to the office staff soon after the move to Botolph House and had completed over eighteen years with the WEA when (as Moira Jedynak) she left in 1985. Her colleague Kathryn Coles, who arrived in 1969, had exceeded this by 1988. Both have shown to the full the commitment, competence and cheerfulness which have traditionally characterised the District's administrative staff. Tutor-organisers' patterns of employment also began to change. The new WEA constitution agreed at the special National Conference in December 1966 included a clause that 'districts should recognise their tutor-organiserships as career posts and encourage their tutor-organisers to regard them as such', and it was indeed at around this time that some of the Eastern District's tutor-organisers embarked upon lengthy periods of service. Hitherto most had stayed for between two and five years. None of those in post at the end of 1954, for example, were still employed at the end of 1958; none in service at the end of 1957 still in the job at the end of 1963; none at the end of 1961 still there at the end of 1966. In this respect, the appointments of John Ridgard as tutor-organiser for Suffolk in January 1965 and of Reg Carnell as tutor-organiser for Industry a few months later were highly significant. Both remained in their posts long-term: Ridgard was still in office in 1988, Carnell stayed until 1978, after which he returned in 1980 to become tutor-organiser for development and ultimately District Secretary. Previously it had been conventional wisdom to regard a tutor-organisership as a relatively-short-term job: a stepping stone to better-paid employment elsewhere. Indeed, Frank Jacques retained this as a personal opinion into his retirement. From the WEA's point of view, a regular turnover of tutor-organisers ensured fresh injections of enthusiasm and constant variety in the subjects offered for teaching; it also benefited the District's finances because tutor-organisers normally did not stay long enough to reach the top of the salary-scale. But with longer periods of service, tutor-organisers have been able to offer greater authority, experience and maturity. To some extent, the longevity is a reflection of the change to a more static pattern of academic employment generally: there is no longer the buoyancy and mobility of the 1960s. But this is not the whole story: many tutor-organisers have chosen to put down roots in their local communities and the WEA has usually profited from the stability this has brought. John Ridgard, for instance, has become a recognised authority on Suffolk history, participating in a new edition of the *Household Book of Dame Alice de Bryene of Acton Hall* (1984) and producing a study of *Medieval Framlingham* (1987) in the Suffolk Records Society series. The same can be said of David Yaxley, appointed to Norfolk in 1972, for he has written a readable and well-illustrated landscape history of his county, *Portrait of Norfolk* (1977), and contributed to the Norfolk Archaeological Unit's report on *Excavations in North Elmham* Park, published in 1980.

Naturally, the change in employment patterns did not come overnight and for some years in the late 1960s and 1970s both county tutor-organisers and their colleagues in Industry continued to come and go. John Lowerson, appointed to Northamptonshire in 1967, left three years later to become a lecturer in social history in the Department of Continuing Education at the University of Sussex; Colin Rochester, who arrived in Hertfordshire in 1968, became the WEA's national development officer in 1971; John Howard, who served as one of the tutor-organisers for Industry from 1972 to 1974, went on to the National Union of Tailor and Garment Workers as a full-time official. This was the familiar pattern. But Derek Tatton, appointed to Bedfordshire in 1968, stayed until 1979 when he became warden of Wedgwood Memorial College, Barlaston. Charles Middleton remained in Northamptonshire from 1974 until 1987, when he returned to his native USA. Roger Moore, who became tutor-organiser for Industry in 1976, was still in post in 1988. Indeed, when the District celebrated its seventy-fifth anniversary, every one of its full-time tutor-organisers had at least ten years' service behind him.

On the subject of personnel, a few words should be said about one great friend of the Eastern District who died during these years. John Hampden Jackson was employed by Cambridge University Board of Extra-Mural Studies first as resident tutor in Norfolk and then as a staff tutor. In addition, he was from its inception in 1946 a director of studies of the training course for new WEA tutors held as part of the annual Cambridge Summer School. He edited the Association's journal, *The Highway*, from 1950 to 1954 and enhanced its reputation beyond the confines of the WEA. Well-known and admired over much of the Eastern District, particularly in Norfolk, for his courses on international affairs, he also served quite voluntarily as an academic adviser, giving his opinion on tutors' applications and syllabuses, and visiting classes to observe teaching in progress. At the first District Executive Committee meeting following his death in November 1966, it was agreed that a memorial should be raised: the original intention was for a bronze bust but it was finally decided in June 1967 to give his name to the committee room in Botolph House. District Office meetings have continued to be held in the John Hampden Jackson Room ever since.

Into the Seventies

In the period reviewed in this chapter, it can fairly be claimed that the Eastern District combined a commitment to pioneer work with a healthy traditional branch structure. *Into the Seventies*, the annual report of the WEA National Committee for 1969–70, showed the Eastern with 168 branches, more than twice the number in any other District. On the other hand, its neighbour to the north, the East Midland, ran 819 courses and enrolled 14,072 students, while to the south London District ran 775 courses with 12,312 students: on these counts, both were larger than the Eastern District, which had 489 courses and 9,095 students.[22] The different structural pattern which underlay these figures a host of one-class branches in the Eastern District, fewer multiclass branches elsewhere – was but one illustration of the diversity in Districts' policies and practices which had arisen since the early years of the century.

Some aspects of that diversity worried the Working Party on Structure, Organisation, Finance and Staffing when it reported to the special National Conference in December 1966. These differences, the report explained,

> are concerned with such matters as the balance of programmes (types and subjects of courses promoted); the extent and nature of the demand made on universities for provision of WEA work as compared with the WEA's independent provision; the degree of coverage by full- time tutors; the use of non-academic organisers; efforts towards selective recruitment of students; attempts to break new ground in harmony with changed social attitudes; and disposition to be imaginative and experimental.

The Working Party was in favour of greater cohesion, of more authority for the WEA at national level to ensure that policies agreed at Conferences were implemented at grass-roots. For this reason, the report recommended that, in future, Department of Education and Science grant should be allocated to the National WEA for subsequent distribution to the Districts, rather than to Districts direct, a system which would of course have given the centre more control over local practice. Such a proposal obviously posed some threat to Districts' freedom of action and Jacques, who had been prepared to argue for unilateral treatment of the Eastern District in pursuit of 90% Ministry grant-aid only six years earlier, had grave reservations about the idea. Nevertheless the recommendation was accepted at the special National Conference: it was agreed that the WEA would seek approval from the DES for a block grant which a national committee would then disburse to the Districts.

The opportunity to press this case came in 1969 with the establishment of another Committee of Enquiry into adult education, soon known as the Russell Committee after its chairman Sir Lionel Russell, former chief education officer for Birmingham. A small WEA subcommittee was set up to prepare evidence. Cecil Scrimgeour, whose surveys of WEA work in the midlands had been cited in *Unfinished Business*, was appointed secretary of this WEA group; having been a staff tutor with both Oxford and Keele Universities, he had recently retired to live near Cambridge and was now an Eastern District member and part-time tutor. Frank Jacques also served on the sub-committee. Their statement of evidence, presented in December 1969, did not specifically mention the Eastern District, but as a summary of the WEA's progress over the previous decade most of it was as applicable to eastern England as to any other part of the country. The statement stressed the importance of voluntaryism, a principle which had been upheld during the steady expansion accomplished by the branches. It drew heavily on examples of experimental work in Industry and with disadvantaged groups (mainly in urban areas) and emphasised the WEA's continuing commitment here. It pointed to the enduring value of joint committee work with universities, while acknowledging a decline in Tutorial Classes and a growth in separate WEA provision.[23] It called for extra grant to enable more full-time tutors to be appointed. And (despite Jacques's opposition on this point) it duly pleaded for the block grant which the National WEA could then apportion among the Districts, as recommended by the Working Party three years before.[24] In the event, the Russell Report when eventually published in 1973 simultaneously paid tribute to what had been achieved in the past and offered a considerable challenge for the future by taking the WEA at its word.

Jack Nobbs teaching at Bludeston Prison c.1966

208

WEA students on a field study excursion, c.1980

NOTES

1) Jacques was quoting, in turn, from the preface to H. W. Nevinson, *Words and Deeds* (1941): 'the battle of Freedom is never done and the Field is never quiet'. He used Nevinson's words frequently in addresses to branches; they also occur in his article, 'What's the Use?' *Highway*, April 1954, pp.252–56.

2) Department of Education and Science: *Survey by HM Inspectors of Industrial Classes conducted by Responsible Bodies in Greater London, Hertfordshire and Essex during 1963 and 1964* (1964).

3) In 1967–68 the courses were 'Understanding Ourselves' (through sociology in the mornings, through literature in the afternoons); in 1968–69 they were 'Current Affairs' and 'Mass Media' followed by 'Social and Political Problems of Africa' and 'African Literature'; in 1969–70 'The Future of Society' was paired with 'Contemporary Arts'.

4) R. E. Pahl, *Adult Education in a Free Society* (1962), pp.16- 17.

5) *The Guardian*, 5 March 1964.

6) Committee on Higher Education: *Higher Education Report . . . under the Chairmanship of Lord Robbins, 1961–63* (1963). Paragraph 518 was devoted to Extra-Mural Departments, the WEA and LEAs, all of which 'have contributed much to the general education of the community . . . if this country is to maintain its proud record, further support for this kind of study will be needed in the future'.

7) On the basis of 1963 = 100, the Retail Price Index rose from 90 in 1959 to 159 in 1972 (D. Butler and A. Sloman, *British Political Facts 1900–1979*, 4th edition, 1975, p.307). The decimal equivalent of the 1s. 0d. fee of 1959 was 5p., compared to the 16p. of 1972.

8) Figures for the Retail Price Index, in the same series and from the same source as in the previous note, were 100 in 1963, 103 in 1964, 148 in 1971 and 159 in 1972. For the other data, see Department of Education and Science, *Adult Education: a Plan for Development* (1973) (hereafter *Russell Report*), pp.257, 271, which shows that several WEA Districts charged higher students' fees than the Eastern during the 1960s.

9) B. Jennings, *Knowledge is Power: A Short History of the WEA 1903–78* (1979), p.57.

10) A memorandum relating to the National Working Party, produced by Jacques in 1965 and derived from figures for 1963–64, showed 65% of all Eastern District students becoming branch members, compared to 86% in Northern Ireland, 70% in North Western District but only 33% in all 21 WEA Districts put together.

11) On the issue of branches' stability, cf. an analysis conducted by the District Office in 1976. This showed that of 183 branches active in July 1975, only 44 had an unbroken record of existence since 1945.

12) Population figures are taken from the subsequent 1971 Census. Although these obviously differ from those of 1969, they are a more accurate guide to that year than the figures available at the time the Development Plans were written.

13) The fact that there was a branch at Ware by 1970–71 (below, p.) only goes to show that the best-laid Plans were open to amendment!

14) Cf. the figures for branch-distribution in Suffolk given by tutor-organiser Cooper in 1956 (above, p.)

15) N. E. McIntosh, J. A. Calder and B. Swift, *A Degree of Difference* (1976), pp.90, 246–47. 'Non-professional workers' are regarded as those categorised as 'technical personnel', 'skilled trades', 'other manual', 'commercial and transport', 'clerical and office workers' and 'shop and personal services' in the OU tables, and as those listed as 'manual workers' and 'non-manual, technical and supervisory workers' in Eastern District Annual Reports.

16) E.g. C. C. Taylor, *The Cambridgeshire Landscape* (1973), p.74; C. C. Taylor, *Village and Farmstead* (1983), p.247; cf. B. K. Roberts, *The Making of the English Village* (1987), p.127.

17) R. L. Greenall, ed., *The Population of a Northamptonshire Village in 1851* and *The Parish Register of Long Buckby, 1558–1689* (Vaughan Papers, Nos.16, 17, 1971).

18) E.g. J. R. Seabrook: 'Contemporary Drama', Long Terminal at Rushden (1964–65) and 'Social Change', Short Terminal at Long Buckby (1971–72); R. P. Bagnall-Oakeley: 'Natural History', Extension course at Ludham (1969–70); J. M. Brearley: 'Philosophy', Sessional at Hertford (1967–68).

19) Mrs. Norman's words are quoted in 'Notes of a discussion at the District Council Meeting, 10th March 1962' subsequently circulated to members of the District's Finance and General Purposes and Executive Committees.

20) *Cambridge News*, 7 October 1963.

21) N. Pevsner, *Cambridgeshire* (Buildings of England series, 2nd edition, 1970), p.242 gives a brief but very favourable description.

22) According to *Into the Seventies* there were 83 branches in East Midland District and 80 in London District. Figures for students include those attending schools and single lectures.

23) In 1959–60, 569 Tutorial Classes had been provided by universities in collaboration with the WEA, in the UK as a whole; Cambridge University had run 29 of these. By 1969–70 the figure had fallen to 390 (Cambridge 15) and by 1972–73 to 300 (Cambridge 9). There had, however, been some increase in one-year Sessionals run in conjunction with the WEA: 728 in 1959–60 (Cambridge 28, Leicester 18), 1,089 in 1972- 73 (Cambridge 49, Leicester 25). See *Universities Council for Adult Education Annual Report, 1959–60*, p.26; *1969–70*, table 5; *1972–73*, table 6.

24) *Evidence presented on behalf of the Association to the Russell Committee on Adult Education, December 1969 and Summary and Short Statement of Evidence to the Russell Committee on Adult Education* (1970)

CHAPTER 7

RESPONSES TO RUSSELL
1973–83

The announcement that a Committee of Enquiry into non-vocational adult education was to be set up, was made in the House of Commons on 4 February 1969. Among the fourteen members of the committee were Elizabeth Monkhouse, senior staff tutor with London University Extra-Mural Department and one of the Eastern District's full-time tutors during the Second War, and H. D. Hughes, principal of Ruskin College Oxford and a WEA vice-president. There was trade union representation in the person of Jim Conway, general secretary of the Amalgamated Union of Engineering and Foundry Workers. Also included was H. A. Jones, who had succeeded Allaway as Professor of Adult Education at Leicester and so was familiar with the WEA in Northamptonshire. Sir Lionel Russell's initial expectation as chairman was that the committee would need two or three years for its work:[1] in the event, it held fifty-one meetings and did not produce its Report, *Adult Education: a Plan for Development*, until 27 March 1973. So having been established by one Secretary of State for Education and Science, Labour's Edward Short, the committee ultimately reported to another, his Conservative successor Margaret Thatcher.

Russell's terms of reference were first to review existing provision for non-vocational adult education in England and Wales and secondly to make recommendations with a view to obtaining the most effective and economical deployment of available resources to enable adult education to make its proper contribution to the national system of education conceived of as a process continuing through life.

The eventual Report deliberately confined its recommendations to realistic short-term goals, involving relatively-modest increases in local authority and DES expenditure. These included a doubling of adult student numbers to four millions – one in nine of the adult population – by the end of the decade; a quadrupling of full-time adult education staff to over 4,000, with more training provided for them; and the introduction of National and Local Development Councils for Adult Education, to co-ordinate the work of the various agencies in the field. As for the WEA, the possibility of depriving the Association of its status as a Responsible Body was dismissed, as it had been in the Ashby Report nearly twenty years before:

> We cannot accept the view that has been put to us that, in a fully integrated service of adult education, the WEA would be best employed in organising groups of students, in stimulating demand and in exploring needs, whilst the provision was made wholly by universities or by the local education authorities.[2]

Once that had been established, more positive proposals could follow.

The Report recognised that the WEA's voluntary and democratic structure inhibited the redirection of priorities from above:

> The WEA fulfils different functions in different parts of the country and . . . generalisations about its work as though this were uniform may be quite misleading. Moreover any voluntary body must make its own policy for itself. We can only indicate what aspects of its work should be particularly deserving of support from public funds in the light of the place we see for the WEA as a provider of classes in our comprehensive service.[3]

This was the cue, in paragraph 232, for the recommendation that the WEA should give particular emphasis to four areas of work.

1. Education for the socially and culturally deprived living in urban areas . . . The involvement of the WEA would have to be in a strictly educational role and closely integrated with the work of other bodies. It would also have to be of an experimental and informal character, requiring new forms of activity and unfamiliar techniques.

2. Work in an industrial context, especially classes held in factories or other workplaces, and programmes arranged in consultation with the TUC and with individual trade unions, including courses for shop stewards.

3. Political and social education . . . New avenues for activity have begun to appear in courses run in co-operation with OXFAM, SHELTER and similar socially oriented organisations, and in certain kinds of 'role education' for those engaged in local government and in social and political activity.

4. Courses of liberal and academic study below the level of university work . . . This is the area of provision where there is the greatest likelihood of overlapping with the work of the local education authorities as academic studies come to find a place in the programmes of their centres. It is an area in which the role of

214

the WEA may gradually come to include a greater element of promotional work, encouraging and supporting balanced programmes by local education authorities as well as making provision of its own.

It was accepted that there would be 'a weakening of the traditionally close links with the universities in joint committee work, though we would not wish to see that work cease': a scarcely-veiled threat to Tutorial Classes, traditionally the jewel in the WEA's crown but no longer identified as a priority.

According to the Report, the four areas outlined above were those which the WEA itself had pointed to in its evidence to the committee. In fact only the first two were clearly linked to distinct sections within the WEA's written submission, while the third was derived from a more general reading of the evidence. The fourth area really had no place in the WEA's statement, where a close partnership with the universities had been envisaged as continuing alongside an increase in independent provision, and where special mention had been made of the value of courses in science, the local environment and arts appreciation. It could be argued, however, that a move away from liberal and academic studies – whether at 'university level' or not – was inevitable if greater priority was to be given elsewhere. Clearly there was potential for controversy here and the Report itself acknowledged that while 'these tasks would once again cast the WEA largely in the role of educational pioneer' not all branches would be happy with a change of focus:

A shift of emphasis from a wide range of general provision to more specific priorities and a more general role in the promotion of adult education will require a substantial effort of reorientation on the part of branch and district committees. Much of the work we have described will be pioneered by professional tutor-organisers and development officers. It will be important that, wherever necessary, they carry the active lay members with them into these new fields, which would otherwise lose the vital contribution of the Association as a democratic body.[4]

What would happen if the WEA democratically refused to be carried into the new fields laid down for it was not spelled out. Beyond this, there were recommendations that DES grant-aid should cover not only teaching but also organising costs in the four priority areas, that the number of tutor-organisers and development officers should increase, and (as requested by the WEA) that DES grant should be paid to the WEA nationally rather than to Districts individually. Only one paragraph in the whole Report addressed itself to an issue of particular relevance to the Eastern District, the problems of rural areas: this called for locally-organised transport schemes and the provision of community centres attached to village primary schools.[5]

The Report was given a moderately-favourable reception, although there was dismay in some quarters that its proposals had not been more radical. *The Times Educational Supplement* had the headline 'An Overweight Mouse'. Its sister *The Times Higher Educational Supplement* called it 'comprehensive, pragmatic and thorough' but still found the Report 'a profound disappointment': 'within their narrow vision, the committee are cautious to the point of weakness'.[6] There were more positive reactions in the May 1973 issue of *Adult Education*, which devoted several pages to the subject. An editorial 'Commentary' called it 'a realistic but limited Plan' which would serve for the rest of the decade but must not be allowed to set the regulative framework for the next half-century. WEA National Secretary Reg Jefferies wrote,

> It is hard to believe that the four years during which the Russell Committee laboured could not have produced a more spectacular and more ambitious document than that which has been finally published

but then went on to commend the Report as 'workmanlike, realistic and capable of immediate implementation': he welcomed the recommendations relating to the WEA but called on LEAs and universities to co- operate in the difficult priority tasks which had been assigned to the movement. It was left to Thomas Kelly, Director of Extension Studies at the University of Liverpool, to sound a note of warning for the WEA by underlining the significance of a shift away from co-operation with universities in the promotion of liberal and academic studies towards a sharper focus on education for the disadvantaged:

> I think the most surprising thing about this proposal is that it can now be seriously put forward and considered. At the time of the Ashby Report less than twenty years ago, it would have been out of the question. But the WEA has moved a long way since then, and given adequate resources of finance and personnel, the change of direction suggested by the Committee is not impossible. Undoubtedly, however, there will be serious misgivings among the ordinary branch members and if their co-operation is to be assured it will be necessary to proceed with caution.[7]

Herein lay the nub of the problem for the WEA. Nearly all voluntary members were sympathetic to the first three priority areas. But would expansion in these fields be in addition to or at the expense of the traditional work they enjoyed, benefited from and successfully promoted? And was an increase in the numbers of professional staff to develop priority courses a measure to be welcomed or regretted? Was a weakening of the link with universities to be accepted as inevitable? And what did 'below the level of university work' mean: was the internal or extra-mural work of universities the bench-mark here and in any case should the WEA deliberately aim to be less than the best? All this provoked considerable debate at the National Conference in Harrogate in 1973 and at successive meetings of the Eastern District Council and Executive, from all of which it was clear that a reluctance to give ground on the traditional provision of liberal and academic studies was widespread. The District Council of May 1973 was addressed by H. D. Hughes, by then National President; as a member of the Russell Committee he had called enthusiastically for immediate action to implement its proposals.[8] But the Council passed a resolution which fell short of the unequivocal support for the Russell recommendations he would have liked to see:

> The Eastern District WEA, while reserving its position on several points of detail for further consideration, in general welcomes the Russell Report on Adult Education and appeals to all concerned to translate its general recommendations into effective and immediate action.

Typical of voluntary members' worries were the sentiments expressed in an Essex Federation motion to the District Council a year later:

> In negotiations concerning the Russell Report, and in planning our work in the situation that arises from it, we should at all times safeguard the principle that WEA branches should have an absolute right to choose the subjects they wish to study, and that no pressure, moral or financial, should be put upon them to undertake particular types of subject or to provide for particular social groups.

This was defeated but only by 40 votes to 26, a powerful argument against being that because the DES grant-aided the WEA, it inevitably imposed some constraints upon freedom of action already.

There was time for all this reflection because no immediate government response to the Russell Report was forthcoming. 1973 was the year of the phenomenal leap in oil prices, heralding a period of rapid inflation and severe restraint on government expenditure, under both the Conservatives to whom Russell had reported and under their Labour successors from 1974. In this climate, even a modestly-expansionist Report had little hope of adoption and many of the Russell recommendations have never come to pass: the proposed National Development Council, for example, appeared in a modified form in 1977 as the Advisory Committee for Adult and Continuing Education,[9] but nothing has been seen of Russell's projected increases in students and full- time staff. Nevertheless, the government did eventually make a move as far as the WEA was concerned. The Retail Price Index more than doubled between 1974 and 1979, with the annual inflation rate consistently above 25% every month from May to November 1975.[10] All this had a crippling effect on District finances, as the value of students' fees and of DES and LEA grant-aid was seriously eroded. By the early months of 1975, the finances of several WEA Districts were in such a parlous state that the very existence of the Association was threatened: 'we need something like £130,000 just to keep going', National Secretary Reg Jefferies told *The Times Higher Educational Supplement*, and the National Committee followed this up with a pamphlet warning the 1975 Conference that 'the Association is now facing the most severe financial crisis in its history'.[11] The DES rescued the WEA in November 1975 by awarding a special supplementary grant for 1975–76 but warned that some recognisable progress towards the first three Russell priorities was expected. Then in March 1977 the Minister of State, Gordon Oakes, announced further measures. Districts' deficits were wiped out by another supplementary grant, from which the Eastern benefited by some £6,000. At the same time, a new system of government financing was brought in. Instead of grant to the WEA Districts being a set proportion of approved costs (broadly speaking, 75% of teaching expenditure), it would be a cash allocation within which, together with income from students' fees and other sources, each District would be expected to manage its affairs; at least 75% of the Department's grant had to be spent on teaching, and closer government scrutiny of non-teaching expenditure was introduced. The new level of grant to the WEA as a whole was pitched some £100,000 per annum higher than previously, in order to encourage the various Districts to make a decisive turn towards the Russell priorities. Indeed, the Minister stressed the importance of such a reorientation:

> We have made it clear to the WEA that much turns upon their own ability to demonstrate that there is in each of the Districts a coherent plan to shift the emphasis away from liberal and acade- mic studies towards the Russell priorities of work. There was, of course, a time when a change in priorities meant no such thing. What it meant was the existing work continued, receiving just the same emphasis as heretofore, while new priorities were grafted on, and additional expenditure incurred. That is no longer normally

218

possible. Running down old priorities and developing new priorities of course takes time: everyone recognises that. It can only be achieved if there is not only a will to do it, but also a coherent plan for its achievement – and coherent subsumes costed.[12]

In return for this additional help, the WEA was expected by 1978–79 to have achieved 12% growth in Russell area 1 (education for the disadvantaged), 31% growth in area 2 (industrial work) and 12% growth in area 3 (political and social education) compared to levels in 1975–76. But grant would continue to be awarded to Districts direct, not to the National WEA for subsequent distribution as Russell had proposed: Districts' future receipts would depend on how far these targets had been met. The government's figures were skilfully calculated. Although President H. D. Hughes told the WEA National Conference in April 1977 that other adult education bodies were 'green with envy' at the Association's success in negotiating these arrangements, the extra grant was not enough to secure growth on the scale envisaged without some diminution in Russell's area 4, the traditional liberal and academic provision. The general mood of this Conference was that after four years of barking, the Russell recommendations were at last going to bite.

Problems and Priorities

Despite the reservations expressed by many voluntary members about the possible implications of a shift in priorities, much impressive work was in fact accomplished during the mid-1970s which would certainly have met with the approval of the Russell Committee. Adult literacy classes in Corby and Northampton, pioneered in 1973–74; Pre-School Child Development courses at Felixstowe, Halesworth, Stowmarket and elsewhere in East Suffolk, organised in conjunction with and partly financed by the County's Department of Social Services in the same academic year; Luton branch's weekend courses for physically-handicapped students at Maryland College, Woburn which began in April 1975; Bedford branch's daytime courses with creche at the Bunyan School in the more deprived area south of the River Ouse from September 1976; these were among the initiatives which would obviously find a place in the first of the Russell priority categories. Moreover, there was a strong case for saying that wherever the District was running a daytime course with creche, and wherever it offered the only liberal studies available in a remote East Anglian village, it was acting in the spirit of Russell's paragraph 232.1, despite the Report's unfortunate association of 'deprivation' exclusively with urban areas: for the students in these courses would certainly have been 'deprived' if the

WEA provision had been withdrawn.

Similarly, there was a sustained increase in this period in industrial work, as envisaged in paragraph 232.2. Demand for industrial relations courses for shop stewards and other trade union representatives as part of the TUC educational scheme was so heavy by the middle-1970s that the District's tutor-organisers for Industry could have been fully employed doing nothing else. Most of these were on local College premises for representatives from different unions employed by several companies. A minority related to individual firms or unions, such as those run in 1974–75 at Baker Perkins, Peterborough and Vauxhall Motors, Luton, and for the Bakers' Union in Cambridge. The constant need to update material in the light of changes in the law, the contrasts between one group of trade union representatives and another, and the fact that some of these courses were at a basic level, others more advanced, made this provision much less repetitive than District Annual Reports might imply: in 1973–74 there were no less than forty-two courses entitled 'Industrial Relations' (or some variant thereof) and in 1974–75 fifty-three. The vast majority continued to be taken by the District's three tutor-organisers for Industry: by 1974–75 each of them (Reg Carnell, Bert Torrison and David Handley) had a teaching load of between 300 and 400 sessions, well in excess of the contractual minimum. Not surprisingly, the District recruited further full-time staff during 1976, one (Roger Moore) as a successor to Torrison but two (Clive Scarlett and Frank Sykes) as entirely new appointments. All three posts were advertised as tutor-organiserships in Social as well as Industrial Studies, so as to allow a wider brief within the various Russell priorities,[13] although in fact those appointed continued to be heavily involved with day-release courses in Industry. Demand for these courses grew further in the wake of the 1974 Health and Safety at Work Act (with its provision for the appointment or election of safety representatives) and the 1975 Employment Protection Act (which established the Advisory, Conciliation and Arbitration Service and introduced many fundamental reforms in the field of industrial relations). Of day-release courses provided by the District in 1976–77, seventeen were in Health and Safety compared to thirty-two in Industrial Relations. As Carnell put it in his annual report for that year, the growing popularity of Health and Safety courses made further demands on tutors:

> It is an indication of the problems facing industrial tutors in this field that they now need to have at least a basic understanding of Physics, to appreciate the problems arising from Noise, Vibration and Radiation; of Chemistry, to appreciate the dangers of toxic

chemicals; of Medicine, to understand the effects of dust and chemicals on the skin, lungs and other parts of the body; and to have a knowledge of the law in relation to the Acts and Regulations concerned with health and safety at work.

Beyond this, Luton and Peterborough branches both ran evening courses on industrial legislation during 1976–77 as part of their advertised programmes. In 1975–76 three and in 1976–77 six day-release courses were offered by the District on 'Law at the Workplace' for which Reg Carnell, in company with a part-time tutor, Gillian Morris of Churchill College, Cambridge, produced teaching materials subsequently revised and published by the National WEA. Carnell also became a member of the BBC/TUC/WEA team preparing a multimedia 'Trade Union Studies' project to consist of television programmes, course books, postal courses, day schools and evening classes, and he helped write the third-year course book *Democracy at Work* published in 1977; the idea behind all this was that an individual could opt to study the material by whichever method suited him or her best, and could also progress from one type of provision to another. A particularly worthwhile venture was a day-release course on economics entitled 'Work and Wealth' provided for employees of GKN Welwyn Garden City, but held in Cambridge. In all, six of these courses were run for the company, each for one day per week for six weeks, at intervals during 1975 and 1976. The teaching materials consisted of cassette tapes and synchronised slides produced by Cambridge Consultants (Training) Ltd., with supplementary documents prepared by the tutors, but the most distinctive feature was that shopfloor workers, supervisors and administrators were all taught together; they all got to grips with such issues as whether there was a cure for inflation, whether profit was really necessary and whether the economy ought to be managed. One of the part-time tutors who helped with this course, Bill Pedley, edited the *Eastern District Bulletin* during its twice-yearly publication between 1974 and 1979, and he doubtless had this course in mind when he wrote in spring 1978 that the WEA's 'links with Industry need to be extended to include the whole work-force'. In purely statistical terms, the net result of all this activity was that whereas in 1972–73 the District reckoned to have provided some fifty-nine industrial courses for 900 students, by 1976–77 it was running eighty-three courses for 1,289.

As for Russell paragraph 232.3, with its call on the WEA to advance political and social education, there were many relevant weekend and one-day schools which supplemented the normal course provision. These included a Cambridge branch day school on 'Equality' in King's

College in May 1974, a Bedfordshire Federation weekend school on 'Political Theory and Equality' at Maryland College in March 1977, and a day school organised jointly by the Bedfordshire and Hertfordshire Federations concerned with the Bullock Report on Industrial Democracy at Luton College of Higher Education in May 1977. Several schools were also held on the European Economic Community around the time of the national referendum on 5 June 1975; one at Peterborough on the Saturday prior to the vote ended with a mock poll showing 2:1 in favour of remaining within the Common Market, exactly in line with the subsequent national result.[14]

Clearly the District was fulfilling many of the expectations of the Russell Committee in its attention to priority work, so the government's new grant regulations from 1977 onwards, with their targets for expansion in the three key areas, were no cause for undue alarm. Indeed, by 1978–79 the Eastern District had made a very fair contribution to the WEA's success nationwide in meeting the required expansion in the first two priorities. The Association interpreted Russell category one, education for the 'disadvantaged', in a broader sense than a literal reading of paragraph 232.1 would allow, but by including courses for the mothers of young children, for the handicapped and for people in hospital and prison, as well as work with immigrants, illiterates and inner-city residents, it was possible to claim expansion nationally from 11,758 class meetings in 1975–76 to 16,893 in 1978–79: a rate of growth well in excess of the required 12% and one which represented an increase from 16% to 19% of all WEA provision. The Eastern District's own figures, undoubtedly boosted by the rise in daytime courses with creches, showed 37% of all provision in this category by 1978–79, against 24% in 1976–77. As for industrial work, at a national level this represented about 15% of all WEA provision in 1975–76 but 31% of a larger total in 1978–79, the actual number of class meetings having risen by almost 150%. The Eastern District, starting from a 'high base', achieved a less spectacular increase but could still claim 35% of its total provision – above the national average – as falling within this category by 1978–79.[15] But despite the success in these two areas, the District's record in political and social education was not nearly as good. Writing in the *Eastern District Bulletin* in autumn 1978, chairman Cecil Scrimgeour frankly acknowledged that, in this field, the 'shift of provision has not been realised . . . the number of classes in social and political studies has quite sharply declined'. Courses in economics, for example, fell in number from fourteen in 1975–76 to three in 1977–78 and two in 1978–79; taking all courses in this general category together, they amounted to only 9% of the District's total provision in 1978–79 compared to 22% two years earlier. It was true that this was the area which gave the WEA as a whole most difficulty, for there was only a very modest increase nationally from 10,037 class meetings in appropriate subjects in 1975–76 to 11,590 in 1977–78, although a rise to 13,336 in the following year ensured that the 12% target was more than achieved. It was also true that, because of success in other areas, the DES did not penalise the District for its failure in this category when assessing future grant-aid. Even so, the figures were regrettable and prompted radical measures at the District AGM in November 1978.

The decision taken on this occasion was that for an experimental two-year period from January 1979, branches opting for courses in politics, economics and international affairs (the syllabuses for which had been approved by the District Office) would be required to enrol only eight students instead of the usual minimum of fifteen. They were also to be allowed concessionary class contributions, so that for a course of (say) twelve meetings the branch would only have to pay £25 instead of the normal £74; even if the customary fifteen or more students enrolled, the class contribution would be held at £50, appreciably less than the usual sum. There was, however, to be no variation in the fees charged to students – which by 1978–79 stood at 40p. per meeting beyond those already standardised for all the District's courses.

The reaction to this decision was heartening. In 1979–80, the first full academic year in which the scheme operated, a total of sixty branches, including no less than sixteen in Essex, took advantage of the new arrangements to offer sixty-five courses in one or other of the relevant subjects; all but thirteen of these courses secured the necessary enrolments to survive. In the following year a further fifty-two so-called 'Russell courses' were offered at concessionary rates, with Essex (eleven branches) again leading the way. Typical of the courses run successfully in 1980–81 which, but for the scheme, would not have survived and might never have been chosen in the first place, were Terminals at Cambridge (ten students for 'Political Issues in Economics'), Clacton (nine for 'The World Food Problem'), Coddenham in Suffolk (eight for 'The Modernisation of China'), Luton (eight for 'Understanding Muslim Cultures'), Saffron Walden (eight for 'Africa at the Crossroads'), and Yelvertoft in Northamptonshire (nine for 'Understanding Politics'). It is a measure of the success of this experiment in reversing the decline in such priority subjects that while courses in international affairs remained virtually unchanged in number between 1977–78 and 1980-81 (fifteen in the first year, fourteen in the second), those in politics and economics rose from five to nineteen. The scheme was renewed at the end of the initial two-year experiment and has since become an established feature of the District's work.

The experience with political and social education – a serious problem provoking a spirited response – was typical of the District's fortunes during the 1970s and early 1980s, for there is no doubt that these were unusually difficult years. The spring term of 1974 was disrupted by power cuts and the 'three-day-week' during the coalminers' strike prior to the February General Election. A few industrial courses were cancelled as a result, as at Colchester and Luton, but only two of those run by branches had to close for lack of accommodation, the rest finding temporary alternatives wherever local authority premises were closed. Enrolments for this term were actually higher than for the corresponding term the year before and Norfolk tutor-organiser David Yaxley, commenting on the situation in his annual report, wrote that

> The winter fuel crisis, while it can scarcely be called a blessing in disguise, at least showed that the WEA can rise to meet an emergency of this sort. Only one branch in the county found that it could not carry on with the planned course without the use of the school. Most classes met in private houses and a few hired public halls and shivered

although he added that the Norwich branch was fortunate in continuing to meet in Ivory House as usual. Similar problems occurred in the so-called 'winter of discontent' at the beginning of 1979, when industrial action by local authority workers coincided with some of the worst weather in East Anglia and the East Midlands since 1947. Indeed, Frank Jacques was moved to write about it all in the *Eastern District Bulletin* that spring:

> Never before during the 44 years in which I've served you as secretary has any term begun under greater difficulties than those which we've faced in this year of 1979 ... This January every possible handicap, except perhaps a 'flu epidemic, from which mercifully we've been spared, has hit our branches in the enrol-ment weeks of this term. Roads untreated, pavements and paths serious hazards to pedestrians, schools unheated, schools closed; all plans disorganised, all previous patterns destroyed.

But once again, branches had recourse to private houses and there was only a marginal decline in the number of courses they offered compared to 1977–78.[16]

On the financial side, increases in students' fees to take account of inflation became at times an annual event. The minimum 16p. per class meeting of 1971 became 22p. in August 1975, 30p. in August 1976, 40p. in August 1977, 50p. in January 1980, 60p. in August 1980, 75p. in January 1982, 80p. in August 1982 and 90p. in August 1983. So a twelve-week Terminal which in the autumn term of 1973 cost a student a minimum of £1.92 plus 10p. for registration was costing a minimum £10.80 ten years later: the saving grace being that the separate registration fee, which many branch officers had found tiresome to collect from students attending their first meetings, had been abolished following a motion from the Cambridge branch to the District Council in March 1975. The class contributions payable by branches to the District did of course rise by similar proportions: from £25.50 (as agreed in 1971) to £124 in the same ten-year period, an increase of almost 400%. For comparison, the Retail Price Index showed a rise of about 250% from 1973 to 1984,[17] although it should be added that local education authorities also had to increase their fees drastically during these years and by the end of the 1970s were normally charging more per class than the WEA was.

The District treasurer to whom fell the unenviable task of presiding over the escalation of fees during the 1970s was R. C. Smail, another in the line of distinguished Cambridge historians to hold the office and one who also served the WEA as a part-time tutor and as founding-secretary of the Willingham branch (Fenland) from 1970. His patient and lucid presentation of accounts at District Councils were long remembered as models of their kind. He and his equally-competent successor from 1979, Moira Bambrough, deserve great credit for recommending frequent and fairly-gradual increases in fees; the alternative policy of trying to hold fees steady would have led sooner or later to massive rises which might have devastated student recruitment and branch morale. Even so, the upward trend in fees called forth the customary protests at District Councils, pessimism about the dire consequences for future enrolments and occasional 'disobedience' from branches charging lower than the required amounts: an Essex Federation motion considered by the District Executive in October 1975, for example, feared an approaching 'breaking point' if there were any further increases in fees. Analysis of student recruitment figures does suggest that the level of fees had a discernible impact during the middle and later 1970s, but it is less easy to detect a pattern in the early 1980s. The first point to make is that in 1975–76 the Eastern District recruited more students than at any time before or since: 11,696, excluding those on residential and one-day schools and at single meetings. A slow decline thereafter brought the figure to 10,025 in 1986- 87, but this downward trend is largely to be explained by the reduced number of industrial courses. If one counts only students attending courses run by branches (and occasionally Federations), the vast majority of whom paid their own fees, and ignores industrial courses and others run by the District for particular groups, where fees were (on the whole) met by an outside body, a rather different picture emerges.

In 1976–77, following an increase in fees at the beginning of the academic year, branches in the Eastern District recruited 10,438 students, 482 fewer than in 1975–76. A further rise in fees led to branch enrolments of 9,475 in 1977–78. There was no increase for 1978–79 and numbers climbed to 9,909. All this suggests a relationship between fees and student-numbers, but the link is more tenuous thereafter. There were four increases in fees between January 1980 and August 1982, but numbers rose steadily, 9,684 in 1979–80, 9,855 in 1980–81, 10,135 in 1981- 82 and 11,019 in 1982–83: a record level of branch enrolments in Frank Jacques's last year as District Secretary. There have of course been further rises in fees since then – to £1 per class meeting in August 1984, £1.10 a year later and £1.15 in August 1987 – but how far these have been responsible for a fall in branches' enrolments is open to debate: the comparable figures were 10,106 for 1985–86 and 9,840 for 1986–87.

The District faced further difficulties towards the end of the 1970s over its policies towards the employment of tutor-organisers. In March 1973 the District Council passed overwhelmingly a Norfolk Federation motion reaffirming 'belief in the value and effectiveness of the partnership between voluntary and professional workers which has proved itself throughout the history of the WEA'. In February 1977 the report of a Working Party on the structure and pattern of the Eastern District, chaired by Cecil Scrimgeour, reasserted the value of tutor-organisers: every Federation chairman, except in Essex, had been of the opinion 'that classes on the existing scale and relations with other agencies in adult education could not confidently be maintained without the help of such tutors' and the Report concluded that it would be highly undesirable not to replace them as vacancies arose, provided that DES grant was forthcoming. Indeed in the year of this Report, 1976–77, the District had twelve tutor-organisers on the payroll, more than at any other time in its history. But as an economy measure Cambridgeshire was left without a tutor-organiser for almost a year prior to the appointment of Paul Middleton in July 1978: under the chairmanship of Dorothy Humphries, members of the Federation Executive took over much of the tutor-organiser's co-ordinating work on a temporary basis. During this time the District's Finance and General Purposes Committee considered whether to switch from territorially-based tutor-organisers to subject-specialists who could teach in more than one county. When the post was eventually advertised, it was for a tutor-organiser *based in* Cambridgeshire rather than specifically *for* the county as had been normal hitherto, so as to leave options open for the future.[18] In practice, nothing more has come of this and Cambridgeshire has continued to benefit from the presence of a resident tutor-organiser. However, following Julian Batsleer's resignation as tutor-organiser for Hertfordshire in February 1985, the District again found itself unable to afford a replacement. This time, a grant of £3,000 was agreed to enable the Hertfordshire Federation to employ a part-time secretary, and two other tutor-organisers, Tony Dennis (Bedfordshire) and Roger Moore (Industrial and Social Studies) undertook to give emergency help in the county for the academic year 1985–86. Moore continued in this role, with some assistance from the District Secretary, throughout 1987.

In the late 1970s the future employment of tutor-organisers for Industry was also called into question, following discussions between the National WEA, TUC and DES. The TUC was eager for a rapid expansion in the provision of day-release courses for shop stewards and other trade union representatives, an expansion which Jacques estimated would require an increase in the number of industrial tutor-organisers within the Eastern District to nine or ten. In reporting all this to the District Executive in February 1978 and to the District Council in March, he said that he had stipulated that the full cost of such appointments should be met from TUC fees for courses and from DES grant-aid, with no hidden subsidy from the voluntary branch members. This principle was frequently reiterated during the next few years, as tutor-organisers for Industry left and no replacements were appointed. With the departure of Reg Carnell in September 1978 to become General Manager of Peterborough Youth Opportunities Council Training Workshop, and the resignation of three of his colleagues who obtained other posts during 1979, the number of industrial tutor-organisers rapidly dwindled to one. At the same time, local authority colleges were building up their own tutorial staffs to meet the demand for TUC courses – only to find, in the changed political and economic climate which followed the General Election of 1979, that demand began to fall. Indeed, having delayed filling the vacant industrial tutor-organiserships during the summer of 1979, despite DES approval for two replacements, the District found this approval withdrawn as part of the public expenditure cuts of the new Conservative government.

Through such a combination of circumstances, the Eastern District's provision of industrial courses fell dramatically: from an all- time peak of ninety-one in 1978–79 to sixty-two in 1979–80 and twenty-five in 1980–81. Had there been a policy of immediately filling vacancies, or indeed of increasing the number of industrial tutor-organisers as requested by the TUC, there would presumably have been less of a decline: but some downturn would certainly have occurred, for the number of WEA/TUC day-release courses in England and Wales as a whole fell from 723 in 1978–79 to only 441 in 1980–81.[19] There were real dangers for the District in taking on extra staff to please the TUC and so becoming too heavily dependent on one source of income. Those who felt it wisest not to dance to the TUC's tune, even at the cost of running down the cherished industrial work, must have felt vindicated when in 1980–81 the one remaining industrial tutor-organiser found his teaching curtailed by the cancellation of TUC day-release courses because of low enrolments by shop stewards: a fact which led to his being given a more varied programme, including some courses in modern history and economics for the branches, in subsequent years. Of course, the District's record of industrial provision after 1978–79 looked bad on paper when set against the advances made previously in the light of Russell recommendations and DES targets. It was ironic that at the very time that the District was increasing its provision in one Russell priority area, political and social education, it should be losing ground in another. In 1978–79 35% of the Eastern District's pro-gramme had been categorised as 'Industrial and Trade Union' work against only 9% 'Social and Political'; by 1980–81 the figures were reversed, with 9% of provision in 'Industrial and Trade Union' studies, 21% in 'Social and Political'.[20] But purely in terms of grant-aid, this no longer mattered. From 1979, with the coming to power as Prime Minister of the lady to whom the Russell Committee had presented their findings six years earlier, the old Report quickly became a dead letter. Far from the expansion envisaged in 1973, curbs on public spending dealt adult education a severe blow. The cuts in DES grant-aid suffered by the Eastern District during the early 1980s – amounting to some £15,000 in 1981–82 alone – were not a penalty for running down industrial provision but a response to an unforeseen surplus of £30,000 on the year's work in 1980–81, at a time when rigid government economies were being looked for. The early eighties were a time when adult educationists generally dug in and hoped to survive. Many local authorities, obliged to cut spending to meet government targets, tried to make adult education self-financing, with the result that by 1980–81 fees for non-vocational evening classes averaged 41p. per hour and were up to 90p. in places: a 51% increase in fees since 1979- 80 had led to an 11% fall in enrolments. Robin Squire, Conservative MP for Horn-church, told the House of Commons in February 1981 that the adult education service in many parts of the country faced 'the spectre of destruction'.[21] His words rang true later in the year when Cam-bridgeshire County Council, despite its proud record as a pioneer of village colleges, considered axing its entire adult education service and making full-time and part-time staff redundant, as one way to meet its spending targets for 1982–83;[22] the District added its voice to the protests against this measure, which happily did not come to pass. For their part, university extra-mural departments also felt the cold blast of economy, and from 1982–83 both Cambridge and Leicester began to claim from the District a portion of the class contribution for courses taken by their tutors.

New Departures

Against this background of tension and difficulty, the Eastern District still had many achievements to be proud of. A group of day-release students from a second-year course in the 'Trade Union Studies' project, run by the District in Harlow, decided in March 1977 to revive the local WEA branch in order to offer evening courses of particular interest to trade unionists; this venture – the District's first 'industrial branch' – lasted until 1981. The 'Trade Union Studies' project itself moved on in 1977–78 to the point where branches in all parts of the District – Bedford, Cambridge, Hatfield, Kettering, Luton, Northampton, Peter-borough – mounted evening courses linked to television programmes as part of their advertised provision. Some repeated the courses in the following year and several were able to build on them to maintain useful links with the trade union movement. During 1978–79, for instance, Luton branch's 'Health and Safety at Work' course enrolled over eighty students, while at Cambridge former day-release students joined a course run by the branch on 'Labour Movements in Britain, 1890–1970' and were subsequently elected onto the branch council. In autumn 1977 the Cambridgeshire Federation (having changed its name from 'Fenland' on the amalgamation of its constituent counties in 1974) ran a training course for voluntary tutors who were interested in teaching English to immigrants; from these foundations, Huntingdon Area Community Education Department developed the language-teaching scheme to the point where, nine years later, a full-time officer was appointed to supervise the work. In the spring of 1978, a two-day residential course in English was organised for Northampton's Chilean refugees and in summer 1980 Bishop's Stortford branch mounted a course on the English landscape for refugees from Vietnam. In the same term, the District ran a ten-week course on Death, Grief and Mourning for the newly-formed Peterborough branch of CRUSE, the counselling support group for the bereaved, and in autumn 1982 launched its first course for SCOPE (Second Chance Opportunities for Women), organised in Cambridge in conjunction with the Open University and YWCA. A series of courses were also held, from 1979 onwards, for psychiatric day patients in Peterborough and March.

The social problem which caused most widespread concern in the early 1980s was of course rising unemployment. Government statistics for the United Kingdom showed unemployment doubling between mid-1979 (1.2 millions) and mid-1981 (2.4 millions) and topping 3 millions by mid-1984.[23] The District's response to this issue was both well-informed and decisive. Anxious that branches should be fully involved in any provision for unemployed people, the District Executive resolved during 1981 to distribute a discussion paper followed by a questionnaire to every branch. Over fifty branches responded to the questionnaire, all expressing concern and some reporting specific measures: Saffron Walden, for instance, had appointed a member of the branch committee to deal with all matters relating to unemployed students, while Kettering had decided to reduce its fees not only for unemployed workers but also for their spouses. The increased awareness within the District resulting from all this – both of the nature of the problem and of how the WEA might help – led to several important initiatives. Essentially, a two-fold policy developed: on the one hand to run courses primarily intended for the unemployed, on the other to encourage these people to join mainstream courses mounted by their local branch. It was with both intentions in mind that in May 1982 the District Council agreed that branches could, if they wished, charge no fee whatsoever to unemployed students.[24] Attractive posters advertising WEA courses (including the fact that these were free to the registered unemployed) were distributed by the District without charge to branches during 1982: and by 1982–83 some 314 unemployed students were on the registers of ordinary branch courses compared to 138 in the previous year, the highest totals being in Bedfordshire (73) and Norfolk (58). Among courses run specially were those in spring and summer 1982 on 'Britain Between the Wars' and 'The Industrial Revolution' for redundant steelworkers participating in an Adult Basic Education Scheme in Corby, and others variously called 'Benefit Rights' and 'Welfare Rights' provided by the Bedford and Luton branches in local Unemployed

Workers' Centres from the spring of 1982 onwards. Norwich branch gave financial support for two courses at Wensum Lodge, each of two full days, entitled 'Positive Responses to Unemployment and Redundancy', taught by chaplains from the Norwich Industrial Mission during 1981–82; these were redesigned as three-day courses in the following year under the auspices of a 'New Directions Group' composed of representatives of various local bodies, with the District employing the tutor and the Norwich branch meeting other costs. Meanwhile in November 1981 the Ipswich branch opened a drop-in centre on Friday mornings in St. Lawrence's Church Hall, offering free refreshments and welfare advice. This was to develop into a most significant enterprise.[25]

By the spring of 1982 the Ipswich centre was attracting a loyal core of a dozen regular attenders, with many more occasional callers. This encouraged the local branch to attempt a more ambitious programme: in June 1982 a visit to the House of Commons and in the following autumn three WEA courses on different mornings of the week. All three, on 'Social Policy', 'International Affairs' and 'A Positive Approach to Unemployment' ran successfully, despite fluctuating attendances caused in part by gains and losses of jobs. In September 1983 Ipswich Trades Council opened its own Unemployment Centre in converted office accommodation at 12 Museum Street, but the WEA was given rooms on the premises and transferred its provision there: by the spring of 1985 the programme had developed to embrace a 'Creative Writing' course on Monday mornings (from which the branch had already published two anthologies, 'Get That in Print'), a 'Living History Workshop' on Tuesdays, benefits advice and an open-ended discussion group on Fridays, plus a 'Practical Art' class on Wednesdays which because it fell outside the WEA's liberal studies remit was funded by the local authority instead. Indeed, the Ipswich scheme demonstrated very clearly the co-operative goodwill of many different agencies, with the borough and county councils, local churches, Ipswich Trades Council and WEA branches and District all doing what they could to keep courses free to the students through a series of donations and concessions. And in purely educational terms, the venture could hardly be paid a higher tribute than the fact that within three years of its humble beginnings in a church hall, two of its former students were at Ruskin College, Oxford. This commitment to work with the unemployed, both at Ipswich and elsewhere within the District, was striking testimony to the dedication of WEA members to education for the 'disadvantaged': not because the Russell Report had commended it or in the hope of earning more DES grant-aid, because both considerations were outdated by the early

1980s, but simply because it seemed the right thing to do.

Within the field of liberal and academic studies in general, the new decade witnessed a remarkable surge of interest in the most demanding courses, three-year Tutorials. The Russell Committee's ambivalence towards them had seemed to signal their ultimate demise. So had new DES grant regulations in 1975 which, as threatened by the Ashby Report over twenty years earlier, had stressed the relevance of length and quality of courses in determining grant levels but had omitted any mention of Tutorials by name.[26] The 1970s had been a lean decade; in 1972–73 for example eight Tutorial Classes in the Eastern District, catering for 156 students, by 1979–80 seven with 167 enrolled. But in 1980–81 twelve Tutorials were run, attended by 289 students; in 1982–83 there were no less than eighteen (the highest number since 1967–68) with 346 students in all. Ten of these eighteen Tutorials were held in the daytime, examples including 'Painting and Sculpture of the 20th Century' at Berkhamsted (Hertfordshire), 'Greek Civilisation' at Colchester, 'America and Russia in the 20th Century' at Danbury (Essex), 'The Puritan Tradition' at Luton and 'Shakespeare and the BBC' at Norwich. Yet by the late 1980s the trend was again downward: in 1985–86 fourteen Tutorials, in 1986–87 nine, in 1987–88 only five. Although demand for Tutorials was actually a little higher than this,[27] the decline inevitably raised questions over their long-term future.

An alternative indicator of quality is the fact that there were well over twenty publications as a result of branch and Federation courses in the ten years covered by this chapter. As in the past, nearly all were on aspects of local history, among them three volumes on Wheathampstead and Harpenden published in 1973 and 1974, another three volumes on Fressingfield (1977–79), *Rayne – From Early Times to the Present Day* (1977), *In and Out of the Workhouse: the Coming of the New Poor Law to Cambridgeshire and Huntingdonshire* (1978), *Bulmer Then and Now* (1979), *The Story of Aspley Guise* (1980), *The Unchanging Revolution: a Study of Mid-19th Century Gislingham, Thornham Parva and Thornham Magna* (1981), *North Walsham in the Eighteenth Century* (1983) and Wherein I Dwell: a History of Earls Colne Houses from 1375 (1983). Creative writing courses in Cambridge produced a series of *Wednesday Evening Anthologies* from 1973 onwards, and a student in a daytime literature course in Luton wrote an autobiographical account of life in working-class London, published as *Canary Girls and Stockpots* in 1977. Members of Leighton Buzzard branch brought out a *Handbook for the Retired* in 1979. WEA courses also made a lasting impact in other ways by leading to the formation of local societies. This happened, for example, at Bungay, where a 'Workshop for Recording East Anglian Tradition' in 1974-75 led to the establishment of the Suffolk Group for Recording Oral Tradition, and at Castor (Cambridgeshire) where a course on 'John Clare' in 1981 was followed by the launch of a John Clare Society.

Of more passing concern was the District's involvement in the 'Brain Train' experiment, devised by the Mutual Aid Centre based in London. This was a scheme whereby commuters formed themselves into small adult education classes for the duration of their morning journeys – an idea first tried on the 7.17 from Cambridge to Liverpool Street in September 1977.[28] The WEA was brought in a year later to run two courses on archaeology, one before Christmas, the other in the New Year of 1979, each meeting on both Tuesday and Thursday mornings. These were followed by courses on British and European politics and on geology over the next two years, before the District finally withdrew towards the end of 1981 when a course on 'Nature in English Literature' had to close with only three students. The classes were shorter in length (fifty minutes to an hour) and because of accommodation problems enrolled fewer students (six to nine) than was normal in WEA or other adult education courses; they also tended to be distracted in their early days by the attention of the media and later on by unsympathetic fellow-passengers who did not respect the seat reservations. Nevertheless those who took part considered the experiment well worthwhile and the national organiser, writing to Jacques in March 1980, was able to report that sixteen such trains were by then operating throughout the country.

The late 1970s and early 1980s were also a time of growing concern to enhance the quality of teaching and learning within adult education. At national level, the WEA established a training committee in 1977; two years later this began to run schools for tutor-organisers and development officers on topics such as 'Literature', 'Social and Political Education' and 'Sustaining WEA Branches'. The Advisory Council for Adult and Continuing Education produced its own report on training courses for tutors in 1983.[29] Within the Eastern District, the traditional form of tutor-training had been the fortnight's course for prospective part-time tutors held as part of the annual Summer School although newcomers had of course received advice from experienced colleagues on an ad hoc basis and there had been occasional meetings, such as a Hertfordshire Federation Conference, 'Teaching Adults', at Harpenden in 1970. The normal pattern on the Summer School course had been for ten prospective tutors each year to learn something of the structure of adult education and of appropriate teaching techniques, and to give practice teaching-sessions which WEA students at the School had been invited to attend and criticise. Obviously this course reached only a tiny fraction of those active as tutors, and in any case it came to an end in 1983, after which the District ceased to run the Summer School for financial reasons. However Reg Carnell, who rejoined the District in July 1980 as tutor-organiser for development, made it one of his priorities to maintain and where possible enhance the already-good standard of teaching.[30] He spent much of his time visiting classes to observe teaching in progress, organising conferences at which tutors could discuss issues of mutual concern and arranging one-day induction courses for new part-time tutors: the procedure here was for morning seminars to be followed by micro-teaching sessions in the afternoons, with WEA members encouraged to attend and comment.

This work was rich in potential. In March 1983 a District Training Team was established, composed of experienced voluntary members and part-time tutors, plus two tutor-organisers, with responsibility for organising a comprehensive training programme throughout the District. By 1984 the District was offering two one-day induction courses for tutors new to the WEA, plus two conferences arranged by county Federations at which tutors and branch officers could discuss matters of mutual concern; members of the training team also visited classes taken by inexperienced tutors. In March 1985 the DES promised the WEA nationally an additional grant of £50,000 per annum for three years, to finance new tutor-training and staff development initiatives, and the Eastern District was able to use its share of this grant to develop the training programme still further. Carolyn Allen, chairman of the Cambridgeshire Federation and already a voluntary member of the training team, was employed from August 1985 to July 1986 as co-ordinator of training, and helped to ensure that the Eastern District's response to the DES offer was well-organised and constructive. As it progressed from 1985 onwards, the District's training scheme came to embrace not only the now-familiar induction courses and Federation conferences but also meetings of tutors in specialist subjects, support for experienced staff to attend 'Training the Trainers' courses, and the publication of a well-presented handbook for tutors, *Learning with the WEA*, which appeared in 1986. The participation of student-members in much of this work, especially in giving advice to tutors at induction courses and conferences, was a practical demonstration of the WEA as a teaching and learning fellowship; the University Extra-Mural Board also contributed, with two staff tutors, Chris Barringer and Jack Herbert, willingly giving their time on various training days. This apart, the District's part-time tutors were by 1986 also enjoying the opportunity to attend LEA training sessions, and an experimental stage one training course had been held in Huntingdon, run jointly by the WEA and the Cambridgeshire authority. A National WEA survey for the year April 1985 to March 1986 showed the Eastern District to have provided training for more tutors (223) than any other in the country.[31]

The fact that the county Federations became more involved in this activity was symptomatic of their growing importance as agencies within the District's total provision. During the 1970s most Federations held a series of one-day and weekend schools, drawing in branch members from all over their counties and beyond: indeed by 1979 Essex was running week-long Summer Schools in conjunction with the local University. Among other initiatives were Essex's help in launching a county Oral History Group in 1974, Hertfordshire's decision to subscribe to the County Supplies Department in 1975 so as to provide branches with stationery and other equipment at competitive rates, and Bedfordshire's introduction of an essay prize in 1977, enabling the winner to attend the District's Summer School on a bursary. In most counties, voluntary members of Federation Executive Committees took on an increasingly-significant role in advising and supporting their tutor-organisers. Federations could also step in to maintain a WEA presence where a local branch had collapsed, or run courses in new centres in the hope that a branch would be formed. For instance the Cambridgeshire Federation ran courses on archaeology and history at Huntingdon between 1974 and 1976 until the local branch could be refounded, and in 1978–79 sponsored courses at Castor and Manea which eventually led to local branch committees being elected to take over.

The Essex Federation Executive gave much thought in these years to the possibility of leaving the Eastern District altogether. A National WEA Working Group, established at the biennial Conference in 1971, produced a report the following year proposing a revision of District boundaries. Their prime considerations were that there should be less disparity in the size of Districts and that each county, including new ones projected under local government reorganisation, should be placed wholly within one District, not divided between two or more. Under this scheme, Bedfordshire and Northamptonshire would have been transferred from the Eastern District to join Berkshire, Buckinghamshire and Oxfordshire in a new South Midlands District. On the other hand, the southern parts of Essex and Hertfordshire would have switched from the

London to the Eastern District. However neat this looked on paper, there was a widespread feeling within the WEA throughout the country that the reasons for these changes were not sufficiently compelling to upset District budgets and break off longstanding relationships. As for the Eastern District, the AGM of October 1972 passed a motion expressing strong disapproval of the proposed changes. But the Essex Federation Executive had been prompted by these discussions to consider whether to link up with branches in the south of the county to form a separate Essex District: a feasibility study, which suggested that such a District might be viable, was submitted to Botolph House in February 1973. However the National WEA made clear its opposition to the creation of a separate Essex District and the idea was dropped, along with the original proposals for a wholesale revision of District boundaries. Nevertheless, the Essex Federation returned to the issue in 1976, this time with a view to possible transfer to the London District. In October, the District Executive gave permission for Essex representatives to meet the London District Secretary and at the Essex Federation AGM in November it was agreed that such a transfer should be sought. EF, the Federation news-sheet, reported that thirty of the thirty-three branches which had expressed an opinion were in favour of the move, the main reason being that London District courses cost less in students' fees; other factors included the lower minimum enrolments required by London, branches' freedom to set their own levels of fees, the fewer tutor-organisers employed and the better communications links with District headquarters. After further discussions with the London District arising from all this, a special Federation meeting held at Braintree in May 1979 resolved that the Essex Federation should formally apply to join London if 75% of branches voted in favour. In the subsequent ballot, twenty-seven branches declared their wish for a transfer with eight against and six abstentions: this meant that about two-thirds of the branches wanted the move, but not the three-quarters required, so the matter did not proceed further. Thereafter, most Essex branches became increasingly happy with their membership of the Eastern District, and by the time of the seventy-fifth anniversary relations between the Essex Federation and the District Office were in fact better than at any time in the previous thirty-five years.

WEA activists in Essex did not allow the uncertainty over their future to deflect them from their educational work, for expansion in this part of the District continued to be impressive. In 1973–74 there were ninety-two courses run by the branches in Essex, attended by 1,749 students. These figures were exceeded only in Hertfordshire with 100 courses and

1,921 students; just behind came Norfolk with eighty-five courses and 1,598 students. By 1982–83 Essex had 111 courses and 2,407 students, appreciably more than Norfolk (eighty and 1,528) and Bedfordshire (eighty and 1,250). By 1986–87, as the District approached its seventy-fifth anniversary, the figures were 117 courses and 2,734 students in Essex, followed by ninety-one courses (1,710 students) in Suffolk. Bald statistics never tell the whole story, but they are nonetheless a fine tribute to the effort and enthusiasm of the branch and Federation officers in Essex in the period since the last county tutor-organiser resigned in 1957.

It would indeed have been ironic if Essex, as a bastion of voluntaryism, had left the Eastern District, for an enthusiastic commitment to the WEA's voluntary and democratic principles was one of the hall-marks of Frank Jacques's service to the District in almost half a century as Secretary. He is remembered for much else besides: for his passionate insistence on the highest standards of objective teaching and diligent study; for his astuteness both in and out of committee in advancing the District's interests; for his instinctive sympathy and generosity towards the underdog; for his resilience whenever faced with disappointment; for his optimistic forward planning when (in advancing years) many would have been content to dwell in the past. But it was to the theme of voluntaryism that he returned time and again when, at District Councils and in Annual Reports, he praised the ordinary WEA members and encouraged them to meet the challenges ahead. When he eventually retired on 30 September 1983, well into his eighties, he left the District with 180 active branches, exactly nine times the number with which he had started in 1935. It fell to Reg Carnell, who had been appointed his successor as one of forty-eight applicants and four candidates inter-viewed, to write the Annual Report for 1982–83, and he struck the right note in his tribute to Jacques:

> Commitment to the concept of voluntaryism, and in turn the democratic control of their destiny by the voluntary members . . . is the real tribute to Frank Jacques. He was able to achieve that most difficult task, defining and then putting into practice the true role of the professional officer in a voluntary movement. This role required a special form of leadership, which drew the best from the voluntary members, their commitment coming from the know-ledge that they were . . . capable of organising and maintaining their own class programmes through a structure of democratically controlled WEA branches.

The last word on this should go to the man himself, writing his final

District Annual Report, that for 1981–82, and reflecting on the movement he loved.

This District covers a larger area than any other in England and, despite the fact that its wide territory is of a substantially rural character, it is comprised of a very much larger number of branches than any other . . . Although our branches are grouped in County Federations, all still retain the right to direct representation by delegate at the three meetings of their Council held in Cambridge each year; thus they exercise a real and, indeed, absolute control over the policies and practices of the District which they comprise.

There is no unseemly or irrelevant boast in what we have written above; rather it is an attempt to declare the truly voluntary character of this District and to pay tribute to the thousands of voluntary workers in its branches. They have made and sustained its progress against the buffetings of the very varied problems which they encounter and the many disappointments which they suffer . . .

The National WEA is an aggregation of its 21 Districts . . . Similarly if the national association is to deserve and justify its claim that it is a truly voluntary movement, it can only do so because each one of its component Districts can demonstrate that it is made and maintained by its branches, and those in turn by all the voluntary workers who not only do all the ground work but also govern locally and regionally through their District associations.

Without these dedicated branch members there would be neither Districts nor a National Association. So to them be all the honour and glory and, especially in these days of the threat of increasing professionalism, the power. Amen.

Megan Mothersole, Assistant Secretary 1965–87

Reg Carnell, District Secretary since 1983 (standing, front row, second from left) with District Executive Committee, 1987–88. Inset: Sheila Bond, District Chai

NOTES

1) *TES* 7 February 1969.

2) *Russell Report*, para.228.

3) Ibid., para.230.

4) Ibid., para.235.

5) Ibid., paras.237, 238, 240, 307, 390–92.

6) *TES*; *The Times Higher Educational Supplement* (hereafter *THES*), both 30 March 1973.

7) T. Kelly, 'The Russell Report – a university perspective', *Adult Education* XLVI (1973–74), pp.13–14.

8) *THES*, 30 March 1973.

9) Although the new Advisory Committee was given the task of promoting 'the development of future policies and priorities, with full regard to the concept of education as a process continuing throughout life', there was widespread disappointment that its name reflected an advisory rather than a developmental role. See, e.g. Open University, *Report of the Committee on Continuing Education* (Venables Report: 1976), pp.80- 81; *THES*, 28 October 1977. *Adult Education* L (1977–78) p.146 was more optimistic.

10) Central Statistical Office, *Annual Abstract of Statistics* (1987), tables 18.6 and 18.7.

11) *THES*, 14 March 1975; WEA, The Financial Crisis (1975).

12) Quoted in *Eastern District Bulletin*, Autumn 1976. The Minister's expectation that liberal and academic studies would decline was at variance with the sentiments of the WEA National Committee's Report for 1975–77. Reservations about the desirability of running down traditional work were more apparent here than they had been in the years immediately before and after the publication of the Russell Report: 'There are limitations to the extent to which work in liberal and academic studies can be curtailed to enable other work to grow. As a matter of principle and of policy the National Committee reaffirms the value of liberal adult education. The WEA's function, in our view, is to provide liberal education for adults. This is the context within which our efforts of development are made: and in liberal adult education are to be found the values that should inform and distinguish our development work.' (p.8). Cf. p.13 of the National Committee's Report for 1977–79: 'There is now an urgent need to ensure that our liberal and academic studies are developed as the essential basis and springboard for the other categories of work.'.

13) *TES*, 24 October 1975, 21 May 1976.

14) The result of the national referendum on the question, 'Do you think that the United Kingdom should stay in the European Community (Common Market)?' was Yes 67.2%, No 32.8%.

15) *WEA National Committee Report for 1977–79*, pp.12–16, 27; 1979–81, pp.8–9, 29.

16) The District Annual Report for 1978–79 gave a total of 486 organised by branches compared to 491 in 1977–78.

241

17) *Annual Abstract of Statistics* (1987), table 18.6.

18) *TES*, 24 February 1978.

19) *WEA National Committee Report for 1981–83*, p.13.

20) Ibid., *1979–81*, p.29, *1981–83*, p.21.

21) *THES*, 20 February 1981; cf. Hansard for 16 February 1981.

22) *TES*, 23 October 1981

23) *Annual Abstract of Statistics* (1987), table 6.1: figures for mid-June.

24) By 1980, 21% of local education authorities charged no fee to unemployed students attending non-vocational courses, a figure which had risen to 27% by 1982. (*Adult Education* LV, 1982–83, p.429.)

25) The Ipswich branch secretary, Adeline Clarke, to whom much of the success of this enterprise was due, submitted an article on the subject to *WEA News*, published in spring 1983. See also *WEA News*, spring 1985, for a report on voluntary work by members of the Ipswich unemployed group for the Southampton-based charity, Tools for Self-Reliance.

26) Department of Education and Science, *Further Education Regulations 1975*, para-.28(2): 'The amount of any such grant shall be determined by reference to the general standard of the courses included in the programmes (having regard to the syllabuses, the quality of teaching, the length of courses and the arrangements for written work, reading under guidance and other forms of private study to be carried out between meetings), the needs of the area, the activities of other bodies providing further education in the area and the fees paid by students'. Cf. the wording of the 1955 regulations, above, p.

27) Among branches which requested Tutorials for 1987–88, two were given Sessionals because they had just completed Tutorials with the same tutors; another was awarded a Sessional because the tutor could not commit himself to a Tutorial.

28) P. le Pelley, *Go to Work on a Brain Train* (1978).

29)· *WEA National Committee Report for 1979–81*, p.19; ACACE, *Teachers of Adults: Voluntary Specialist Training and Evaluating Training Courses* (1983). In the previous year, the Advisory Council had called for a 'comprehensive new structure to provide training for part-time staff' (ACACE, *Continuing Education: From Policies to Practice*, 1982, pp.168–69.)

30) An analysis by Carnell of a sample 132 tutors' reports on courses taken in autumn 1980 showed 65% with 'good' or 'high' levels of student-reading and 88% with 'good' or 'high' discussion; on the other hand, only 24% were rated 'good' or 'high' for written work.

31) *Report on WEA Training Provision, April 1st 1985 – March 31st 1986*, appendix.

CHAPTER 8

LIVING WITH ESH
1984–88

An assessment of the work of the Eastern District during the middle and late 1980s must await its next historian: perhaps at the centenary in 2013! But it needs no hindsight to appreciate the importance of the new DES funding arrangements, which became fully operational in 1987–88 after a three-year phasing-in period. Under the scheme, DES grant-aid was divided into three elements. First, each District received a Core Grant – initially set at £25,000 – to cover the costs of a District Secretary and certain other administrative expenses. Beyond that, the main grant - around 70% of the total – was based on Effective Student Hours (ESH): every student attending two-thirds or more of a course at least six hours in length earned future grant for the District, the allocation for 1987–88 being based on ESH for 1985–86, that for 1988–89 on ESH for 1986–87, and so on. A third element related to 'Special Activities', various forms of priority work concerned not only with experimental courses but also with measures to improve the quality and efficiency of existing provision. 10% of the Department's total grant to the WEA was allocated to the Association at National level, and a special committee distributed this to the various Districts on the basis of the claims they submitted. However, this was not additional grant for development work: in effect, each District received 10% less from the DES and then had to argue its case with the National WEA for a share of the Special Activities Fund, a share which might or might not – cover the direct grant which had been lost.

This new formula, the outcome of discussions between the DES and the National WEA but essentially reflecting the government's consistent desire for cost-effectiveness in every sector of education,[1] had many significant implications. A uniform Core Grant to every District took no account of different sizes and staffing requirements but at least gave a small element of stability to an otherwise fluctuating government contribution. The Special Activities Fund afforded the National WEA some of the control over Districts' priorities which it had been seeking since the Working Party Report on Structure, Organisation, Finance and Staffing over twenty years before.[2] Most important, the emphasis on Effective Student Hours presented the obvious temptation to offer more 'popular' courses to boost numbers, but also challenged the WEA both to recruit students and to retain them. From the Association's point of view, the least satisfactory aspect of ESH-related funding was that the level of DES grant to the WEA as a whole was predetermined: an individual District which increased its 'effective students' would only receive additional grant-aid at the expense of other Districts. The various Districts were, in effect, being invited to compete with one another in their claims for government finance: in the hypothetical situation of every District increasing ESH by identical proportions, they would receive the same shares of grant as before. In all this, there may be echoes of 'payment by results', introduced as the basis for government aid to elementary schools in 1863, but at least Robert Lowe's 'Revised Code' allowed for total grant to rise or fall according to the overall level of performance: as he told the House of Commons, 'If it is not cheap it shall be efficient, if it is not efficient it shall be cheap'.[3] It remains to be seen whether the DES formula will eventually be amended to allow total grant to increase in real terms, as an incentive to every WEA District to improve its record of Effective Student Hours.

Although the long-term impact of these arrangements cannot be known, they soon had the effect within the Eastern District of altering procedures for the closure of under-enrolled classes. Whereas it had been normal hitherto to allow courses to run for three meetings in the hope that sufficient students would enrol, the fact that if such courses closed the students would have attended for less than six hours, so earning no grant whatever, prompted a change in the rules at the 1986 District AGM. Henceforth, any courses with less than eight students at the first meeting had to close immediately; those with eight or more were allowed to continue to at least the fourth meeting. As for Special Activities, the District's first allocation, for 1987–88, totalled £16,700, most of it to subsidise courses offered free to unemployed students but some to help branches meet the cost of providing creches and to finance day schools on Special Activities in each Federation area.

These financial issues have given the incoming District Secretary and his officers plenty to ponder. Quite apart from the new grant-aid formulae, they have also had to reckon with repeated cuts in the actual level of DES funding, amounting to a fall of 8% in the three-year period to 1986. This prompted during 1984 a campaign of letter-writing by branches akin to the protests of the 1950s and 1960s. But for all the difficulties posed by financial problems, there can also be a great deal of pleasure and satisfaction in working for a voluntary movement. As Reg Carnell wrote in his 1985–86 Annual Report,

> the WEA seems to draw to it those individuals who are reserved and modest about their achievements and still believe in the old-fashioned virtues of integrity and honesty.

It is working with such people that makes the WEA professional's job so worthwhile.

As the 1980s wore on, the District continued to offer high-quality adult education in the liberal studies, while also being ready to innovate and experiment. A glance at the 1986–87 class programme, totalling 520 courses, makes the point. Titles in Bedfordshire ranged from 'Archaeology of the Old Testament' at Luton to 'Spanish Painting' at Leighton Buzzard to 'Health: Alternative Therapies and Complementary Medicine' at Studham. Cambridgeshire offered 'The Norman Conquest and Domesday' at Cambridge, 'Understanding the USA' at St. Neots and 'Nuclear Diplomacy – 1945 to the Present' at Peterborough. In Essex there were courses on 'Greek Civilisation' at West Mersea, 'An Ecologist in the Garden' at Boreham and 'Counselling in the Community' at Colchester. Hertfordshire provided 'Introduction to Astronomy' at Hitchin, 'Power and Conflict' at Hoddesdon and 'The World of Islam' at St. Albans. Norfolk had 'Music in Context' at Burnham Market, 'Post-Freudian and Post-Jungian Psychology' at Norwich and 'Women as Rulers' at Great Yarmouth. Northamptonshire included 'History from the Air' at Great Houghton, 'The 20th Century Novel' at Woodford and 'Ulster in Perspective' at Long Buckby. Suffolk embraced 'Creative Writing' at Great Cornard, 'Western Democracies' at Saxmundham and 'After Chernobyl – Social Change and Alternative Technology' at Leiston. Moreover, there had been some significant additions to branches' programmes in preceding years: courses for School Governors (as at Bedford in 1983–84 and Huntingdon 1984–85) and topics such as 'Peace Studies' (Bedford 1983–84) and 'Women and Health' (Shefford 1984–85, Aspley Guise, Luton and Sharnbrook, all in Bedfordshire, 1985–86). At the same time, the flow of publications was maintained. Local History courses in Luton between 1981 and 1984 led to the appearance of two books on Hightown; Kelvedon branch (Essex) produced *Kelvedon and Feering, 1881 and 1986, A Contrast* in 1986; work at Whittlesey (Cambs.) bore fruit as *Whittlesea Mere* in 1987.

The headquarters of the Eastern District, Botolph House, was repaired in the spring of 1988 with the help of grants from Cambridge City Council and the Georgian Society; the new cupola is believed to have restored the building to an appearance close to the original. Among the staff there Ann Diamond, who had joined as Administrative Assistant in 1980, became the District's Assistant Secretary in January 1988. In the following month, Heather Tinsley and Rosemary Abram began work as part-time organisers for Hertfordshire and Northamptonshire respectively: appointments which represented a significant change in District policy, given that both counties had been served in the past by full-time tutor-organisers. Meanwhile the District Council, having met for thirty-seven years at the Arts' School, Bene't Street, Cambridge,[4] began to use a new venue in the city, Parkside Community College, in May 1987. Accordingly it was at Parkside that the District marked its seventy-fifth anniversary with the Council meeting on 21 May 1988: in the morning a series of discussion groups, in the afternoon an address by Baroness Seear (a WEA vice-president and Social and Liberal Democrat spokesman on education in the House of Lords), and in between a celebration buffet at the nearby YMCA.

Every WEA District is different, with its stronger and weaker points, and a few statistics serve to demonstrate this. Of the 880 WEA branches in England and Wales in 1985–86, no less than 184 were in the Eastern District: over one-fifth of the total and a hundred more than in any other District.[5] In the same academic year, the Eastern ranked sixth in total number of students (11,910 if those on day schools, at single meetings and on residential courses are included). It also had the third highest proportion (69%) of women students in its classes, and the third largest number of creches (69). Only the Yorkshire North and London Districts held more Tutorial Classes: sadly most Districts no longer included them in their programmes. If the Eastern District has enjoyed one advantage, which has helped to maintain the large number of branches and relatively-high number of students, it is that the region it has served has for most of the period since the Second World War been one of buoyant population increase. Between 1961 and 1971, and again between 1971 and 1981, East Anglia (regarded for government statistical purposes at Norfolk, Suffolk and Cambridgeshire) had the fastest population growth rate of any 'Standard Region' of England and Wales. From 1961 to 1971 Essex (although including the metropolitan area outside the Eastern District) was the third fastest-growing county and Bedfordshire the fifth fastest. And in both 1961–71 and 1971–81, every county in the Eastern District had a population growth rate significantly higher than the average for England and Wales as a whole.[6] But any advantage has to be capitalised upon, and if the Eastern District can fairly claim some success as a lively and socially-conscious agency of adult education, this is basically because of the effort, enthusiasm and enterprise of voluntary and professional members alike.

The Eastern District celebrated its seventy-fifth anniversary in an age when General Election campaigns were packaged for television by advertising executives, when three daily and two Sunday newspapers were in the hands of a single proprietor,[7] and when only 14% of the 18–19 age group in Great Britian entered higher education.[8] Was there ever more need of an independent, voluntary, democratic and non-partisan adult education movement, drawing on academic expertise and committed to deepening understanding of the heritage and society we share? Of course, the WEA in any form recognisable today – will never have mass appeal. An Advisory Council for Adult and Continuing Education report in 1982 revealed that as many as 35% of the adult population of England and Wales were not participating in education but wished that they were: yet the vast majority of these people either wanted courses to improve their qualifications and job skills, or plumped for foreign languages, domestic science and practical art,[9] precisely what the WEA does not normally provide! Reaching out beyond these perceived needs, to broaden people's horizons and awaken interest where none exists already, remains a most difficult task for an adult education movement. But anyone concerned that cultural appreciation, environmental awareness, and social and political understanding should be more than the preserves of a privileged minority, will wish the WEA well. For the Eastern District, the seventy-fifth anniversary gave an opportunity to reflect on what had been achieved. But not for long: there was too much work to be done.

NOTES

1) In response to the DES's wish to allocate grant on a more 'cost-effective' basis, the National WEA proposed in 1985 that future grant-aid should have three elements: Core Grant, Output Grant (based on ESH or similar criteria) and a Grant for Priority Work. However the DES's eventual apportionment of grant between these three was very different from that envisaged by the WEA.

2) See above, p.

3) J. S. Maclure, *Educational Documents England and Wales, 1816 to the Present Day* (3rd edn., 1973), p.79.

4) District Councils had consistently been held at the Arts' School, Bene't Street, Cambridge, from the AGM of 1950. It had also been used on previous occasions (e.g. the AGMs of 1939 and 1940), but other venues in Cambridge, such as the Oak Room of the Dorothy Cafe and the Houghton Hall, Union Road, had also been favoured.

5) The next largest number of branches was 81 in London District, followed by 79 in East Midland. This and other data about the WEA in the present paragraph is from *WEA Statistics 1985–86*.

6) The national intercensal population growth for 1961–71 was 5.74% and for 1971–81 0.83%. Growth rate for 1961–71 in East Anglia was 13.60%, in Essex 23.05% and in Bedfordshire 21.31%; for 197181 the rate in East Anglia was 12.11% (Office of Population Censuses and Surveys, *Census 1981: Historical Tables 1801–1981, England and Wales*). After 1981 East Anglia continued to have one of the fastest annual growth rates in the country, although it was overtaken by the South West in 1983–84 (Central Statistical Office, Regional Trends 21, 1986, table 2.1).

7) During 1987, Rupert Murdoch's *News International* added *Today* to its other British national newspapers, *The Times, Sunday Times, News of the World* and *Sun*. The last three were market-leaders in their respective sectors (quality Sunday, popular Sunday, popular daily).

8) *Higher Education: Meeting the Challenge* (1987), p.3: estimated age-participation index for 1986.

9) Advisory Council for Adult and Continuing Education, *Adults: Their Educational Experience and Needs* (1982), esp. pp.89-107; cf. *THES*, 3 December 1982.

SELECT BIBLIOGRAPHY

Books and Official Reports

Advisory Council for Adult and Continuing Education, **Continuing Education: From Policies to Practice** (Leicester 1982)

Advisory Council for Adult and Continuing Education, **Adults: Their Educational Experience and Needs** (Leicester 1982)

Advisory Council for Adult and Continuing Education, **Teachers of Adults: Voluntary Specialist Training and Evaluating Training Courses** (Leicester 1983)

Baker, W. P., **The English Village** (Oxford University Press 1953)

Board of Education Adult Education Committee Reports:

No. 1   **Local Co-operation Between Universities, Local Education Authorities, and Voluntary Bodies** (HMSO 1922)

No. 3   **The Development of Adult Education in Rural Areas** (HMSO 1922)

No. 9   **Pioneer Work and Other Developments in Adult Education** (HMSO 1927)

No.10   **The Scope and Practice of Adult Education** (HMSO 1930)

No.11   **Adult Education and the Local Authorities** (HMSO 1933)

Committee on Higher Education, **Higher Education Report . . . Under the Chairmanship of Lord Robbins** (HMSO 1963) i.e. Robbins Report

Department of Education and Science, **Adult Education: A Plan for Development** (HMSO 1973) i.e. The Russell Report

Draper, W. H., **University Extension: A Survey of Fifty Years, 1873–1923** (Cambridge University Press 1923)

Fieldhouse, R., **The Workers' Educational Association: Aims and Achievements, 1903–1977** (Hull 1977)

Headlam, J. W. and Hobhouse, L. T., **Certain Tutorial Classes in Connection with the Workers' Educational Association** (Special Report No.2, Board of Education, HMSO 1910)

Jennings, B., **Albert Mansbridge and English Adult Education** (Hull 1976)

Jennings, B., **Knowledge is Power: A Short History of the Workers' Educational Association, 1903–1978** (Hull 1979)

Kelly, T., **A History of Adult Education in Great Britain** (2nd edn., revised, Liverpool 1970)

le Pelley, P., **Go to Work on a Brain Train** (London 1978)

Lowndes, G. A. N., **The Silent Social Revolution: An Account of the Expansion of Public Education in England and Wales, 1895- 1935** (London 1937)

McIntosh, N. E., Calder, J. A. and Swift, B., **A Degree of Difference** (Guildford 1976)

Maclure, J. S., **Educational Documents England and Wales, 1816 to the Present Day** (3rd edn., London 1973)

Mansbridge, A., **University Tutorial Classes** (London 1914)

Mansbridge, A., **An Adventure in Working Class Education** (London 1920)

Mansbridge, A., **The Trodden Road** (London 1940)

Ministry of Education, **The Organisation and Finance of Adult Education in England and Wales** (HMSO 1954) i.e. The Ashby Report

Ministry of Education, **General Area Survey of the Study of Public Affairs by Youth and Adult Groups in Hertfordshire, 1948–49** (London 1950)

Ministry of Education, **A Survey of the Adult Education Provided by Responsible Bodies in Norfolk** (London 1952)

Ministry of Reconstruction: Adult Education Committee Final Report (Cmnd. 321, HMSO 1919)

Open University, **Report of the Committee on Continuing Education** (Milton Keynes 1976) i.e. Venables Report

Oxford and Working Class Education (Oxford University Press 1908) i.e. The Oxford Report

Pahl, R. E., **Adult Education in a Free Society** (London 1962)

Price, T. W., **The Story of the Workers' Educational Association** (The Labour Publishing Co. Ltd., London 1924)

Raybould, S. G., **The WEA – The Next Phase** (WEA London 1948)

Raybould, S. G., **The English Universities and Adult Education** (WEA, London 1951)

Raybould, S. G. (ed.), **Trends in English Adult Education** (Heinemann 1959)

Ree, H., **Educator Extraordinary** (Longmans 1973)

Royal Commission on Oxford and Cambridge Universities (HMSO 1922)

Shearman, H. C., **Adult Education for Democracy** (WEA 1944)

Stocks, M., **The Workers' Educational Association, the First Fifty Years** (Allen and Unwin 1953)

Tawney, R. H., **The Acquisitive Society** (Bell and Sons, London 1927)

Tawney, R. H., **The Future in Adult Education** (WEA 1947)

Tawney, R. H., **The Radical Tradition** (Allen and Unwin 1964)

Universities Council for Adult Education, **Annual Reports**

Waller, R. D., **A Design for Democracy** (Max Parrish 1956)

251

Welch, C. E., **The Peripatetic University: Cambridge Local Lectures 1873–1973** (Cambridge 1973)

Articles, Pamphlets and Other Material

Annual Reports of the WEA Eastern District, 1918–87

A Record of Thirty Years' Service (WEA 1933)

Cole, G. D. H., **Workers' Education** (Highway, Vol.XV, May 1923)

Douglas-Smith, A. E., **The WEA in the Countryside** (Highway, Vol.X-XIV, February 1934)

Educational Reconstruction (WEA 1917)

Eastern District Workers' Educational Association (Souvenir programme of celebrations at Cambridge, Eastern District 1924)

Eastern District Supplement (Highway, Vol.XXVIII, December 1935)

George, R., **Unconventional Approaches to Adult Education** (WEA 1919)

Greenwood, A., **The Education of the Citizen** (WEA 1920)

Jennings, B., **The Oxford Report Reconsidered** (Studies in Adult Education, Vol.7 No.1, 1975)

Light, G. D. V. and Ross, D. A., **WEA Policy and Problems: Rural Areas and County Councils** (Highway, Vol.XVIII, November 1925)

Martin, H. A. J., **This Grant Grabbing Racket** (Highway, Vol.XXV, March 1935)

Morris, H., **The Village College** (Memorandum, Cambridge University Press 1925)

Newlove, J. G., **Prospecting in Broadland** (Highway, Vol.XIII, March 1921)

Pateman, G. H., **The Teaching of History** (Highway, Vols.X and XI, 1918)

Pateman, G. H., **Adult Rural Education** (Highway, Vol.X, August 1918)

Pateman, G. H., **The Light in the East** (Highway, Vol.XIII, April 1921)

Poole, H. E., **Going Well, 1938–1944: A Report on the Eastern District** (Pendragon Press, Cambridge 1945)

Poole, H. E. (ed.), **The Workers' Educational Association in Norfolk: Report for the Session, 1938–39** (WEA Eastern District 1939)

Rural Reconstruction, Interim Report (WEA 1918)

Shearman, H. C., **The WEA in Rural England** (Highway, Vol.XX, February 1928)

Shearman, H. C., **What the Villager Wants** (Highway, Vol.XXIV, February 1934)

Shearman, H. C., **Impressions of the Rural Conference** (Adult Education, Vol.7 No.1, September 1934)

Temple, W., **The WEA: A Retrospect** (Highway, Vol.XVI, Summer 1924)

The Adult Student as Citizen (WEA 1939)

The Local Authority and Adult Education (British Institute of Adult Education 1926)

Universities Extra Mural Consultative Committee Reports and Memoranda, 1926–1939

University Reform: Recommendations of the WEA submitted to the Royal Commission (WEA 1920)

What Labour Wants from Education (WEA 1916)

Wimble, E. W., **WEA Finance** (Highway, Vol.XII, September 1920)

Workers' Educational Association, 1903–24 (WEA Eastern District)

APPENDIX A

CHAIRMEN AND TREASURERS OF THE WEA EASTERN DISTRICT

Chairmen

1913–20	S. J. Hutley
1920–22	Mrs. C. Rackham
1922–23	J. W. Seamark
1923–24	F. J. Fletcher
1924–34	H. Wash
1934–36	H. C. Shearman
1936–47	A. C. Allen
1947–52	P. V. Daley
1952–53	Mrs. E. M. Tipple
1953–56	J. Chear
1956–59	S. A. Robinson
1959–66	Miss J. Roberts
1966–73	A. G. Addison
1973–80	C. A. Scrimgeour
1980–87	D. G. H. T. Emery
1987 to date	Mrs. S. Bond

Honorary Treasurers

1918–31	F. R. Salter (Fellow, Magdalene College, Cambridge)
1931–41	H. L. Elvin (Fellow, Trinity Hall, Cambridge)
1941–47	D. M. Thomson (Fellow, Sidney Sussex College, Cambridge)
1947–53	E. Miller (Fellow, St. John's College, Cambridge)
1953–58	T. P. R. Laslett (Fellow, Trinity College, Cambridge)
1958–68	B. H. Farmer (Fellow, St. John's College, Cambridge)
1968–79	R. C. Smail (Fellow, Sidney Sussex College, Cambridge)
1979–87	Mrs. M. Bambrough
1987 to date	D. G. H. T. Emery

APPENDIX B

WEA EASTERN DISTRICT FULL-TIME TUTORS, ORGANISERS AND TUTOR-ORGANISERS TO 1988
(T = Tutor; OT = Organising Tutor; OS = Organising Secretary; TO = Tutor-Organiser)

1919–39	S. Green (T, Kettering and District)
1920–26	J. G. Newlove (T, Norfolk)
1927–30	H. C. Shearman (T, Bedfordshire)
1930–34	W. Whiteley (T, East Suffolk)
1938–41	H. E. Poole (OS, Norfolk)
1941–42	E. B. Leather (OS, Norfolk)
1941–46	P. N. Molloy (OS, Hertfordshire)
1941–46	P. Hyde (T, Essex)
1941–43	E. Monkhouse (T, Norfolk)
1941–49	L. M. Springhall (T, Norfolk)
1942–45	D. Parry (OS, Norfolk)
1942–46	E. Freeman (T, Essex)
1942–46	E. Floyd (T, Norfolk)
1942–50	S. G. Thicknesse (T, Norfolk, also OS Norfolk 1945–48)
1942–44	A. Tatlow (T, Northamptonshire)
1942–45	G. Jolliffe (T, Hertfordshire)
1943	M. Clarke (T, Norfolk)
1943–44	A. Spicer (T, Northamptonshire)
1943–46	J. Walters (T, Northamptonshire)
1943–46	H. Collingwood (T, Northamptonshire)
1943–44	A. Frimston (T, Norfolk)
1943–44	H. Atkinson (T, Suffolk)
1943–44	J. Hadfield (T, Cambridgeshire)
1943–45	K. Savage (T, Hertfordshire)
1943–47	M. Hodgson (OS, South Suffolk and North Essex)
1945–48	R. Young (T, Norfolk)
1945–46	R. Rowles (T, Suffolk)
1945–47	A. L. Basham (OT, Fenland)
1947–49	W. J. A. Harris (OT, Fenland)
1948–51	A. F. J. Brown (OT, Essex)
1948–51	C. G. Stuttard (OT, Hertfordshire)
1948–51	L. A. Smith (OT, Norfolk)
1948–54	H. Fearn (OT, Suffolk)
1949–52	G. W. Pattison (OT, Fenland)

1950–54	R. P. B. Davies (TO, Northamptonshire)
1951–54	F. M. J. Elliott (TO, Hertfordshire)
1951–55	R. Hallett (TO, Norfolk)
1952–54	J. Walters (TO, Essex)
1953–56	F. Cossey (TO, Fenland)
1954–56	B. M. Cooper (TO, Suffolk)
1954–57	K. Collingwood (TO, Essex)
1954–58	H. W. Parris (TO, Northamptonshire)
1955–56	H. McClellan (TO, Hertfordshire)
1956–60	H. J. Smith (TO, Norfolk) ·
1956–60	R. A. Johnson (TO, Suffolk)
1956–59	E. Richards (TO, Bedfordshire)
1956–63	J. T. Dodd (TO, Hertfordshire)
1957–58	R. L. Butler (TO, Industry)
1958–66	M. J. Carthew (TO, Industry)
1958–62	M. L. Colgan (TO, Northamptonshire)
1959–61	R. J. Darby (TO, Fenland)
1959–63	A. J. Scull (TO, Bedfordshire)
1960–63	G. N. A. Guinness (TO, Norfolk)
1961–64	R. A. Holland (TO, Suffolk)
1961–66	D. M. Wheatley (TO, Fenland)
1962–67	T. M. Jackson (TO, Northamptonshire)
1963–64	G. R. Crosse (TO, Industry)
1963–68	J. L. Alexander (TO, Hertfordshire)
1963–64	J. A. Thrower (TO, Bedfordshire)
1965 to date	J. M. Ridgard (TO, Suffolk)
1965–68	E. O. Evans (TO, Bedfordshire)
1966–69	A. Lenney (TO, Fenland)
1966–71	M. F. Surman (TO, Norfolk)
1966–78	R. C. W. Carnell (TO, Industry)
1967–70	M. E. Friesner (TO, Industry)
1967–70	J. R. Lowerson (TO, Northamptonshire)
1968–71	C. Rochester (TO, Hertfordshire)
1968–79	D. Tatton (TO, Bedfordshire)
1968–69	B. M. Kaye (TO, Industry)
1969–71	N. J. Harden (TO, Fenland)
1969–71	W. P. Kitson (TO, Industry)
1970–75	A. E. Torrison (TO, Industry)
1970–75	J. M. McDonald (TO, Daytime)
1970–73	P. R. Smith (TO, Northamptonshire)
1971–74	S. C. Maddison (TO, Hertfordshire)

1971–72	G. P. Sherriff (TO, Industry)
1971–77	G. J. White (TO, Fenland; from 1974 Cambridgeshire)
1972 to date	D. C. Yaxley (TO, Norfolk)
1972–74	J. A. Howard (TO, Industry)
1973–74	J. M. Neeson (TO, Northamptonshire)
1974–85	J. S. Batsleer (TO, Hertfordshire)
1974–79	J. A. Dennis (TO, Luton)
1974–77	D. A. Handley (TO, Industry)
1974–87	C. P. Middleton (TO, Northamptonshire)
1976 to date	R. Moore (TO, Industrial and Social Studies)
1976–77	C. Scarlett (TO, Industrial and Social Studies)
1976–79	F. Sykes (TO, Industrial and Social Studies)
1977–79	D. Bennett (TO, Industry)
1978–79	D. L. Vulliamy (TO, Industry)
1978 to date	P. S. Middleton (TO, Cambridgeshire)
1979 to date	J. A. Dennis (TO, Bedfordshire)
1980–83	R. C. W. Carnell (TO, Development)
1988 to date	H. M. Tinsley (Part-Time Organiser, Hertfordshire)
1988 to date	R. Abram (Part-Time Organiser, Northamptonshire)

APPENDIX C

" The best we can do for any man is to help him to be his own best self, to reach his own highest possibility."

THE WORKERS' EDUCATIONAL ASSOCIATION.
HALSTEAD BRANCH.

REPORT AND BALANCE SHEET FOR 1920-21.

DEAR SIR OR MADAM,

In submitting this report to you we trust that your interest in the above Association will still be maintained.

The Association is non-Political and non-Sectarian in that its relations with other organizations are limited to such mutual activities as further its aims and objects ; which are to stimulate and to satisfy the demand of working men and women for education ; and generally to assist the developments of a national system of education, which shall ensure to all children, adolescents and adults such education as is essential for their complete development as individuals and as citizens.

Last year the committee arranged six lectures by visiting and local speakers. We have every assurance they were all appreciated. A University Tutorial Class has also been formed with the assistance of the Local Education Committee for the study of "The Evolution of Government." Mr. J.R.M. Butler, M.A., Fellow and Lecturer of Trinity College, Cambridge, being the Tutor. The aim of this class is to continue a course of study for three winter sessions, each consisting of twenty-four weekly lessons. Each lesson consists of an hour's lecture followed by an hour's joint discussion by the Tutor and the students. Books recommended by the Tutor are loaned to the students free of charge for their private study. Although we did not get as many students as we desired, we feel sure those who have attended will have benefited with the instruction given. The last two lectures of the session will be given on Fridays, April 22nd and 29th, when the Tutor will review the winters work. Mr. Butler would welcome any of our Members or Friends who desire to come to the lectures on the aforementioned dates.

We are greatly indebted to the following Speakers for their kind services, which in every case were voluntarily given :—Mrs. C.D. Rackham, Rev. T.H. Curling, M.A., Mr. Arnold Mac Nair, M.A., Mr. Morton Mathews, Mr. E. Pike, Rev. A.E. Lett, B.A., B.D., and Mr. J. R. M. Butler, M.A., also to those Ladies and Gentlemen who so kindly gave hospitality to the visiting Lecturers. Our heartiest thanks are also due to all those who helped us during the session to make it a success.

The ANNUAL MEETING will be held on Tuesday, April 26th, 1921, in the Co-operative Rooms at 7.45 p.m., prompt. Kindly attend if possible as an encouragement to the Officials of the Local Branch in their efforts, as we wish to hear your desires.

The Secretaries will be pleased to answer any communication.

Signed on behalf of the W.E.A.

52, Tidings Hill.

W. KNOWLES,
C. BARTHOLOMEW, } Hon. Secs.

259

LIST OF SUBSCRIBERS, 1920-21.

	£	s.	d.
S. Courtauld, Esq., J.P. -	2	2	0
Mr. T. Brough, J.P., - -	1	0	0
Sir Cecil Beck, M.P.,	1	0	0
Mr. L. Widdop - -	1	0	0
Mr. A. Foster - -		10	6
Miss Brookes, M.A., - -		10	0
Miss Jardine- - -		10	0
Mr. E. Doubleday - -		10	0
Working Mens' Club -		10	0
Halstead Co-op Society -		10	0
The Moulders' Union -		7	6
Miss Brown - - -		6	0
Carpenters & Joiners Asstn.,		5	0
Workers' Union (No. 1 Branch)		5	0
Womens' Co-op Guild -		5	0
Mr. & Mrs. M Goodey -		5	0
Mr. & Mrs. H. North -		5	0
Mr. & Mrs. Bartholomew -		5	0
Power Loom Overlookers Asstn.		5	0
Mr. & Mrs. Booth - -		4	0
Mr. & Mrs. J. Barnes -		4	0
Rev. T. H. Curling, M.A., -		3	0
Miss H. Harboard - -		3	0
Miss Inman - - -		2	6
Miss Inman - - -		2	6
Miss E. Spurgeon - -		2	6
Rev. A.E. Lett, B.A., B.D., -		2	6
Mrs. Cargill - - -		2	6
Miss Cargill - -		2	6
Mr. & Mrs. G. Clark -		2	6
Mr. A. Yerbury - -		2	6
Miss E. Yerbury - -		2	6
Mr. E.C. Edgar - -		2	6
Mrs. Steed - -		2	6
Miss E. Duval - -		2	6
Mr. Morton Mathews -		2	6

	£	s.	d.
Mr. E. T. Dean - -		2	6
Mr. W. Knowles - -		2	6
Mr. C. Harrington - -		2	6
Mrs. Matthews - -		2	0
Miss E. Matthews - -		2	0
Mr. W. Harrington - -		2	0
Mr. Constable - -		2	0
Mr. F. Rowland - -		2	0
Miss B. Legge - -		2	0
Mr. J. Harrod - -		2	0
Miss Tiffen - -		2	0
Mr. W. Cocksedge - -		2	0
Mr. F. Shelley - -		2	0
Mr. W. Tyler - -		2	0
Miss Coles - -		2	0
Miss Short - -		2	0
Mrs. Pountney - -		1	6
Mr. & Mrs. Gibbons- -		2	0
Mr. & Mrs. Plaistow -		2	0
Miss Wash - -		1	0
Miss Bonnet - -		1	0
Mr. S. Cobbold - -		1	0
Mr. J. Cooper - -		1	0
Mr J. Monk - -		1	0
Mr. H. Willings - -		1	0
Mr. F. Stapleton - -		1	0
Mr. J. Moule - -		1	0
Miss L. Bearman - -		1	0
Mr. F. Beadle - -		1	0
Miss A. Cooper - -		1	0
Mr. E. Mizon - -		1	0
Mrs. Reynolds - -		1	0
Mrs. Constable - -		1	0
Miss Constable - -		1	0
Mr. A. Rayner - -		1	0
	£15	12	6

BALANCE SHEET.

RECEIPTS.		£	s.	d.
Balance from last year ...	...	4	17	11
To—Subscriptions ...	...	15	12	6
„ Collections ...	...	4	1	7
„ Annual Social ...	...	1	19	2
„ Interest ...	...	0	1	2
		£26	12	4

EXPENDITURE.	£	s.	d.	£	s.	d.
By—Printing—Mr. Root	9	17	0			
Mr. Barry	2	7	9			
Mr. Carter	1	3	0			
				13	7	9
„ Speakers' Expenses—						
Mr. C. D. Rackham	0	10	0			
Mr. Morton Mathews	0	12	6			
Mr. Pike	1	1	0			
				2	3	6
„ Lantern Expenses				0	8	0
„ Delegates to Cambridge ...				1	0	0
„ Rent of Rooms				2	3	6
„ Receipt Book				0	1	2
„ Printing for Tutorial Class ...				0	18	6
„ Postage and Stationery ...				0	14	6
„ Affiliation Fee. W.E.A. ...				2	12	0
„ Cash in Treasurer's hands ...				3	3	5
				£26	12	4

April 18th, 1921.

Audited and found correct,
A. J. YERBURY.

TOWARDS A

BRIGHTER

COUNTRYSIDE.

WORKERS' EDUCATIONAL ASSOCIATION

Eastern District.

N.B.—Do not destroy this. Please pass it on to anyone likely to be interested.

FOREWORD.

By a Rural Student.

As a village man having a thorough knowledge of the Workers' Educational Association, I most heartily commend this scheme.

There must be many men and women in this county who were obliged, as I myself was, to leave the village school at an early age, and who now desire to understand better the things around us. This scheme will bring to them opportunities, hitherto confined to towns, of free and open-minded inquiry into all those subjects which most immediately concern our appreciation and enjoyment of life.

There are scattered throughout the country many people whom the W.E.A. has assisted to appreciate the past and understand the present. It has brought us into the fellowship of learning and made us eager both to find truth and to share it with others. I am glad this work is to be extended and sincerely hope that the men in the country parts will back it up, and secure in the meetings the same pleasure and profit that I have found in them myself.

I commend it in the confident hope that it will be warmly welcomed, and ask for it the friendly aid and co-operation which it so richly deserves.

Renhold Green,   E. W. GURNEY.
Bedfordshire.

TOWARDS A BRIGHTER COUNTRYSIDE.

The opportunities set out in this pamphlet are now, for the first time, being brought in reach of all in the villages and smaller towns within a radius of about twenty miles round Bedford. Openings for pleasure and profit which were confined, not so long ago, to the favoured members of the Universities, are being extended to the country districts.

The Workers' Educational Association provides lectures on topics of real interest, closely related to our every day life. The subjects treated vary widely and there is something for everyone. No standard of education is necessary in order to take advantage of the scheme: it should therefore prove especially attractive to those whose schooling finished in early life.

Though hitherto chiefly confined to the towns, the W.E.A. has attracted keen villagers who have often travelled under difficulties in order to attend its classes; and the interest aroused by lectures already given under the W.E.A. in some villages has led to the appointment of a Resident Tutor for this rural area.

HOW TO ENTER UPON THE SCHEME.

The W.E.A. is an organisation relying largely on voluntary local effort for support and development. In all centres the local branch has been started as a result of the efforts of one or two individuals, seeking opportunities for themselves and their fellows.

Anyone can take the lead—either a clergyman, minister, schoolmaster, or trade union secretary, or the man or woman at the plough, in the shop, or in the home.

Show this pamphlet to your friends; discuss it with them: try to get a few to join with you in a request for one of the lectures or courses in this programme, and write without delay to the Tutor, Mr. H. C. Shearman, Sedes Mea, Willington, Beds. Mr. Shearman welcomes enquiries and will endeavour to pay a visit to anyone who would like to see him in connection with the scheme.

Meetings can be held in a schoolroom, village hall, or in any place where people are accustomed to gather. There are no rules and restrictions; smoking is allowed, and free discussion is welcomed.

The W.E.A. is responsible for the main costs of the scheme, and only a small part of the expense will fall on the village.

Books bearing on the subject can be borrowed from the nearest County Library branch; some suggested titles are given under each lecture, and a fuller list may be had from the County Librarian, the local librarian, or the Lecturer.

SINGLE LECTURES.

(Nos. 1 to 3 are Lantern Lectures).

---

1. The Story of our Village Churches.

Their unknown builders ; changing fashions in style and decoration ; what the building tells us of the past life of the village.

Books : J. C. Cox—The English Parish Church ; Consitt—Outline of Architecture.

2. Travelling and Wayfarers in other days.

When roads were quagmires ; when the bridge fell down ; wandering merchants and chapmen, carriers, pilgrims, scholars, and minstrels five hundred years ago ; from pack-horse and pilgrimage to motor bus and aeroplanes.

Books : Harper—The Great North Road ; Parkes—Travel in England in the Seventeenth Century.

3. Village Life of Long Ago.

Old methods of farming ; the fallow field, the plough ox, the goose on the common ; the Manor Court ; quaint customs ; Merry England.

Books : Clark—Working Life of Women in the Seventeenth Century ; Quennell—History of Everyday Things in England ; Coulton—Chaucer and his England.

4. The Place Names of Bedfordshire.

What they tell us of the early settlers ; how they have changed in process of time ; deceptive place names ; place names as a clue to problems of history.

5. A Day in the Life of a Member of Parliament.

Mr. Speaker takes the Chair ; the Member puts a question on behalf of one of his constituents ; a Private Bill ; a big debate ; the Division Lobbies ; the Committee Rooms ; Eleven o'clock—"Who goes home?"

Books : Ilbert—Parliament ; Masterman—How England is governed.

6. The Co-operative Movement.

Origins—Owen, Rochdale pioneers ; producers' co-operation and its failures ; co-operation in other lands ; problems and questions.

7. Thomas Hardy: Poet and Novelist of Country Life.

"Far from the madding crowd": Farmer Gabriel Oak; Lambing under the stars; the rick-burning; the Fair; Tess and the Milkmaids; "Under the Greenwood Tree": the Christmas carols; Jude the Obscure and the University.

Books—Hardy's Novels, Selected Poems; Abercrombie—Thomas Hardy, a critical study.

8. Three Novelists of Country Life.

Balzac's "Eugénie Grandet": a French village miser; Knut Hamsun's "Growth of the Soil": a pioneer farmer in Norwegian backwoods; Sheila Kaye Smith's "Sussex Gorse": a phase in English rural history. These three writers bring out the strength and weakness of the "successful" man, whose outlook is limited to his work.

Books: The three novels are in the County Library.

9. Tolstoy and his novel "War and Peace."

Tolstoy, the greatest of the Russian novelists, was a prince who became a peasant; an idealist who describes men and women as they really are; an ex-soldier who preached peace; and his great novel of the war with Napoleon is full of meaning for us, with our memories of a greater war.

Books: This and other novels and stories by Tolstoy.

10. Dante and his Vision.

Dante, the greatest poet of Italy, and one of the three or four greatest of all poets, died 600 years ago. Into his "Divine Comedy," an Epic Vision of the future world, he put all his deep and wide experience of this world; of men, of defeat and exile; of poverty and dependence; and also his hopes and ideals for world peace and harmony.

Books: Cunnington—Stories from Dante; Howell—Dante, his life and work.

11. A Day in London.

The Tower; Bank of England, Guildhall; St. Paul's; Newspaperland; Law Courts; Trafalgar Square; Whitehall and Downing Street; the Cenotaph; Westminster and Houses of Parliament.

SHORT COURSES.

(Some of the Lectures below can also be taken as single lectures if desired).

A. How We are Governed.

1—The Government and its Servants: Whitehall and the Civil Service, and the place of the permanent official in the smooth running of the state.

2—The Government and its Masters: the Cabinet and its dependence on Parliament and the Electorate.

3—The Courts of Law: The Magistrate, the Jury, the Courts of Appeal, the House of Lords.

4—Local Government.

Books : Masterman—How England is Governed ; Ilbert—Parliament.

B. Problems of the Modern World.

1—The Cost of Living: Why prices rise and fall and how the "cost of living" is estimated.

2—The Poor Law: The relief of the poor was formerly the duty of the church and the trade-guild ; how the problem became too big for local effort, and the state organised poor-relief ; probable changes.

3—Unemployment.

4—New Ideals in Education : the infant; the boy and girl; continuation schools; adult education.

Books : Lawrence—Why Prices Rise and Fall ; Pigou—Unemployment ; H. Jones—Social Economics ; Montessori—The Montessori Method ; Russell—On Education ; Wells—Sanderson of Oundle ; Mansbridge—An Adventure in Working Class Education.

C. The New Europe.

1—Nations and Empires: a sketch of the development of Europe in the last hundred years.

2—The Peace Treaty of 1919. It was an attempt to realise certain ideals and to create a lasting settlement of Europe, but it was also to some extent a compromise between conflicting ideals and claims.

3—Europe since 1919. The "growing pains" of new nations.

4—The League of Nations: Earlier schemes for world peace; the growth of arbitration ; " The Parliament of Man, the Federation of the World" ; problems of the League.

Books : Gooch—History of our own Times.

D. Democracy.

1—The Winning of Democracy: Democracies have existed, in some form, at various stages of history; modern democracy was achieved in England by a slow process, changing the old House of Commons into a popular assembly, by the pressure of public opinion and the gradual education of the people.

2—Democracy and its Leaders: How our national leaders and party leaders are chosen ; the English Premier and the American President ; do leaders really "lead ? "

3—Problems of Democracy. .

4—Democratic Ideals: Liberty, Equality of Opportunity, Progress. How can they be realised ? " Short cuts versus Education.

Books: Jenks—History of Politics ; Brown—The Meaning of Democracy ; Trevelyan—British History in the Nineteenth Century.

E. Life and Work in Bygone Days.

1—The Village Community : Food and dress in the "good old days" ; sports and amusements ; the Manor Court—making "the punishment fit the crime " ; marriage; women's life and work when food, clothes, and houses were all "home made."

2—Fields and Fallows : Methods of cultivation before the days of hedges ; pastures, root crops.

3—The Coming of the Hedges : how the countryside came to be what it is—a patchwork of enclosed fields, some ploughed and some grass.

Books : Ditchfield—Old Village Life ; Hartley—Life and Work of the People of England in the Fifteenth Century ; Waters—Economic History of England ; Quennell—History of Everyday Things in England.

F. Life and Work in Modern Times.

1—New Methods in Agriculture: "Turnip Townshend" ; new breeds of cattle ; the beginnings of scientific seed and soil study ; large farms and small holdings.

2—The Coming of Machines : the rise and rapid development of our industries, based on coal and steam.

3—The Labour Movement : the new Industry in its effect on the life of the workers ; their organisation in the new large towns—trade unionism and co-operation.

4—The State and the Welfare of the People : Factory Laws, Education, Insurance.

Books : Fordham—Short History of the English Agricultural Labourer ; Townsend Warner—Landmarks in English Industrial History ; Waters—Economic History of England ; Ashby—Economic Organisation of England ; Stone—A History of Labour.

G. An Introduction to Literature.

1—On Reading the Newspaper : Why we read the newspaper ; how newspapers began in war-time ; "Tidings" in Bible days : the instinct of curiosity—we want to know more about our fellows and the world about us.   Literature helps to satisfy the higher forms of this instinct.

2—The Reading of Novels : Novels generally contain a story, a plot, and some character study, just as newspapers often give us news, mysteries, and personalities.   How far is fiction "true ?"

3—The Study of Poetry : at first Poetry was compounded of telling a story and singing ; the story gave us the great Epics, and song gave us the Lyric.   The difficulties of poetry : it uses uncommon words and phrases—the language of emotion.   "Of what use is poetry ? "

4—The Art of Writing.   How to write a letter ; two questions – what to say, and how to say it.   How to write an essay.   Conclusion—Reading and Expression as the beginning and the end of education.

Books : Lamborn—Rudiments of Criticism ; Quiller-Couch—Art of Reading ; Canby—Better Writing ; Hudson—Introduction to the Study of Literature.

H. An Introduction to Shakespeare.

1—Shakespeare and his England.   The days of Good Queen Bess ; the Stratford youth ; the London stage ; his sonnets.

2—Shakespeare's Comedies : What is a Comedy ? " Twelfth Night "—a typically complicated love story ; some comic characters.   In the comedies we laugh at men's weaknesses and foibles.

3—The great Tragedies : these men's failings entail terrible results ; common human motives, like jealousy and ambition, are made the basis of crimes which recoil with deadly effect.

Books : Lamborn—Shakespeare and his stage ; Masefield—Shakespeare ; Dowden—Shakespeare.

I. Some Countryside Poets.

1—Robbie Burns, the ploughman-poet of Scotland.

2—William Cowper, of Olney.

3—John Clare, of Helpston, near Stamford ; the poet who began life at the plough and wrote his best verses in the asylum.

4—Wordsworth.

Books : Roy—Cowper and his Poetry ; Kellow—Burns and his Poetry ; Hudson—Wordsworth and his Poetry.   Poems by John Clare.

J. Some great books of other lands.

1—Dante's "Divine Comedy."

2—The Spanish Novel, " Don Quixote."

3—Three great Russian novelists : Turgeniev, Dostoievsky, Tolstoy.

In each of these, as well as in other cases, the greatest literature of the nation is closely connected with a crisis in the nation's history.

Books : Cunnington—Stories from Dante.   The Story of Don Quixote.

The above Lectures and Courses are being given by MR. H. C. SHEARMAN, M.A.   It is hoped that some other Lecturers will also be available for other subjects from time to time.   Enquiries for Lectures on subjects not mentioned in this list will be welcomed.